ISLAMIC REPUBLICS AND NATIONS

ISLAMIC REPUBLICS AND NATIONS

A H Mastan

MD PUBLICATIONS PVT LTD
NEW DELHI
www.mdppl.com

Published by :

MD Publications Pvt Ltd
"MD House", 11, Darya Ganj,
New Delhi - 110 002
Phone : +91-11-45355555
E-mail : contact@mdppl.com
Website: www.mdppl.com

ISBN: 978-81-7533-301-7

Published and Printed by Mr. Pranav Gupta on behalf of **MD Publications Pvt Ltd** at Times Press, Delhi.

PREFACE

The term "Islamic republic" has come to mean several different things, some contradictory to others. Theoretically, to many religious leaders, it is a state. A state is a political social contract with effective sovereignty over a geographic area and representing a population. These may be nation states, State or multinational states under a particular theocratic form of government.

A republic is a state or country that is not led by a hereditary monarch but in which the people have an impact on its government. The word originates from the Latin term res publica, the penal code. An Islamic Republic is a form of government, known as a theocracy, advocated by some Muslim religious leaders in the Middle East. Under the rule of an Islamic Republic the laws of the state are the religious laws of Islam, as dictated by the Koran. The head of state and sole ruler is a high-ranking religious cleric, who rules by divine right with a group of religious leaders and spiritual advisors.

Islamic republic is the name given to several states in the Muslim world including the Islamic Republics of Pakistan, Iran, Afghanistan, and Mauritania. Pakistan adopted the title under the constitution of 1956. Mauritania adopted it on 28 November 1958. Iran adopted it after the 1979 Islamic Revolution that overthrew the Pahlavi government. Afghanistan adopted it after the 2001 overthrow of the Taliban. Despite the similar name the countries differ greatly in their governments and laws.

Though there have historically been many regimes that could be interpreted as primitive Islamic Republics, in the modern era there have been very few. The Islamic Republic of Iran (1979-) is currently the only nation that operates under a self-proclaimed status as an Islamic Republic. However, many believe that since the death of the republic's founder Ayatollah Khomeini Iran's traditional religious infrastructure is crumbling, and the nation is slowly edging away from its strict Islamic principles.

Today, the creation of an Islamic State is the rallying cry for many Muslims, including those described as Islamists, all over the world. However the term itself has different meanings among various people. Many advocate the abolition of the monarchies. A monarchy is a form of government in which supreme power is absolutely or nominally lodged in an individual, who is the head of state, often for Life tenure or until abdication, and "is wholly set apart from all other members of the state." The person who heads a monarchy is called a monarch of the Middle East, regimes which they believe to be overly authoritarian or otherwise repressive to Islam, in some cases, to be replaced with a unified and monolithic Caliphate.

I am very grateful to Mr. Pranav Gupta, Director of MD Publications Pvt Ltd, New Delhi, for his kind cooperation and support for this book.

A H Mastan

Contents

1

Islam in Jordan, Central Asian States and Rural Malays

ISLAM AND JORDAN

INTRODUCTION

Both scholars and policy-makers alike represent the relationship between Islamic movements and the state in terms of political conflict. Whether manifested as militant groups or moderate reformists, Islamists are labeled as part of the "opposition." The alternative discourse of legitimization sponsored by Islamists is seen as a central challenge to the stability and survival of incumbent Arab regimes. As a result, a great deal of scholarship attempts to elucidate the potential consequences of Islamic movements for state power.

While it is clear that Islamic movements frequently mobilize against regimes and that the state apparatus is often utilized to circumscribe Islamic activism, such characterizations oversimplify the relationship between Islamists and the state. As several scholars have noted, Islamic movements are not monolithic entities.They are multifaceted and constituted by a variety of different Islamic groups. Struggles over sacred authority, tactics, and Islamic interpretation create important internal movement differences and disagreements. Such divergences, in turn, engender alternative patterns of state-movement interaction, only some of which are predicated upon conflict and struggle. During the 1970s, for example, regimes throughout the region supported Islamists during elections to professional associations to combat the power of Nasserists, Ba'thists, and leftist movements. More recently in Egypt, the Mubarak regime has provided financial support to Islamic Non-Governmental Organizations which focus upon the provision of basic goods and services rather than revolutionary change. And in Morocco, the government supports Sufi groups as an alternative to more radical Islamism. All of these examples indicate that the relationship between Islamic movements and the state is not based simply upon conflict. It is more complex and nuanced than the image of "Islam against the state" implies.

Using the Muslim Brotherhood in Jordan as a case study, this article argues that the dynamics of Islamic movement-state relations may be characterized more by cooperation than conflict when there is a conjuncture of interests. In Jordan, the regime benefits from Muslim Brotherhood success because as a moderate reform movement it checks other more confrontational social movements and channels Islamic activism into a non-violent agenda. The Muslim Brotherhood, on its part, benefits from organizational opportunities produced by the incumbent regime. State support allows the movement to extend its reach in society and enables the Brotherhood to more effectively deliver its religious message. Though the movement may disagree with policies or articulate opposition, it continues to act through the institutions of the political system without challenging the raison d'être of state or Hashemite power. In effect, the Brotherhood acts as a "loyal opposition."

This creates what Thomas Schelling refers to as a "coordination game." In this game, each actor cooperates with the other to achieve different ends. The regime seeks to perpetuate its power and control by supporting moderate Islam, while the Muslim Brotherhood hopes to promote a more Muslim society with state support. The Jordanian case study indicates that not all Islamic groups are unequivocal enemies of the state and that mutual interest can lead to cooperation. This support is not constant and the relationship is dynamic, but a complete understanding of state-movement relations necessitates elucidating points of cooperation as well as conflict. The Muslim Brotherhood's moderate approach to religious change, its history of support for the regime, concomitant movement opportunities in society and the state and independent Islamist views of the Brotherhood-regime relationship been outlined.

REFORM, NOT REVOLUTION

The Muslim Brotherhood is an Islamic reform movement founded in Egypt in 1928 by Hassan al-Banna. Although it initially began as a movement for the reform of the individual and social morality, its broader political significance grew to challenge secular leadership in Muslim societies. Its strategy of change was to facilitate a more Muslim society through grassroots programs in education, charity, and social activities. Over time, branches of the Muslim Brotherhood were founded in other Arab countries, including Saudi Arabia, the Sudan, Kuwait, and Jordan. Although the various Brotherhood branches are connected through shared symbolic and ideological linkages, historical experiences differ and each enjoys administrative independence.

The Muslim Brotherhood in Jordan, founded in 1945, is not seeking to destroy the current political system. It proposes reform from within. Statements by leaders and working members of the movement reflect this outlook. Abdul Majid Thunaybat, the current leader of the Muslim Brotherhood, describes the movement's approach to change:

> Our approach to education is to begin with the individual and then move on to the family and then ultimately the Islamic government that rules as provided for in God's *sharia*. Our mission does not envisage an overthrow of the regime in the sense of holding the reigns of power regardless of people's temperament or whether they approve of this regime or not. We seek the creation of faithful grassroots that receive these instructions and this order, and government by Islam comes later.
>
> We renounce violence and say that the alternative is political

reform and respect for Islamic *sharia*, which constitutes the base of powers as approved by all Arab and Islamic constitutions.

Thunaybat's views are echoed by other members of the Muslim Brotherhood. In his outline of the Islamic position on political involvement, Ishaq Farhan, a leader in the Brotherhood, reemphasizes the movement's support for the stability of Jordan and argues that "no matter how much the political stands differ between the Islamic movement and the official stand, things must never end up with using violence and the opposite violence [counter-violence]." Of paramount importance is that the movement supports the "state of law and institutions while adopting the gradual reform means in order to shift towards the application of the Islamic *sharia* in society." Elsewhere Farhan states that the Brotherhood "will not spill one drop of blood or vandalize any public or private property." This derives from a belief that "Sometimes words speak louder than swords." The Muslim Brothers articulate a gradualist agenda for change that begins with "the Muslim individual, up to the Muslim family, the Muslim community, and then the Muslim State."

The Brotherhood's method of change is not the erection of a new system of politics; it is a reformist strategy of working through the current system to imbue it with more Islamic tones. Leaders in the movement characterize themselves as "reformists, not revolutionaries," and argue that the strategy of change is "evolution, not revolution." It is an attempt to renew the system, not to radically change or alter it. Members of the Brotherhood view themselves as partners with the government in providing social and moral guidance. Bassam Umush echoes these sentiments when he argues that any change should be pursued by "making an effort toward reforming government rather than through an attempt to overthrow the regime." Various members of the movement have labeled their relationship with the regime as one of "peaceful coexistence."

Movement outsiders recognize the peaceful nature of this relationship as well. In a series of articles in the Jordanian

Arabic daily, *al-Ra'y*, numerous observers outside the Muslim Brotherhood describe the relationship between the regime and the movement as one of mutual cooperation. Many further argue that there has never been any real contradiction or confrontation because peaceful coexistence brought "mutual benefit" for both parties. As the next section explains, this rhetoric of moderation is supported by a history of cooperation and loyalty to the political system and regime.

THE HISTORICAL RECORD OF LOYALTY

The Muslim Brotherhood in Jordan has never seriously challenged the legitimacy or power of the ruling regime. While the Egyptian Brotherhood experienced violent clashes with President Abd al-Nasser and has been repressed by Presidents Sadat and Mubarak, the Jordanian movement has enjoyed a relatively cordial and cooperative relationship with the Hashemite monarchy. Although moments of tension have surfaced over the years, the relationship has remained one of mutual understanding and cooperation, reinforced by common interests and institutionalized through repeated episodes of interaction. Though earlier years in the relationship witnessed serious disagreements and mutual suspicion, conflict diminished as the result of extended interactional experiences. Each actor has, in essence, learned the limits and objectives of the other. Despite its advocacy of a more Islamic society, the Jordanian Muslim Brotherhood has never sought a radical or revolutionary change in political arrangements that would threaten the survival of the regime, nor has it sought the dissolution of monarchical rule. On the contrary, it has actively supported the regime and its claims to legitimacy, and has served as a source of stability throughout Jordan's tumultuous history.

Its relationship with the regime began when the movement was founded in Jordan on 19 November 1945. King Abdullah I, the founder of the kingdom, provided patronage for the inauguration of the general offices and granted the movement legal status in January 1946 as a charitable society. The king was a personal associate of the Jordanian

Brotherhood's founder, Abdul Latif Abu Qura, and included the movement's secretary, Abdul Hakim Adin, in the government's cabinet, proclaiming that "Jordan is in need of the Brotherhood's efforts." Abdullah allowed the Brotherhood to establish branches throughout the kingdom, enabling the movement to extend its influence during the initial period of state-formation. The Brotherhood became an active participant in the construction of the new Jordanian entity and has maintained an important role in shaping the affairs of the country. King Abdullah supported the religiously-conservative agenda of the Brotherhood and viewed the movement as a strategic ally in combating leftist and communist forces in the kingdom. The Muslim Brotherhood, on its part, supported the King's annexation of the West Bank and respected the religious credentials of the Hashemites. The mutual amicability and cooperation was colored by periods of tension but established the foundations for a long-lasting relationship.

Throughout its history, the Muslim Brotherhood has consistently supported the regime during periods of crisis. During the height of the regime's confrontation with Arab nationalists and the coup attempt in the 1950s, the Brotherhood openly declared its loyalty to King Hussein, supporting martial law to combat destabilizing movements such as Nasserists, communists, leftists, and Ba'thist forces. The Brotherhood objected to the atheistic nature of these movements, while King Hussein feared erosion of his power and control. The Brotherhood's support for the king was reaffirmed during the 1970-71 civil wars when the movement reinforced its allegiance and commitment to stability by staying out of the conflict.

More recently, during the 1989 and 1996 riots which erupted over subsidy reductions, the Muslim Brotherhood was careful not to criticize King Hussein, focusing its attacks on the cabinet and not the system of power or legitimacy. The Brotherhood actively worked to ease tensions and looked to the king as an unbiased arbiter during the crisis, publicly praising his wisdom and political acumen. In 1996 during a public speech, the king publicly recognized the Brotherhood's restraint during the riots.

In another instance, the regime directly requested Muslim Brotherhood assistance to promote political stability after unrest exploded in the Palestinian refugee camps following a 1990 incident in which Israelis killed twelve Palestinians near a Tel Aviv train station. Because of the Brotherhood's political influence in the camps, the regime approached leaders and asked them to use their influence to regain order. The Muslim Brotherhood complied with the request and order was subsequently restored.

The Brotherhood's moderate stance has also served to counter radical Islamic groups. From the perspective of regime survival, the Muslim Brotherhood's most important function is that it marginalizes more militant Islamic groups which propose revolutionary changes in the political and social system. During the 1960s and 1970s, the Muslim Brotherhood acted to counter the more radical Hizb al-Tahrir (The Liberation Party). As a moderate, supportive, and legal Islamic movement, the Brotherhood was viewed as a means of absorbing the increased religiosity that began in the 1970s to divert it away from more radical groups such as Hizb al-Tahrir. At times, the Brotherhood uses its high profile and legitimacy to delegitimize the claims and ideologies of groups that espouse violence in the kingdom. Any new, more radical Islamic group, which might construct a material or ideological challenge to the regime, would first need to successfully diminish the Muslim Brotherhood's status in the community. This creates a legitimating buffer that protects the regime from revolutionary discursive challenges. The Brotherhood, in effect, serves as a mechanism of internal social movement discipline that prevents the growing power of more threatening Islamic groups.

Despite this cooperation, the relationship has experienced downturns as well. In 1956, the Muslim Brotherhood organized protests against policies that permitted a substantial British presence in the country. Later, divisions between the movement and the crown emerged over the regime's policy towards Iran. Before the 1979 Iranian revolution, King Hussein used his prestige, in an attempt to bolster the faltering

Shah, by visiting Iran three times in 1978. Since the majority of Jordanians supported the Iranian revolution, the king's actions in support of the Shah were used by the Brotherhood as an opportunity to attack the government's policies as un-Islamic. King Hussein's later support of Iraq during the Iran-Iraq war further emphasized these differences.

Another clash occurred during Egypt's rapprochement with Israel. Despite King Hussein's public condemnation of the peace efforts, he refused to break ties with Egypt, continuing economic relations after the Camp David Accords in 1979. The Muslim Brotherhood expressed dismay at what it viewed as inadequate action against Egypt's independent break with the united Arab front against Israel.

Still another breakdown in relations occurred when political circumstances between Syria and Jordan improved. Prior to the mid-1980s, the king allowed the Brotherhood to organize and launch attacks against the Asad regime from Jordanian territory. After relations between Jordan and Syria improved, the regime cracked down on the Brotherhood to prevent further military attacks. This included an assortment of measures designed to repress the movement's foreign operations as well as domestic activities. Other areas of confrontation have emerged over issues such as economic liberalization, relations with the West, the peace process, and the election law. In all of these disagreements, the Brotherhood disagreed with particular policies without challenging the regime's ultimate authority or power.

Regardless of any differences, the Muslim Brotherhood has remained loyal to the political system and the Hashemite regime. It has never operated underground, attempted to destabilize the kingdom, or used violence. Though there have been disagreements, it is like any relationship and has experienced ups and downs. The historical record has demonstrated the movement's loyalty to the system, and a long history of interaction has created a predictable relationship in which the actors are well known to one another. As Hilmi Asmar, member of the Muslim Brotherhood and former editor of the Islamist weekly, *al-Sabil*, argues,

> There is an accumulation of trust-building because we have been dealing with decision-makers for a long time. There is a gentleman's agreement between the royal court and the Muslim Brotherhood. The first headquarters of the Muslim Brotherhood in Jordan was opened by King Abdullah so trust started from the beginning. There was no real conflict between the Muslim Brotherhood and the regime...We are partners; we are not revolutionaries. We have disagreements, different points of view, but we do not go boxing.

Although there is a growing ideologically oriented faction within the Muslim Brotherhood, known as the "hawks," the Brotherhood leadership remains predominantly realist and loyal to the political system. Rather than staunchly opposing structures of power, the Brotherhood works from within the system to produce changes. It acts within the rules of the game, even when these rules are monopolized by the regime. Most importantly, it has never challenged the legitimacy of the state or the Hashemites. While the movement has opposed specific government policies, it has never opposed the right of the regime to govern or threatened the capabilities of the state.

OPPORTUNITIES FOR GRASSROOTS ACTIVISM

As a result of this cooperative relationship, the Muslim Brotherhood has been awarded maneuvering room for social movement activism. Beginning in the 1950s, the Brotherhood expanded through a variety of grassroots activities while all other movements were repressed. Peaceful coexistence, based upon a history of system loyalty and experience, has led to a number of opportunities unavailable to other political actors in the kingdom.

The Brotherhood's greatest expansion has been through Islamic Non-Governmental Organizations (NGOs). Islamic NGOs are non-profit organizations that provide basic goods and services to communities in a manner Islamists claim are consistent with the Quran and Sunna. Examples of Islamic NGO activities include schools, health care, religious lessons, and youth programs, all designed to promote Islamic values and behavior. As points of contact between the Muslim

Brotherhood and communities, these NGOs create vehicles for developing a clientele and support for the Brotherhood cause. It is important to note that Law 33 of 1966 provides the state with absolute discretion as to which social groups can mobilize through NGOs, and it has used this power to prevent opposition groups from utilizing grassroots organizations. The Brotherhood, however, has been provided ample space for NGO activism.

Most of the Brotherhood's grassroots activities operate through the Islamic Center Charity Society, which was licensed in 1963 and serves as the charitable arm of the movement. During the martial law period, the Brotherhood was the only political movement allowed to operate in civil society, and it took advantage of this status to institutionalize itself as the dominant social movement in the kingdom. The Center's activities grew during the 1970s with the influx of oil-related revenues and financial support. With expenditures in 1993 of JD 1,148,573 (approximately $1,640,820), the financial resources of the Center dwarf those of all other NGOs, except those sponsored by the royal family.

The Center runs a variety of organizations. One of its best-known enterprises is its system of schools. The society operates a network of kindergartens and schools, including the reputable Dar al-Aqram and Dar al-Aqsa schools (the latter had 17 branches throughout Jordan as of 1993). These schools combine the mandatory national curriculum with special religious classes and hold special Islamic events, such as Islamic book festivals. Non-religious classes, such as biology, are imbued with an Islamic dimension by explaining scientific information in terms of the Quran and *hadith* (the written record of sayings and traditions attributed to the Prophet Mohammed).The society also built the Islamic Community College in Zarqa and Zarqa University. The University institutes norms of gender segregation in classes and promotes Islamic behavior. Other organizational activities through the Center include health clinics, sewing centers, Quranic reading courses, orphanages, scholarships for students, and financial and in-kind distribution for the poor.

The Center's most successful charitable project is the Islamic Hospital in Amman. During the initial phase of state-building in Jordan, most health and educational institutions were operated by missionaries and foreign nationals. Following the 1967 war with Israel, members of the Muslim Brotherhood decided to establish their own health care facilities. Construction of the hospital began shortly thereafter in 1970 and it was opened in 1982. Today, there are 1,100 employees and virtually every medical specialty is available at the hospital. Treatment is better than at many private hospitals and the cost is less because all profits are reinvested.

At the hospital, the Brotherhood attempts to promote Islamic values through a variety of activities. Nurses must wear the *hijab*, all employees are required to pray five times a day, and the hospital tries to implement norms of gender segregation. In practice, these requirements are not always possible and exceptions are permitted. There are also religious lessons for employees, including weekly lectures on the meaning of the Quran, *hadith*, *fiqh* (Islamic jurisprudence), and Quranic recitation. Patients are exposed to Islamic values through employee practices and special activities. The staff is encouraged to discuss Islam with patients, and religious programming is shown on all hospital televisions. Books and pamphlets on Islam are also readily available to patients.

Because of the Muslim Brotherhood's relationship with the regime and its consistent support for working through the system, it has enjoyed special treatment in organizing through the Islamic Center Charity Society. Not only was it permitted to organize when all other political organizations in the country were banned during the martial law period, but it has been allowed to expand the scope of its activities, broadening the reach of its appeal. For example, the law requires that NGOs first obtain permission to open branches. Though the Center has opened only four official branches, it has side-stepped regulations by opening 32 "committees." These committees are not a secret; they are well known to the state apparatus and their existence is due to state tolerance and tacit approval, an acceptance that is not forthcoming for many other social movements. In addition, while the Ministry of Social Development strictly monitors the financial records of NGOs through annual audits, the Islamic Center Charity Society has frequently been exempt.

The tacit state support of the Center Society provides the Brotherhood with greater opportunities for garnering support. It is a point of contact with communities and an opportunity to publicly display movement achievements through concrete projects. As Ra'if Nijim, the engineer responsible for the construction of the Islamic Hospital and former director of its fund for the poor, observed,

> All of these projects-cultural, political, and social projects-prove this movement is helping the people that these projects are for the people. So when you do such projects, it is better than being only an association talking to people, calling them to Islam, calling them to pray, calling them to go for pilgrimage. This is how they succeed and because of this they have succeeded. Not because they are the only Muslim movement, but because they have done a lot of projects for the country.

Although the Islamic Center Charity Society does not directly engage in politics, there is a political effect. Beneficiaries provide political support to the Brotherhood because of its social services. Zaid Abu Ghamineh, an administrator at the Islamic hospital, argues that,

> Our success is in building a practical model for how Islam can serve. It has raised the confidence of the community that Islam can solve people's problems. That is why people now support the Islamic movement and this is reflected. Poor people, especially those served by the hospital, they pay us back in elections and meetings. They interact with us. The hospital has influenced them... This influence is not direct. We do not require that people either support the movement or we will not help... It is not a requirement that they become members of the Muslim Brotherhood. They voluntarily find themselves morally indebted to the movement and that is why they do not pay us [immediately for charitable work]. When the

movement is in elections or needs support, they repay the debt.

The Islamic Hospital also serves as a source of movement patronage. According to Ra'if Nijim, the vast majority of employees at the hospital are members of the Brotherhood; a fact which he believes brings down the quality of service:

> Now the hospitals here, the Islamic Hospital, all the employees there, all the doctors, are members of the Muslim Brotherhood, regardless of their knowledge or the ability for work. I go and visit the hospital always and I can see with my own eyes. There are many workers and many employees [who] do not deserve to be employed in that hospital because this is a big, standard hospital in the country and should employ better staff. They do not employ anyone who is not a member of the Muslim Brotherhood.

In reality, there are non-Muslim Brotherhood employees as well, but Nijim estimates that 90% of the staff is from the movement. This provides an employment incentive for Brotherhood loyalists.

Following political liberalization, the Muslim Brotherhood expanded its NGO presence into the cultural arena through the Society for the Preservation of the Quran. Founded in 1990, the society engages in a variety of activities intended to promote the application of the Quran because of a belief that "there is no way man can be happy unless they take their knowledge from the Quran, read it, and understand." The society teaches Muslims, especially younger Muslims, to read and memorize the Quran. It also educates participants in fields related to the Quran, such as the *sharia*, *fiqh*, and the Sunna. In July, it holds the National Project for the Conservation and Learning of the Quran which encourages children to participate in Quranic education and activities. During the month of Ramadan, the society holds a national contest for students who have memorized more than five parts of the Quran. Members of the society also bring people in from the streets for general Quranic lessons.

As is the case with the Islamic Center Charity Society,

this society enjoys an amicable relationship with the state. While a similar cultural society comprised of more critical Islamists was routinely denied permission to open branches, the Society for the Preservation of the Quran has successfully opened 100 centers throughout the kingdom, far exceeding the Ministry of Awqaf's own 26 cultural societies. This provides access to a variety of neighborhoods in different cities. It is the strongest and best organized of the nine Islamic cultural societies. While other Islamic cultural societies are routinely denied permission to form branches without an explanation, the only barriers for this society are "financial, strictly financial." It enjoys a good relationship with the regime and the state apparatus. As the director of the society states, "The Ministry of Culture understands perfectly the goals of the society. We have all the moral support we need from the Ministry of Culture. The only obstacle is financial, and we keep the Ministry informed of our activities." In fact, the society's bylaws, approved by the Minister of Culture, state that it can open branches whenever it wants and informs the Ministry after the fact. In most cases, NGOs require prior permission to open branches. In addition, the society often works directly with the Ministries of Culture, Education, and Awqaf, often-utilizing state-owned facilities such as the Islamic Center at King Abdullah mosque in Amman. Given this supportive relationship, it is not surprising that the director of the society is also an employee at the Ministry of Awqaf. Other Brotherhood-run NGOs, such as the Yarmuk Sports, Social, and Cultural Club, the Islamic Studies and Research Association, the International Institute for Islamic Thought, the Green Crescent Society, and the Al-Afaf Society, have also received favorable treatment.

The Muslim Brotherhood's activities in organizations and its grassroots operations are well known. It is not an insidious political scheme to uproot the regime. The history of the Brotherhood demonstrates otherwise. It is a grassroots attempt to promote a religious message through formal organizations in civil society. The movement has supported the state, and the state, in turn, has reciprocated by allowing the Brotherhood to organize effectively.

MUSLIM BROTHERHOOD ACCESS TO THE STATE AND GOVERNANCE

As a result of its moderate and pragmatic approach, the Muslim Brotherhood has also enjoyed access to institutions of governance, including Parliament, cabinets, national consultative bodies, and various ministries. This allows the Brotherhood to augment its grassroots campaign with influence through the state.

One of the most notable instances of Brotherhood accesses to state institutions is through employment opportunities. Numerous members of the movement have been employed by the government. This includes appointments to positions of leadership within the state apparatus. Ishaq Farhan, for example, served as Minister of Education in 1970 and later as the Minister of Awqaf from 1983-1985. He was also the Director of Curriculum and Textbooks (Ministry of Education), the Director of Teacher Education (Ministry of Education), and the President of Jordan University, which is controlled by the government. From 1989-1993, he was appointed as a Senator in the Upper House of Parliament. Abdul Latif Arabiyyat, another prominent leader in the Brotherhood, was the Director General of the Amman Educational Department from 1980-1982 and the Secretary General of the Ministry of Education from 1982-1985. He was also the Speaker of the Lower House of Parliament from 1989-1993 and a member of the Senate from 1993-1997.

Aside from high level leaders such as Arabiyyat and Farhan, other members of the Brotherhood are also employed at state institutions. According to a study of the Islamic Action Front Party (IAF) membership, 21% of the founding members, most of them from the Brotherhood, work at the Ministry of Education. Still other members are employed at state controlled institutions such as universities and public schools. In 1993, 40% of the members of the IAF shura council were government employees.

Leaders in the Muslim Brotherhood have also been appointed to various national consultative bodies by the regime. For example, Ishaq Farhan was appointed as a member of the National Consultative Council, formed in the 1970s as an alternative to recalling Parliament. Arabiyyat and other members of the Brotherhood served on the National Charter Committee formed to draft the National Charter in 1991 that served as a blueprint for political liberalization. During the National Charter negotiations, committee members, including the Muslim Brothers, stated as one of their primary objectives to assure the continued legitimacy of the Hashemite monarchy and support for the king.

The Brotherhood's experience in state institutions and its ubiquitous grassroots presence through NGOs placed the movement in a strong position to benefit from political liberalization, which began in 1989. Because all other political movements were repressed during the martial law period, the Brotherhood emerged as the most organized and well-known movement in the kingdom. As a result, it faired well during the parliamentary elections. In 1984, by-elections were held to fill vacant seats in the Lower House. The Muslim Brotherhood won three of the six seats reserved for Muslims. In the 1989 elections, the Muslim Brotherhood won 22 of the 80 seats. In 1993, the movement captured 16 seats and continued to act as a formidable parliamentary actor.

In 1991, at the onset of the Gulf War in January, members of the Muslim Brotherhood and independent Islamists were invited to participate in the cabinet, a decision that is made by the king and his appointed Prime Minister. The Muslim Brotherhood was given the most influential domestic portfolios, including the Ministries of Education (Abdullah Akaileh), Health (Adnan Jaljuli), Justice (Majid Khalifeh), Social Development (Yusuf al-Athm), and Awqaf (Ibrahim Zayd al-Kilani). These Ministries were viewed as effective mechanisms for implementing the movement's social objectives. The participation of the Muslim Brotherhood in the cabinet only lasted six months, but the domestic portfolios provided the movement with a high profile and offer a glimpse at the kinds of changes they seek through governmental institutions. None of the changes initiated by the Muslim Brotherhood during this period of cabinet participation challenged the structure of the system or the legitimacy of the regime. In fact, Islamists outside the Muslim Brotherhood have characterized the Brotherhood changes as "trivial" and "insignificant." In one ruling, the Minister of Education prohibited fathers from watching their daughters in sporting events because they would see other girls immodestly dressed. In another ruling, alcohol was banned from being served on Royal Jordanian flights and at government functions. Though such policies engendered outrage from less conservative quarters in society, they never challenged the system of power. All the policy changes were aimed at regulating individual behavior and were not designed to initiate political reforms that would have altered the structure of political power in the kingdom.

Access to state institutions and NGOs creates Brotherhood opportunities for religious change from above and below. Although the movement's ability to promote its agenda is limited by the ultimate concerns of the regime, points of mutual interest have led to a cooperative relationship. The Brotherhood's strong presence in society is to a large extent due to this coordination.

OTHER ISLAMIST VIEWS OF THE BROTHERHOOD-STATE RELATIONSHIP

This cooperation and participation has been criticized by more radical groups within the broader Islamic movement. These groups argue that the Muslim Brotherhood has compromised its ideological and religious message for political and social power. From this perspective, the pragmatism of the Muslim Brotherhood has superseded its original intent. Layth Shubaylat's objections to the movement reflect the view of many Islamists outside the Muslim Brotherhood:

I do not think they are serious. I think they are part of the regime. I think they are not serious and they are tame. And their duty is to tame the new followers. They give them a lot of rhetoric and tell them to obey, and they say this is why and that it is the wisdom.

An Islamist from the Mutazileh movement lamented that the Muslim Brotherhood is concerned with "small, trivial things, like preventing alcohol from being served on planes or stopping pornographic movies; but these are very trivial matters and are not effective in social movement." Another Islamist complained that "their nature, their very thought, is pragmatic," and argued that the Muslim Brotherhood will never affect real Islamic change in Jordan because it has been "captured by the system."

Even radical members of the Muslim Brotherhood itself articulate this perspective, charging that the leadership is more concerned with political power than with producing an Islamic society. Despite such internal disagreements, however, radical members of the Brotherhood do not propose a violent or confrontational approach that would threaten the power of the king or the political system. Their approach is more one of non-participation, which includes boycotts and statements opposed to government policies. They believe that the Brotherhood should remain outside Parliament and the cabinet, and that the movement should pursue change through other venues such as grassroots projects. This wing of the Brotherhood, which is not a majority, fears that cooperation could lead to co-optation and the "domestication of the opposition" (if this has not occurred already).

Such critiques highlight internal movement disagreements about whether Islamists should coordinate with incumbent regimes. While the majority of the Brotherhood believes that they can coordinate their tactics and goals with the regime to more effectively produce results, other independent Islamists question the efficacy of cooperation. Regardless of these differences, the Brotherhood's experience in Jordan demonstrates that movement-state interactions are not always characterized by political conflict.

This case study indicates that Islamic movement-state relations cannot be unequivocally characterized in terms of confrontation or struggle. Just as the Islamic movement is not a monolithic entity, state-movement interactions cannot be singularly characterized in terms of political conflict. Rather than assuming a diode of conflict, students of Islamic movements should examine the range of interactions, which include both conflict and cooperation.

The Jordanian Muslim Brotherhood's success is to a large extent the result of its relatively congenial relationship with the regime. Throughout its history, it has supported the Hashemite regime and political stability during various crises. Its rhetoric of moderation is thus matched by a history of loyal opposition and participation in the political system. As a consequence, the regime has provided ample room for Brotherhood organization. This includes both grassroots organization through Islamic NGOs as well as access to the state apparatus and government employment.

The benefits of the Muslim Brotherhood's special relationship with the regime, however, may decline with the consolidation of democracy. As political participation and civil liberties are institutionalized, state support will become less important for movement success. Previously repressed and marginalized movements are slowly gaining greater freedoms, independent of regime cooperation. The relative weight of the Brotherhood in society thus may decline as other movements become more organized in the new democracy. In addition, the regime's need to cultivate the Brotherhood's support will most likely become less important (though certainly not irrelevant) as legitimacy shifts to democratic values and practices.

Despite any such changes, the cooperative relationship has institutionalized itself over a long period of history and is unlikely to devolve into antagonism. The Brotherhood may vocalize opposition to government policies and the regime may be less willing to give into Brotherhood demands, but both sides recognize the value of negotiation and coordination over conflict. Islamic movements and the state are not necessarily natural enemies; cooperation is possible and oftentimes in the best interest of both parties, as the Jordanian case demonstrates.

ISLAM AND POLITICS IN CENTRAL ASIAN STATES

INTRODUCTION

The role of Islam and Muslim traditions in Central Asian societies is becoming increasingly important for assessing the situation in and around the region. More correctly formulated, the object of research is not simply Islam per se but rather the 'Islamic factor', a notion that comprises: (*a*) Islam's impact on social and political life; (*b*) the use of Islam as a political instrument by the ruling elite as well as by the opposition; (*c*) Islam as an instrument in foreign policy; and (*d*) Islam as a means to strengthen the authority of Central Asian states in the Muslim world.

Experts differ on the details of this multi-stage definition. Islam's impact on society can be assessed as an absolute or it can be disregarded. In other words, for some researchers the 'Islamic factor' is something artificial, something thought up by scholars of Oriental culture and cultivated by some politicians interested in continued socio-political tensions. For others, it is a natural dominant idea of Muslim society, something that determines material and spiritual life.

All this has a direct bearing on the situation in the emergent states of Central Asia- Kazakhstan, Kyrgyzstan, Tajikistan, Uzbekistan and Turkmenistan- for which Islam is one of the factors regulating their internal life and to some extent their external orientations. This circumstance should be neither ignored nor considered an absolute- both extremes are dangerous, especially in making political decisions. Thus, it is especially important to separate the spheres in which Islam's influence is limited from those in which its potential is far from exhausted.

Islam has always been a main factor of the religious and cultural identity of Central Asia, even if this self-identification existed unofficially under the Soviet Government. In the official ideology, religious and national traditions were viewed separately. Today, dual self-identification as Uzbek Muslim, Tajik

Muslim, and so on, has come back with a vengeance, and these terms sound as natural as Arab Muslim or Persian Muslim. In the mid-1990s, 78.8 per cent of the Kazakhs, 95 per cent of the Kyrgyz, and more than 90 per cent of the Uzbeks considered themselves Muslims.

Islam's role as an ethnocultural factor of self-identification is axiomatic, as is its role as one of the regulators of social relations. In the absence of this role, Muslim society loses its fundamental generic characteristics. Islam has always played this role, even under the communists. This is true of the countryside, which has preserved the rules of communal relations that became adapted to the collective-farm system. It is also true of the towns, where the *mahallah* remained the smallest unofficial social unit in which traditions of relationships between people were made sacred by Islam, where people always performed the main religious observances, and where clerics enjoyed prestige and were influential by virtue of their knowledge.

The tremendous importance of Islamic tradition to families is sometimes overlooked in assessing the overall influence of religion on society and the political sphere. This is perhaps a mistake: the conviction is stamped into the mind of the individual from childhood that tradition is of absolute importance and cannot be broken, together with the belief that the right thing for the individual is to follow tradition. The growing individual extends the importance of tradition to family relationships and everyday life, to public and political spheres. We do not speak of tradition as an absolute but rather of its being regarded as one of the appreciable legitimate factors underlying political affairs.

As society evolved, tradition could not remain the sole regulator of public life. Under the Soviet Government a political elite, Europeanized in the Soviet fashion, and a stratum of technocrats emerged. These people, despite a considerable influx of personnel from the rural regions, comprise the 'first echelon' and the present day elite. However, neither group has ever broken the cultural and generic link to tradition. Most of these people are characterized by a 'double standard' of conscience and thinking. Under different circumstances a politician or public figure can be an equally sincere European and orthodox Muslim. (This seems to be a fundamental difference between the Muslim politicians of Central Asia and their Russian counterparts: Uzbek President Islam Karimov looks more natural on the prayer rug in a mosque than Boris Yeltsin, taper in hand, in a church.)

The distribution of political and social roles between families, clans, tribes and regional groups in Central Asia still relies strongly on tradition. Notably, all the medium and top ranks of the administrative hierarchy are taken by persons originally from families and clans traditionally connected with religious cult. In particular, those having influence among members of the Tajik and Uzbek nomenklatura are Fergana *khojas* who are lineal descendants of the 'rightly guided' caliphs (the four caliphs who ruled after the Prophet's death in the 7th century AD). The continued existence in the region of the Sufi Brotherhoods (orders) merits separate mention, especially the biggest of them, the Naqshbandiyyah, whose members have great prestige and influence on decision making in secular spheres.

Remaining one of the regulators of social relations, Islam is inevitably a factor in political life. Drawing on the historical experience of Christianity, and secularized Western societies, many experts find this unnatural. The desire to see a strictly religious cult aspect in Islam is also characteristic of the proportion of the Muslim clergy who are under the patronage of the authorities and fear that they may lose their influence in the event of Islam's politicization. Nevertheless, the fusion of religion and politics is inherent in Islamic civilization, and Islam lacks the division into things religious and secular that is typical of Christian societies. Islam is a 'total' religion, in the sense that it covers all the aspects of social existence and incorporates its own regulating precepts. The *Shari'ah*- a code of laws grounded in divine revelations and holy books, laws that regulate the life of the individual and society- is unique to Islam. History indicates that the tendency to build an Islamic state has existed in Muslim societies at various stages of their development. Rooted in Islamic values and ideas, economic and political programmes and activities intended to bring them into effect are an inalienable part of the sociopolitical life of the entire Muslim world. Central Asia is hardly an exception.

Alongside the general reasons rooted in the special nature of Muslim civilization there are concrete short-term reasons for the strengthening of the Islamic factor- the state of society, the objectives and tasks of some political forces or other, and so on.

Every political group, be it the establishment or the opposition, is guided by its own egoistic considerations. They are all active in a social and cultural environment which has to some extent been prepared to accommodate Islam in politics, and which is sensitive to Islamic slogans. At the same time, Muslim society is not homogenous. The predisposition to Islamic motives in politics varies according to social affiliation, occupation, gender and age. Sociological studies of views of Islam and how far it is a political factor have been conducted in all Central Asian countries except perhaps Turkmenistan, where this sort of survey is rather difficult to conduct because of the extremely tough regime, even by the standards of the region. Studies reveal recognition of the steady growth in the role of Islam in the public and political affairs of the countries and that fears are being voiced in this connection. For example, 86 per cent of the population in Kyrgyzstan polled in the mid-1990s was sure that Islam's role in public affairs would grow, and more than 50 per cent of Uzbeks believed that 'Islam alone is the solution to Uzbekistan's many problems'.

The social reasons for politicizing Islam lie in the general crisis of the system, the difficulties of economic rebuilding of society and the lowering of the status of entire social strata- this leads to persistent disaffection among the people and spurs them to look for a way out of the current situation via the authentic ethnic and religious values that were lost in the Soviet era and have not been reconstructed in the post-Soviet period. We speak of a search for an 'Islamic alternative'. While this seems to be a Utopia, more and more people from many different sectors of society are turning to it.

This tendency is based on the desire to restore social justice backed by strong authoritarian rule and directly connected with direct appeals to the 'genuine' Islamic tradition of the Prophet's era in which, Muslims believe, social justice and strong religious and political authorities are inseparable.

The turning to Islam by the establishment has a complex and controversial character. On the one hand, all the Central Asian states are secular in accordance with their constitutions. Religion is separated from politics. In response to a question on whether Uzbekistan corresponds to 'the standards of the Muslim world', its president, Islam Karimov said a categorical 'no': 'We are out of keeping with the Muslim standards because we are a secular state.' Turkmenistan's head Saparmurat Niyazov thought along the same lines: 'We have firmly proclaimed the principle that Turkmenistan is a secular state. . . . We have no grounds to think that someone intends to change this principle'. The Resolution approved by the conference of religious figures of Turkmenistan in 1994 speaks of the 'inadmissibility of interference of religion in organizational and state affairs'.

As Kazakh researcher Alma Sultangaliyeva rightly observed, 'practically none of the countries have avoided registering a special attitude to Islam on the part of the official authorities, including the top-level people of the states.' There are three circumstances that impel the ruling elite to turn to Islam.

First, the desire to press religion into service to consolidate the indigenous Muslim peoples and simultaneously use it as a source of a national ideology. This is more characteristic of Tajikistan, Uzbekistan and Turkmenistan where, it should be noted, the size of the non-Muslim population has sharply and steadily declined. The use of Islam in the official ideology is virtually ruled out in Kazakhstan and Kyrgyzstan. In Kazakhstan the Russian-speaking community is almost as numerous as the Kazakh ethnic group, and the cosmopolitanism and pro-western views of the local top people led by Askar Akayev in Kyrgyzstan are well known.

Second, the ruling elite is trying to seize the initiative of using Islam from their opponents, whose increasing criticism of the authorities stems precisely from religious positions. The ruling quarters of Uzbekistan are making the greatest efforts in this regard because the religious movement there is gaining more influence. The desire to monopolize Islam in the early 1990s emerged as one of the main tendencies in the development of the internal Tajik conflict, during the course of which the Islamic opposition succeeded in getting seats in the government and become a legitimate part of the establishment. It can be assumed that the ruling quarters of Kyrgyzstan and, to a lesser degree, those of Kazakhstan, are getting gradually involved in the 'struggle for Islam'.

A characteristic sign that Islam is being used for political ends is the establishment of state control over the activities of the Muslim clergy. Authorities meddle in the appointment of *imams* and *mullahs* and try to 'edit' their sermons. The conformist part of the clergy is paid salary by the state. One of the tried and tested methods in this regard is the creation of institutions under state patronage, such as those founded in Turkmenistan in 1994, the Gengeshi (council) for Religious Affairs under the country's president; the Interdepartmental Council for Religious Affairs founded in Kyrgyzstan in 1997; and the Council for Religious Affairs in Kazakhstan.

Third, the authorities turn to Islam in order to firm up their prestige in the Muslim world. Contacts between the former Soviet republics and Muslims in other countries have appreciably strengthened in the past decade. The Central Asian leaders are constantly obliged to refer to their shared religious identity and sometimes to demonstrate, albeit in a specific form, adherence to the idea of Islamic solidarity. (This subject arose in April-May 1999 in connection with the conflict in Yugoslavia during the course of which Uzbekistan and Turkmenistan went on record to say that, unlike Russia, they shared the cause of the Muslims in Kosovo.) The Central Asian countries, members of the influential Islamic Conference, are trying to get financial assistance from the Islamic Development Bank, and so on. Another significant fact is that, without exception, all the presidents of the Central Asian states have been on the pilgrimage (the *hajj*) to the holy cities of Mecca and Medina, which every Muslim must make.

Such appeals to Islam by Central Asian politicians are a

way to flaunt their independence from Russia. Former Turkestan is returning on the historical landscape from which it was plucked in Soviet times.

At the same time, this departure is by no means always a sure sign of worsening interstate relations. Paradoxically, under certain circumstances the Islamic factor can promote closer relations between Russia and Central Asia, for example, in the case of the threat of Islamic radicalism spilling over from neighbouring Afghanistan, and Uzbekistan's and Tajikistan's fears in 1996 of Taliban expansion. The 1998 joint statement by the Russian and Uzbek presidents referred to the 'explosive situation' in Afghanistan and said that 'further escalation of tension in that country fraught with the spread of religious extremism and terrorism, the growing arms and drug smuggling, refugee exodus threaten the national interests and security of the states in the region'.

At that time this view was shared by the other presidents of the Central Asian republics with the exception of Turkmen leader Niyazov, who hoped for normal relations with the Taliban movement and to be able to act as mediator in the internal Afghan conflict.

People in the region seem less afraid of Afghan Taliban campaigns of conquest than of their successes in setting an example to local Islamists and spurring them into more resolute action.

We can assume that Central Asian states have an axe to grind in cooperation with Muslims in other countries, or we can interpret this primarily as a diplomatic game or, on the contrary, as a sincere desire for cooperation. At any rate, Central Asia identifies itself with the Muslim world which, for its part, recognizes Central Asia as its component part.

Whereas for the ruling circles turning to Islam is probably tactical in character, the Islamic factor is decisive for some parts of the opposition. These groups openly state that the above-mentioned 'Islamic alternative' is the only possible solution if the present situation in society is to be radically improved. This opposition is variously described as fundamentalism,

Islamism, extremism or 'Wahhabism'. Analysing the overall Islamic movement (not in Central Asia alone) shows clearly what is behind these terms. Fundamentalism implies attitudes that idealize the 'golden age of Islam' and an ideology that gives reasons to believe in the inevitability and need of going back to the past, restoring values and rules of social and personal behaviour on the basis of the *Shari'ah,* which in the final analysis is only possible in an Islamic state. Nevertheless, a life-long fundamentalist can be simultaneously a law-abiding citizen who does not participate in any political activities.

Islamism is political action that aims to establish an Islamic state, that is, to achieve the main goal of the fundamentalist ideology. Are fundamentalism and Islamism present in society and on the political stage of Central Asia? They are, beyond any doubt. Their followers are shaping a trend in public opinion and are fully fledged participants in the political process. It is useless and even dangerous to try to ignore this fact and even more so to fight fundamentalism and Islamism as a sociopolitical and ideological phenomenon. We know from the experience of Muslim countries- Algeria, Turkey, Sudan, Egypt, Indonesia and others- that persecutions of political Islam result in the radicalization of its followers and the appearance of extremists. This destabilizes the situation in society and can even lead to civil war, happened in Algeria in the wake of the 1992 attempt by the authorities to destroy the Islamic Salvation Front, the leading opposition force.

The word 'Wahhabism' originated in the 18th-19th centuries and is connected with the name of Muhammad ibn 'Abd al-Wahhab, who conceived the idea of recreating an Islamic state of the Prophet Muhammad times in Arabia. Given the entirely specific nature of his ideology and practices, this can be described as a special case of 'proto-fundamentalism' and 'proto-Islamism'.

Islamism in Central Asian states and regions is of an enclave nature. The extent of the influence of Islamic opposition in society depends on how traditionalist society is, on the opportunities to conduct corresponding propaganda and, finally, on the opposition's ability of self-organization. It is possible to single out three broad stages of Islamist activities during the 1990s. The first stage was at the start of the 1990s, when political Islam was developing in the general context of an Islamic renaissance. It was a time before the disintegration of the USSR, when Islamic political organizations were being created, including republican branches of the All-Union Islamic Renaissance Party (IRP) founded in Astrakhan in 1990. In addition to the local IRP branch in Uzbekistan, there was the Adalat movement, the Islamic Party of Turkestan and the Party of National Freedom, and the Islamic Cultural Centre (leaning toward politics) in Kazakhstan. It proved impossible to found an Islamic organization only in Turkmenistan, and a harsh regime was established almost immediately after the declaration of an independent state.

The majority of the Islamic structures of those times were not fated to become stable political organizations. Some proved no more than educational groups, while others could not establish a strong organizational centre. Still others did not go beyond one-time actions, even if these were rather clamorous. Some organizations disbanded, while others were crushed by the state.

The Islamic Renaissance Party of Tajikistan proved the most successful of all, making it to the government in 1992 and later playing a key role in opposition. The *Adolat* movement, for example, enjoyed great popularity in the Fergana Valley but was finally brought down by President Karimov.

The second period, between 1992 and 1996, led to the impression that Islamists were unable to really compete against the ruling regimes anywhere but Tajikistan. This was actually a lull during which Islamism was restructuring. The breeding ground for Islamism remained, however he worsening economic situation, growing unemployment, general disappointment caused by failed reforms and the renaissance of Islam was only a matter of time.

The beginning of the third period, marking a fresh spiral of Islamist activity, came somewhere between 1996 and 1997. This was a time of success for the United Tajik Opposition (UTO), in which Islamists form the foundation. As a result of a negotiating process, the UTO won a number of key positions in the coalition government. At the same time, in Uzbekistan, the radical organizations 'Warriors of Jihad', 'Hizbollah' and 'Akramiyyah' grew more active. The section of non-conformist clergy was consolidated and many mosques, primarily in the Fergana Valley, became centres of political Islamic opposition. Islamism began to be strengthened in Tashkent. One can endorse the view of reputable journalist Igor Rotar, who believes that Islamists are the 'main competition' to the Uzbek establishment.

(According to other views, Islamism or, to use official Uzbek terminology, Wahhabism, plays no essential role in politics and poses no threat to the regime, whereas the authorities skilfully use it as a bugbear and a pretext for further curtailment of freedoms.)

Be that as it may, Islamists and generally all those who occupy the positions of non-conformist Islam are being systematically harassed. They face criminal trials, many clergymen who crossed over to join the opposition are in prison, and some have vanished without trace. The authorities have closed down several mosques, which they claim had become centres of anti-government propaganda. Furthermore, Oliy Majlis, Uzbekistan's Parliament passed a law in 1998: 'On Freedom of Conscience and Religious Organizations' and on stricter punishments for violating the rules of teaching religious subjects, and for preparing and disseminating materials containing ideas of religious extremism. The regional committees of the authority received lists of questions to help identify 'Wahhabites' or those sharing 'Wahhabite convictions' in the different regions. Item 6 of this document, for example, requires the committees 'to discover residents connected with Wahhabites, determine the composition of their families, who of them are employed, where, or what they do . . . to report sources of their sustenance'.

Political Islam is gradually gaining a foothold in Kyrgyzstan and southern regions of Kazakhstan. In Kyrgyzstan, primarily in the cities of Osh and Dzhalal-Abad, as well as in Batken, a number of Islamist groups were trying to secure official registration with the Justice Ministry. In and around Osh where, according to official figures, there are more than 1000 mosques, there is a perceptible influence of fundamentalist ideology, transmitted mainly by the local Uzbeks and agitators from Tajikistan. In 1996-97 there was a propaganda campaign in the republic for founding an Islamic party.

In Kazakhstan, although the majority of specialists agree that 'the Islamic fundamentalist ideas have so far not become widespread', many factors indicate that the tendency towards political Islam is becoming more and more evident in the south of the country, in Chimkent, Turkestan and other towns and regions. (Interestingly, the Archbishop Aleksiy of Almaty and Semipalatinsk warned the author way back in 1994 of potential danger of Islamic fundamentalism in Kazakhstan.)

The activities of political Islam are hampered by the absence of a single guiding or coordinating centre in individual countries, let alone in Central Asia as a whole. It is also important to note that in order to be successful any Islamic political movement needs authoritative, or better still, charismatic leaders. There is no such leader to be found in Central Asia today, and there is no suitable candidate. This is mainly because the Islamic movements and organizations currently active there are practically national, that is to say, their objectives do not go beyond their own countries, or even regions.

Nevertheless, Islamism in Central Asia is stable and relatively dynamic. Its stan-off with secular authorities has become a regular part of the political scene. It is obvious that the current unwillingness on both sides to reach a compromise could culminate in a conflict.

The importance of the Islamic factor for the sociopolitical affairs of Central Asia is limited, and there are spheres in which it plays no appreciable role. First, it is not a unifying factor for the overall society. The ethnic Russian population accounts for nearly 34 per cent in Kazakhstan, 17 per cent in Kyrgyzstan, 6.5 per cent in Uzbekistan, 8 per cent in Turkmenistan and 4 per cent in Tajikistan. If, in the name of national-state consolidation, the ruling elite starts systematically and intensively to appeal to only one religion, this would not only completely sour its relations with the non-Muslim population but also prove to be yet another irritant for Russia and cause bewilderment abroad, where mixing Islam and politics provokes negative reactions.

Second, Islam is unable to play a consolidating part on the ethnic and national levels. Regional, clan, ethnic and tribal interests nowadays has precedence over adherence to a common religion. For example, the civil war in Tajikistan was between Muslims from various regions and clans. In Kazakhstan, to be a member of the *zhuz* is in practical life incomparably more important than professing Islam. Finally, in the interethnic conflicts in Central Asia, in Fergana in 1989, in Osh in 1990, and so on, those involved were Muslims.

Naturally, as society and especially the ruling elite go back to their traditions the Islamic factor will contribute to a consolidation of society.

Third, Islam is not a factor of organizational development of the state. The Central Asian republics are secular states. The problem of recognizing Islam as the official religion is being debated only in Tajikistan. Religion is separated from the state and it is impossible to speak of the participation by the religious institutions- councils of *'ulama*, *Shari'ah* courts and so on- in state activities. On the other hand, however, legitimization of some *Shari'ah* laws and blending them with secular norms is most likely a matter for the near future. (A similar problem is being debated in Russia's Muslim regions, let alone separatist Chechnya, which has been proclaimed a republic. See the chapter by Leonid Sykiäinen in this volume.)

Fourth, Islam is not a factor of political stabilization. There are two approaches to Islam in society. One reflects the views of the political and Europeanized (mostly Soviet-style) intellectual elite, which confines Islam's role to the religious and cultural sphere and as a regulator of relationships between people in everyday life. The other reflects the view of 're-Islamization' of Central Asian societies has not been completed. Such views are widespread among traditionalist intellectuals, Islamic opposition politicians and a considerable proportion of Muslim clerics who share the views of the former and cooperate with them. Those advocating either approach are so far in opposition to each other, and tensions in society will continue unless both reach a compromise.

Fifth, Islam is not a factor for the mobilization of Central Asian societies for purely secular accomplishments- the creation of modern economy, infrastructure, expansion of agriculture, etc. as compared with Algeria, Libya, Iran and many other Muslim states in which Islamic rhetoric was widely used to interpret their economic and social strategies. Many people know that Algeria's President Houari Boumedienne (1965-78) proposed that economic reform be seen in the context of 'big *jihad*', or activities directed at improving the position of the Muslim community. The five-year economic development plan drafted in the 1960s opened the *b-ism il-lah*, 'in the name of God' prayer formula. No Central Asian state has a similar interpretation of economic development, and it is impossible in the lifetime of the current elite.

Sixth, appeals to Islam do not promote consolidation between states in the region. The elite discuss the religious communality of Central Asian states on extremely rare occasions, and the subject practically never arises in foreign affairs.

Despite its limited role, the Islamic factor is a social and political reality in Central Asia which cannot be denied today. Its importance varies from country to country. Islam is constantly influencing the sociopolitical processes, shaping the concepts of values and regulating relations between people. Islam is undoubtedly a political tool, whose role will grow to probably intensify the struggle between the various parties and groups, primarily between the regimes and oppositions.

On the other hand, there are influential forces in Central Asia which insist on abridging the role of religion and taking it out of the sphere of politics. The best solution to this dichotomy is to reach a compromise between things purely secular and Islamic, in the absence of which the worsening of social, interethnic and religious conflicts will constantly threaten Central Asian societies.

ISLAMIC RESURGENCE ON THE BELIEF SYSTEM OF RURAL MALAYS

THE OVERT PICTURE

A foreigner paying a visit to a Malay village may notice certain recurrent features in the manner and topic of conversation introduced by the villager towards the foreigner. One of these is the recurrent emphasis on their Islamic identity and adherence, with regards to both belief and practice. This is not unexpected, if we consider the pressure and movement towards Islamic orthodoxy experienced by the Malay population in recent decades. No doubt, there has been a noticeable consciousness-rising among the Malays in this period towards searching for the true Islam and cleansing their culture of non-Islamic elements. This process has been accompanied by a genuine drive to become better Muslims, as the religious identity of the Malays is of paramount importance. Traces of this resurgence seem to be found in the behaviour and attitude of people living in even the remotest villages of the peninsula. Nevertheless, in order to complete the picture of the religious beliefs of the Malays, it is necessary to go beyond the overt picture facing the newcomer which is carefully presented to her by the village population.

This paper will examine the impact of this latest wave of Islamic resurgence on the religious beliefs of the Malays. In the course of the discussion it will also be necessary to question what belief is, and to point out that it is not necessarily equivalent with what Giddens denotes as 'discursive consciousness' (1984: 41-45, 374-375).

ISLAMIC RELIGION VERSUS TRADITION

As a theoretical point of departure, a distinction should be made between great or formal religions, and informal traditions. While formal religions are based on scriptures and possibly claim to have universal applications (sometimes be missioning), smaller religions refer to polytheistic/animistic belief systems belonging to local oral traditions. I will reserve the term 'religion' for the former, and tradition or extra-religious beliefs for the latter. This dicotomy is much akin to Robert Redfield's twin concepts great and little traditions (1958: 70).

Extra-religious beliefs often exist prior to formal religions. As the latter are introduced to a region, they partly replace the existing beliefs. Such a replacement is quite often the explicit aim of those adhering to the new religion, which therefore brings it forward through a variety of means. But the notion of extra-religious belief as used here also includes liberal interpretations of the religion itself, as when Christian elements such as Bibles and crosses are used for divinational purposes, or when the prophet Mohammad is used for propitiation. Such a body of *folk magic* seems in fact to accompany the history of the monotheistic religions (Weber 1968: 415-416; Hurgronje 1906: 33).

Whatever the official religion of a people is, if any, the fact remains that the total belief system tends at local level to be a mixture of the elements of formal religion as well as of other elements: what is commonly known as syncretism. Although these domains cannot always be clearly separated in practice, it may sometimes be useful to do so for analytical purposes, so as to determine the identity they provide, the area of ritual practice they pertain to, their internal logical and power of explanation, and even their psychological and social functions.

In times of revivalism of the official religion, however, a strengthening of it seems to occur both through the search for correct interpretations of dogma and in proper religious behaviour. The position of the traditional or folk elements is, on the other hand, weakened, as they are sought eliminated by the forces calling for more orthodoxy among the religious adherents.

I agree with the idea of the relative displacement of the two 'systems' or areas of belief, i.e. that one are strengthened at the expense of the other. However, this picture needs refinement. My contention is that the extra-Islamic belief elements are not simply eliminated as to a matter of degree, but are partly also relegated to a somewhat different and perhaps less visible area than before.

My argument will be drawn from a case study of Malay fishermen and their belief system. The focus will be on the relative change during the last two-three decades in the position of their official religion, Islam, in comparison to the local tradition. This period has in Malaysia been dominated by a revival of orthodox Islam, known as as the Islamic Resurgence (Chandra Muzaffar 1987: 1-12). The following analysis therefore pertains to a particular setting, where the official religion is Islam, in a country where the historical, political and ethnical conditions create a unique situation compared to the religious revivalism of other syncretic religions. There are reasons to believe, however, that the basic structure of the emerging pattern is not qualitatively unique. It may be found as a covert reality in other societies where certain basic conditions for maintaining extra-religious elements of belief and magic exist, in spite of pressure to the contrary.

THE STATUS AND IMPACT OF ISLAM IN MALAYSIA

Let us first examine certain features characteristic of the social situation in Malaysia. This country is highly multiethnic, with the Malays (48.6%), Chinese (31.7%) and Indians (8.4%) constituting the three biggest groups respectively (Population 1983: 17). The Chinese community as a whole is considered to be economically superior, while the Malays hold the political power in the country. The great bulk of the Chinese and Indians are descendants of people who arrived in Malaysia at the end of the last or at the beginning of this century, i.e. during British colonial rule. The Malays, on the other hand, are together with some smaller minority groups defined as native to the region and have been given the special status of *bumiputra*. This category, which constitutes slightly more than half the population, is assigned certain economic and other privileges in order to redress the economic imbalance between the ethnic groups of the country.

Islam is the official state religion, although all have the constitutional right of freedom of profession and practice of their own religion. Although 53% of the population is Muslim, the Islamic religion is closely identified with the Malay community. Virtually all Malays are Muslims, and in local speech being Malay and becoming Malay are synonymous with being a Muslim and converting to Islam.

Religions, and also more traditional beliefs, seem universally to meet certain needs. Among other things, they provide their adherents with an identity, accompanied by moral guidelines for behaviour; explanations; and security and comfort, through the prescription of a normative set of rules for behaviour and through postulating a fair system of rewards and punishments.

This is also the case with the Islamic religion, and the meaning it holds for the Malays. In this special case, the meaning of the religion must be seen in the light of the ethnic situation in the country. The economic prosperity of other ethnic groups is now and then explained as the result of their adherence to religious traditions of a morality inferior to Islam. In other words, many Malays see the prosperity of others as obtained partly by the use of immoral techniques. The religious identity of the Malays is therefore much coloured by their identity vis-à-vis other ethnic groups in their country, and thus a linkage between religious and ethnic identity is enforced. Although a call for religious orthodoxy is found all over the Islamic world today, the directions of the movement differs form country to country. Muzaffar says that while the resurgence in, for instance, Indonesia deals with economic issues like poverty and exploitation, in Malaysia the movement seems to be more concerned with identity (Chandra Muzaffar 1986: 6-7). This fact is of crucial importance for understanding the local contents and direction of the Islamic revivalism in Malaysia today. The ethnic dimension will strengthen the identity aspect of the religion and influence how it is communicated and emphasized both outwards in society, but also inwards towards one's own self.

BELIEF AND PRACTICE AMONG RURAL MALAYS

THE TRADITIONAL WORLD VIEW

The traditional world view among the Malays is based on what is commonly referred to as animism. Various elements in nature have an immanent force called *semangat*, and this force can under certain instances decrease so that the host is weakened. In addition to the *semangat*, there exists a range of spirits in the surroundings, many of which are invisible. These spirits sometimes affect the lives of human beings. But human beings can also intentionally seek to influence or manipulate both forces and spirits in order to achieve a desired result. Such magic can be both black and white, i.e. intended to harm other people or not.

The description that follows is based on the particular case study of the fishermen of Pulau Tuba, Langkawi. This is a small island community of 1,300 people, virtually all Malays although some of the land is owned by Chinese. The economy is directly or indirectly based on small-scale fisheries, supplemented by wet-rice farming, horticulture and the collection and utilization of jungle products as well as coastal resources (especially shellfish). In portraying their traditional world view, the emphasis will be on the role of spirits and forces in the context of economic activities.

It is difficult to present a brief and general account because of the seemingly disparities of views regarding the spirit world that exist between people. In addition, the same persons seem to express different and mutually incompatible beliefs in different contexts, without this seeming to cause much disturbance among the holders of the beliefs themselves. Not even when these discrepancies are pointed out to them, for instance by the field-worker eagerly searching out a logical system in their beliefs, does this seem to puzzle people. Pointing out that the belief element expressed is contrary to Islam will, however, spur a reaction and feeling of discomfort among the fishermen, but only because of its un-Islamic connotations.

This said, it is generally believed that there is one spirit associated with the land and one with the sea, but each of these spirits may have many appearances and sometimes divide into separate entities each with significant attributes. Both the land and the sea spirit seem to have human qualities, but again these two apparitions are generally thought to be identical with *Syaitan,* or Satan. Thus the various spirits are in the end linked to an Islamic concept. Although the interaction between people and spirits can potentially be of many kinds, the most important issue is to appease the latter in order to avoid their displeasure and mischief. This is because most economic activities take place somewhere in nature, on land or at sea, and people therefore intrude into the domain of the spirits. Thus people resort to magic rituals where incantations play a prominent part.

As all the objects and matters are believed to contain *semangat*, so also are the means of production. Thus the fishermen's boats, nets for catching fish as well as birds, bird flutes, etc., are believed to have this vital force whose assistance, or at least co-operation or good-will, should be sought. And attempts should be made to control the *semangat*, or rather "soul" of the animals involved in the economic activity. The fish and the bird must be attracted towards the fisherman or hunter and lured into his net, or insects and rodents damaging a rice field or honey bees in their hives must be driven away in order to secure the products. Again rituals with incantations are used.

Even if the use of magic is not acknowledged by the sources of Islam, this does not prevent elements of the Islamic religion from being separated from their original contexts and used for the purpose of magical rituals. Sometimes Islamic prophets, and other persons associated with the history of Islam, are appealed to in rituals through the use of incantations. Throughout history these beings have become associated with various objects or parts of nature which are pertinent as means of production to the fisherman. Thus Noah is the prophet of the boat, Solomon of the net and Khir of the sea. By seeking their cooperation, the outcome of an expedition at sea is more likely to succeed. The reference to Islam creates a sense of legitimacy in the use of magic.

It is further believed that some of these beings (spirits, prophets, Satan) can be manipulated to cause harm to other people, that is to prevent a big catch for another fisherman or hunter, or to cause him other harm such as illness. Bad luck at sea, especially in comparison to others fishing close by in the same waters, like repeatedly getting roots and branches from trees into the net, may understandably result in suspicion of such black magic.

A prominent feature of the traditional world view on this group of islands must finally be mentioned. That is the phenomenon of something being *keramat*, or 'sacred'. On Tuba, there are a number of assumed graves which are considered sacred. One of them has been identified as belonging to Tok Bagus, the first person to clear land on the island and therefore considered to be the ancestor of most people living there. He is considered to protect the community. It is generally believed that some of the deceased have certain powers, and thus can help the people of the community in various ways, among others in securing the economic outcome. Special rituals can be performed in order to contact their souls and ask for their assistance, usually at the graves. Such rituals commonly involve sacrifices.

THE IMPACT OF THE ISLAMIC RESURGENCE

But according to orthodox Islam, most of these beliefs, and especially the ritual practices, are heresy. There is only one, undivided god. Adherents of the religion should believe in, worship and pray to him only, and not via prophets, for instance. It is true that Islam postulates the existence of certain supernatural beings such as *Jin, Syaitan* (Satan) and *malaikat* (angels). But the character of the spirits in Malay tradition clearly shows their origin in Hindu, Buddhist and other pre-Islamic religions or traditions. And in any case one should not seek to manipulate them in a fashion not prescribed by Islam. The *imam* of Tuba explained that people could protect themselves against such spirits, but not actively seek their help in order to achieve certain ends, disregarding the purpose. The Islamic personal prayer, *do'a,* is the only means by which human beings should put forward their requests.

The interesting point is that at a certain level of consciousness most people in the community are aware of this. There is discernible evidence of the work of propagators in recent last decades who have been calling for a return to orthodox Islam in Malaysia. Many Tubans will emphasize in their conversations with people outside their community that previously, or in the olden days, they were traditional and did not know better. But today they are modern and aware of the right doctrine. During my stay in the island community such utterances were regularly heard among people eager to present themselves in a favourable light to the outside world. Sometimes my inquiry into traditional beliefs would spark off such a reaction. It is interesting to note that the various people I chatted with would use much the same examples and modes of expression when pointing to their current beliefs and practices, seen against the mistaken previous practices conducted by them or their ancestors. Thus upon careful inquiry into the kinds of skills that could be found among the islanders regarding ritual observations or spirit propitiations, most people would deny that such existed. Or they would add that previously people might have had such knowledge, but now they pray to God only (*sembahayang kepada Tuhan sahaja*), pointing upwards while saying the last words. This act I observed several times. Some people would also go to the point of listing some of their traditional ways of being un-Islamic and therefore wrong.

One such institution was the tradition of *bersanding*, which is the climax of the wedding ritual. The bride and the bridegroom are made to sit on a dais for some minutes with the guests as cheering on-lookers. The couple should try to remain seemingly unmoved during the act, staring in front of them with their hands placed in their laps. This ritual is derived from court traditions and is clearly of Hindu origin. The overt intention of the ritual is to protect the newly-weds from forces in the environment and to strengthen their *semangat*. But the ritual is today more a hallmark of Malay tradition as such and therefore felt to be a necessary part of a "proper" wedding.

The *bersanding* thus signifies various dimensions to the Malays. It is thought to be traditional and therefore a hallmark of Malay identity. But the ritual is nevertheless associated with un-Islamic propitiation of spirits, and therefore improper for true Moslems and therefore Malays. And thirdly, one can speculate that the Hindu origin of the ritual associates it with traditions belonging to another ethnic group present in the Malaysian society, and therefore to an identity Malays are eager to delimit themselves from.

The two concepts 'modern' (*moden*) and 'traditional' (*tradisi*) therefore carry special connotations among the Malays. To be modern is the opposite of being backward and unenlightened, labels the Malays seem to fear and be touchy about. To have knowledge of the tenets of orthodox Islam is considered enlightened, and therefore modern. 'Traditional' can therefore also be seen as the opposite of 'modern' and in this sense carries a negative significance. Thus 'traditional' can be charged with both positive and negative connotations.

Returning to the similarities in how people respond to the mentioning of spirit belief and the use of magic, we can detect the work of people belonging to what is commonly known as the *dakwah* movement. The term *dakwah* is derived from the Arabic word *da'a,* which means to call or to invite, that is with reference to the obligation of all Moslems to try to bring negligent followers of the faith back to the right doctrine as well as to convert non-believers to the faith.

In the Malaysian context *dakwah* relates in everyday speech first and foremost to the work of certain Islamic organizations or movements (Nagata 1984: 81-83). The members and followers of this *dakwah* movement advocate a more pious life-style and correct interpretation of the Holy Scriptures among people. Through home visits, distribution of pamphlets, etc., village people come into contact with their ideas. But the *dakwah* movement has also put pressure on the village people to observe the teachings of the Qur'an in indirect ways: through its impact on the religious authorities, the mass media, the religious teachers and the educated children of the villagers.

It should be noted, though, that Islam is disseminated to the Malays from the moment they are born. Not only are they reminded of their religious identity through the observance of and participation in practical conduct like prayers, food restrictions, greetings and the use of such outward signs as clothing and wall decorations with Islamic texts, but the children are from an early age taught religion in organized groups and classes, both in school as well as in private fora. Later in life people can seek religious instruction from knowledgeable people in the village, from religious programmes on radio and televison, and from the *dakwah* missionaries visiting the home.

Thus at all stages of life the heresy of traditional beliefs and practices is pointed out to people. And it was obvious that certain formulations and examples were pointed out. The *bersanding* ritual is a case-in-point. People would inform through much the same wordings that the performance of this ritual had ceased among the Malays or within the close family only because it was Hindu and did not follow Islam. In practice, however, all the weddings on Tuba included the *bersanding* as a public ritual. Whether the scale and extent of the ritual had diminshed throughout the years, I am not able to judge. But on a discursive level (see Giddens 1984), *bersanding* has become an important hallmark of being "un-Islamic", although the symbolic significance of the ritual is not unambiguous and points to the dual connotation of tradition.

Another practice which was frequently pointed out by the fishermen of Tuba as an example of heresy was the ritual feast of *puja pantai*, or offerings on the beach to the sea spirit. This ritual was previously held annually in order to appease this spirit, who was otherwise inclined to damage the fishing gear or afflict the fishermen with illnesses when at sea. This feast, which is known from various fishing communities in Malaysia, has been banned by the religious authorities in the past couple of decades. It was pointed out to people that the image of the spirit had been identified as pre-Islamic, and propitiations of spirits are in any case wrong. It is interesting to note that some people, who quickly pointed out this ritual as an example of backward or heretic behaviour which has now disappeared due to the enlightenment of modern Malays, would state the public dancing in connection with the feast and the resulting contact between the sexes as the undesirable element seen from Islam's point of view when asked to explain why. People, and sometimes also religious officials, were therefore quite certain that this ritual was wrong according to orthodox Islam, but gave various answers as to why.

INDIVIDUALIZATION AND PRIVITIZATION

Thus, as a result of the Islamic resurgence and the work of the *dakwah* movement, some changes have occurred in the significance of traditional spirit beliefs and use of magic during the past two or three decades. The traditional rituals can be said to have diminished along two dimensions. First, they have become individualized. From communal offerings on behalf of the whole community they have been reduced to the individual propitiations of spirits on behalf of one person or household. Previously people in the community would join forces to organize rituals of which the purpose would be in the interests of all. The colourful event of *puja pantai* has already been mentioned. This would gather lots of people on the beach and include a communal meal. Although the offerings were performed by ritual specialists, the intention was to safeguard the expeditions of all fishermen casting their nets in the nearby waters, as well as other villagers travelling across the sea.

Similar communal rituals were previously held if the village was plagued by outbreaks of epidemics and pestilence. In this case the guarding spirit of the village was appealed to. This spirit would be identical with the *keramat* of the founding father of the village, Tok Bagus. A public ceremony was performed involving the ritual slaughtering of an animal and offerings given to the spirit. This would act as protection for the village as a whole.

Secondly, the magic rituals have been privatized. Public rituals with a big audience are hardly ever found any more. Magic is executed mostly by a person alone and partly out of sight of others. A discontented fisherman may seek the assistance of a traditional ritual specialist in order to identify and then satisfy the mischievious spirit who is believed to have been at work. The specialist will most probably quietly perform rituals to the special sea spirit without the surrounding people being notified. Or sometimes it is believed that the trouble at sea stems from the weakened *semangat* of the fishing boat. It can then be brought ashore and its vital power strengthened. Such rituals are sometimes also performed before a new boat is launched. Some fishermen will themselves make discrete petitions to the Prophet Khir before leaving the house and in the morning and going to sea in order to ensure a safe and bountiful expedition. The most common use of magic is not an active attempt to influence an agent towards something, but to protect oneself from it through the observances of taboos or prohibitions, like not wearing shoes on board boats. Traditional rituals are therefore relegated to a much more private domain than previously.

As we shall see, individualization and privatization make the traditional magic less visible and unnoticeable. To the degree it still exists, it does not lend itself to much reflection by the people. The foreigner making a casual visit to the community will think the local Muslims are rid of such exotic spirit beliefs. She may not be able to spot any traces of magic being performed, and people normally deny its practice. Of course spirit beliefs are generally not discussed due to their association with heresy and backwardness, and because they relate to unknown and possibly dangerous forces. These are, however, not the exhaustive reasons for rejecting their existence. The villagers themselves are today mostly unaware of the place of their tradition on a conscious and discursive level and genuinely believe when bringing the matter forward that its occurrence is little more than folkloristic relics of the past. Some people are, of course, minimally involved in the performance of personal rituals. Others, even if they do employ ritual specialists, may, due to the small scale and discrete performance, not ponder about what they are doing and identify this with heresy. They remember the concrete acts and formulations presented to them by religious teachers and missionaries, but are genuinely unaware of the presence of such traditional elements in their everyday lives.

THE QUESTIONS OF WHY AND HOW

My contention is that these remnants of traditional elements are not mere leftovers from pre-Islamic times. They continue to exist in spite of pressure to the contrary precisely because people employ them in order to meet certain cognitive *needs* in their present lives. People continue to believe, at least periodically and to a certain degree, in the existence of forces and spirits with intrinsic power, and in people's ability to influence these agents in a desired direction. Some people also apply magic themselves, or employ traditional ritual specialists to do so.

Islam, the religion, and the traditional beliefs, have the dual qualities of offering comfort, especially in times of uncertainty, and of explaining why events happen the way they do. The qualities found in the religion and those found in the tradition do not, however, overlap. Islam provides explanations of events as the result of Allah's will, the promise of a fair judgement and possible reward in the afterlife. The traditional beliefs provide an explanation and the possibility of interaction with and manipulation of spirits in the surroundings. The latter area of beliefs differs from the religion in offering a multitude of possible explanations and, not least, potential for manipulation. In Islam there is only one almighty agent whose will is absolute and unambigious, although it may be unintelligible to ordinary mortals. People may end their daily prayers with personal petitions to the Lord, but accept that whatever happens is according to his will. Not so within the area of traditional beliefs. We here encounter a multitude of spirits and forces in a variety of apparitions.

The hapless fisherman who has met with misfortune may look around for explanations. He may have prayed to God for a safe and bountiful journey at sea, but is not able to settle with the thought that the outcome should be accepted as God's will and that any rewards will not come until later. Such an idea is hard to accept if bad luck continues for longer periods. This is when the fishermen of Tuba turn to magic. In the area of traditional beliefs one can attempt to identify the cause of misfortune by trying out one spirit after the other as a causing agent. This provides the fisherman with seemingly more control, as he can continue searching without having to accept the situation as something final. Moreover, he is not left to perform a silent personal prayer, as to God, but can seek to influence the spirits through active manipulation. The explanations and manipulations are more down to earth, causal and pertain to notions of being capable of something as tangible as mastering a technique. The concept of magic may therefore bestow on the believer a sense of being in control.

Instead of describing the two cosmological areas as pantheons with spirits belonging to separate domains, it seems perhaps more reasonable to render them as constituting different logical domains. The Malay fisherman always carries with him the belief, or at least notion, of the almighty Allah and accepts the idea that certain other non-human forces are present in the environment, which is not contrary to the Holy Scriptures. What separates the "approaches" to the spirit world is the *nature* of the interaction between man and the members of the supernatural realm.

The extra-Islamic elements, i.e. the manipulation of forces, spirits and prophets for concrete ends, and the orthodox Islamic doctrine, therefore seem to play partly different roles in the lives of people and to appear in partly separate contexts. Despite their being logically speaking contradictory, this does, however, not result in much mental conflict. This is due to the existence of certain qualities or "mechanisms" inherent in the traditional belief system.

PARTICULARISTIC AND CONTEXTUAL NATURE

One major characteristic of the traditional beliefs on Tuba is the dispersed manner in which they appear. Along with the average villager, I came to hear about spirits and their misdeeds through fractional and 'incomplete' stories told at intimate gatherings. Often the assumed behaviour of the spirits, as well as people's reaction to them, were only hinted at in such a way that each person listening could interpret it in her or his own fashion.

The general nature of the spirit world was seldom discussed. The spirits were usually referred to in practical situations, when attempting to avoid their mischief or when discussing the misfortune of a villager. Thus, the traditional beliefs are normally only activated in specific contexts, and not on an abstract level. They hardly form a system in which the elements are assigned a fixed and unambiguous place in relation to each other.

The traditional world view of the Malays is therefore seemingly characterized by being expressed, used and learned in 'bits and pieces.' Ordinary villagers acquire the knowledge of traditional beliefs from childhood on by a process of deduction from their informal exposure to stories about spirits, and to incidents assumed to be the work of spirits. Islam, on the other hand, is as mentioned taught to children- and sometimes adults- in a range of fora. The child is also taught religious norms in practical situations, which can be accompanied by an explanation that this is according to religion. While the suspected work of spirits is mostly hinted at, religious explanations are on the contrary stressed: people seem to experience a certain relief if they can ascribe their own behaviour to being in accordance with the moral norms of Islam, and they will tend to make a point of this to others.

The "visible" qualities of the Islamic religion enable it to stand out as the religion, well defined towards other religions and belief systems with which the Tubans do not identify. It is associated with the mosque, the imam, the Qur'an, the wearing of special clothes, verbal expressions and other markers of identity. The people in the island community thus identify strongly with Islam as their religion vis-à-vis other formal religions.

INDIVIDUALIZED NATURE

It was stated above that the propitiation of spirits associated with economic ventures has become more privatized and individualized. It is carried out by the interested party alone, or by a ritual specialist employed by this party. As a result, the set of knowledge and beliefs held by each person tends to differ. The spirit beliefs not only appear unsystematically and dispersed in the mind of the individual; there are also disparities and inconsistencies between the beliefs held by various people. Due to their hidden nature, they are not systematically compared from person to person. Only in special instances may a person start to learn the acts of a traditional ritual specialist. But such instruction is again transmitted privately between pairs of persons.

Since knowledge is conveyed privately and between two people only, there is no external agency to control and correct the information. And ordinary people are normally none too eager to 'compare notes'- the spirits are basically harmful and should therefore not be mentioned explicitly. The whole matter is possibly best left alone, which of course does not mean that people are indifferent to the work of these unknown forces.

So in comparison to Islam people are not particularly enthusiastic about arriving at an acknowledged, standardized ritual for conduct. The traditional beliefs are not brought to the fore in interaction and communication between people. The result is again a lack of visibility, which would have been a reminder of its existence.

DISTANCING

It can be argued that the majority of villagers in fact have a *passive* relationship with the traditional beliefs. These Tubans sometimes participate in the conversation revolving around spirits and their work. They may inquire carefully about the details of a story, without commenting upon it. If they do involve themselves actively in the conversation, there is a tendency for them to distance themselves from the narratives. They will frequently open their accounts with the expression *'orang cakap...'* or 'people say that...', thus detaching themselves from the story and not committing themselves to testifying to its truth. Or they may clearly state that what they are telling is not their own belief, but according to *kepercayaan disini* or local belief, as opposed to religion. The important thing to note is that following such an objectification of the narratives, people may switch to an emotional statement of what happened to them personally.

When speaking about Islam, the fishermen of Tuba tend to make a point of the fact that Islam is their religion, that they are followers of Islamic practices, that the religion offers the best moral tenets, etc. People describe Islam in unambiguous terms, and express a strong feeling of identity with it. In contrast to the traditional beliefs, the overriding importance of the religion is expressed and perhaps overemphasized. We can speak of a presentation of identity, a process known from, for instance, ethnic situations (see Eidheim 1974: 53). The very fact that Islam is a practical religion, and that it is further embodied in personal and communal rites executed on a regular basis, helps people to internalize a feeling of nearness and belonging to the exclusion of other religions or belief systems.

DIFFUSE CATEGORIES

The last identified "mechanism" relates to a certain diffuseness when referring to traditional beliefs and practices. A peculiarity that struck me when discussing these beliefs was the tendency to avoid stating the clear presence of something. People would instead admit that there was a little bit of of something among them, with referrence to, for instance, *keramat* places or traditional ritual expertise on the island.

A further diffuseness is found in reference to the identity of both spirits and practitioners. It has been mentioned that people tend to use the generic term *hantu* for a range of spirits and forces when asked what they are referring to. Quite often, though, people refrain from using any noun at all, and - if so required- apply pronouns like 'something' or 'it.' People are also reluctant to refer to God directly, as can be expected when touching on the subject of a powerful and respectful image. They will use the term *Tuhan* (Lord) or *Tuhan Allah,* or simply point upwards towards heaven. But generally speaking there is less reluctance to refer to God directly than there is with spirits.

And due to the unity of God, there is no ambiguity in what or whose power or will is referred to.

The religious leader of the community is always referred to and addressed as *Tok Imam* by everybody in the village except his closest relatives. This is therefore a twenty-four-hour title as it is used in non-religious contexts also. The same can in some cases be said about the religious teachers (*ustaz/ustazah*) and those who have made the pilgrimage to Mecca (*haji/hajjah*). This is contrary to the traditional specialists, who are only referred to by their proper name when indiciating particular persons. None of these persons are working as full time specialists, and their fellow villagers are not reminded of their special skills in everyday life.

A series of qualities inherent in popular spirit beliefs, and in the manner in which people relate to them, functions as a mechanism to veil their existence, or at least their significance in the life of the villagers, both from outsiders and not least from the people themselves. The very fact that Islam tends to be far more visible due to its communal and public nature, and that due to the ethnic situation and the Islamic revival people identify strongly with it, result in its overwhelming pervasiveness and predominance in people's minds. With its strict insistence upon monotheism and the unity of God- constantly insisted upon by present-day religious scholars- the idea of the spirit world tends to be relegated to the depth of people's consciousness. Uncomfortable feelings occur whenever specific institutions or actions are explicitly pointed out as heresy, which has clearly been the case time and again for the last 20-30 years. The composition and magnitude of traditional beliefs have therefore changed, but they seem to have settled into a less visible place in the background. From here they are able to provide people with a certain amount of consolation by offering an alternative or supplementary approach to explaining and dealing with their misery in times of distress, when the feeling of impotence and meaninglessness becomes predominant.

For the great majority of Tubans, the spirit world is not a matter for daily concern. In fact, when reminded of it, many people will use the notion of popular beliefs to accentuate their own religious belonging as a contrast to it, thereby dissociating themselves from it. Magical beliefs and practices may then be branded as backward and ridiculed. Still, the fact remains that a general idea of the existence of a variety of unknown forces in the environment is inherited and stored in people's minds. This idea which under most circumstances is no more than a latent reservoir of diffuse knowledge suddenly gains importance and meaning when insecurity, instability and incomprehensibility prevail. Although its significance does not always emerge on a conscious or at least discursive level (or at least not immediately), people are granted a feeling of the presence and power of spirits, and may react accordingly. Thus spirit beliefs still play a lively role in the culture of the fishermen on Tuba.

2

The Islamic Movement in Israel

RAPHAEL ISRAELI

On the eve of the High Holidays in Israel in September 1999, just days after the Sharm al-Sheikh Accord was signed by Israel and the Palestinians to relaunch the peace process between them, two car-bombs exploded in the northern cities of Haifa and Tiberias, injuring innocent passers-by. Within days, the Israeli security authorities had arrested six Israeli Arabs, all affiliated with the northern faction of the Islamic Movement in Israel, who were apparently recruited by Hamas in the West Bank for the purpose of wrecking both the accord and the Jewish holidays.

TENSIONS IN NAZARETH

The radicalization of Muslims in Israel may also be seen in the tensions making headlines in the Arab city of Nazareth in the Galilee. On December 21, 1997, just four days before Christmas, Muslim zealots in Nazareth invaded the plaza at the foot of the Basilica of the Annunciation, the major Christian shrine in the city. They fenced off an area, declared the land to be a holy Muslim endowment (*wakf*), and began to erect a mammoth tent as a provisional mosque prior to the construction of a permanent mosque with a planned 86-meter-tall minaret which would tower above the adjacent Christian shrine. Israeli authorities have sought to resolve the controversy by peaceful means, thus unwittingly consecrating the Muslim claim and complicating the resolution of the issue.

In November 1998, the local elections in Nazareth brought into office a city council dominated by the Islamic movement. The campaign had revolved around the controversy over the mosque, whose supporters won a majority of the vote. In addition, the present mayor, Ramez Jeraysi, is likely to be the last Christian mayor of the city. Jeraysi is a representative of the former communist Hadash party, and the Islamists are, by definition, anti-communist. Furthermore, as a result of thetensions surrounding the mosque, Jeraysi was physically attacked by assailants in mid-October 1999.

Just prior to the attack, the Israeli government approved the construction of a mosque of more modest size at the site, outraging Christians who warned that in response the pope may cancel his visit to Nazareth scheduled for Spring 2000.

In Nazareth, a Christian city during most of its history, the now outnumbered Christians appear to have lost confidence in their ability to maintain their long-standing coexistence with their Muslim neighbors, and many have left the city for neighboring Christian villages or other mixed Israeli cities where they can escape from Muslim hegemony. Others have immigrated from the country altogether, much like the Christians of Lebanon, Bethlehem, and other locations in the Muslim world. This is a sign that the Christian minority living in Israel believes that the Jewish state is either unable or unwilling to protect them any longer, or that the Israeli authorities, themselves menaced by mounting fundamentalist Islam, are more concerned with their own protection than they are with the plight of the Christians.

The trend is clear; Nazareth will soon become a Muslim city. Though it is part of Israel, and the government in Jerusalem still wields some influence through its funding of the local government, major decisions are being made within an intensely Muslim ambiance with regard to the Christian holy places, urban priorities, city planning, and the position of non-Muslims in the community, casting a long shadow on the future of the remaining Christians. Perhaps now that the events of Nazareth, Haifa, and Tiberias have converged to illustrate the dangers that lay ahead, new measures will be required to meet the challenge of the Islamic movement in Israel.

A MILLION MUSLIM ISRAELIS

While the Muslim population within Israel is now approaching one million, it is difficult to gauge the sentiments of this community. Most of its members embrace a quietist attitude toward Israel, enjoying the benefits they draw from their Israeli citizenship, and refraining from overt acts of disloyalty. They are indeed on record as condemning the recent acts of violence by the Islamists, and are wary not to wreck the rather comfortable boat in which they find themselves. However, in contrast to the current misconception that they are "loyal" to their country, one should recall the near-consensus among them that shuns Independence Day celebrations in Israel and terms that day the *nakbah* (disaster). They also side automatically with their Palestinian brethren in any confrontation with Israel, and express a growing desire for practical steps toward autonomy. The quietist majority among Muslims also identifies itself as Palestinian rather than Israeli, and regards itself as a national rather than an ethnic, linguistic, or religious minority in Israel. All of these perceptions and self-perceptions are pregnant with the potential for dissent, unrest, disobedience, and hostility, though they generally do not yet transcend the boundaries of legality.

THE WORLDVIEW OF RADICAL ISLAM

The range of cleavages between the Jewish majority and the Arab minority in Israel is often bridgeable by common language, economic interest, and neighborly relations. But Islamic fundamentalism, which has injected massive doses of Islamic symbolism into the Arab-Israeli dispute, has often lent to it a religio-cultural nature, thus turning it into a qualitatively insoluble dispute. In turn, Muslim fundamentalists in Israel, who would otherwise accept their minority status and adjust to the vagaries of life under a Jewish authority, once imbued with the general mode of thinking of other Muslim radicals, tend also to exacerbate their anti-Israeli rhetoric and attitudes.

The Arabs of Israel, even more than other Muslims who may feel resentment and frustration at their inability to retrieve the Holy Land of the Muslims with Jerusalem at its heart, sense in a more immediate fashion the humiliation of being ruled by an erstwhile *dhimmi* (inferior) people which had itself submitted to Islamic rule, and which had projected a questionable reputation and status in Islamic tradition. As pious Muslims, these Arabs cannot disregard the vehement anti-Israeli arguments advanced by masters of radical Islam all around them.

The Israeli Arabs felt thrust aside by Israeli society, which relegated them to something less than the accepted norms of equality in the country, and they also felt that they were looked upon suspiciously by other Palestinians because they were Israelis. For some, Islamization was the way out, not only in order to escape the margins and set themselves in the center stage, but also to signal to both the Israeli and Palestinian societies which had alienated them that they, together with other Palestinian fundamentalists in the West Bank and Gaza, constitute the core and the vanguard of the future. Indeed, after 1967, Arab Muslims in Israel began inviting renowned Palestinian clerics from those areas to deliver sermons in mosques, schools, and social gatherings. Thus, the ideologies of the Muslim Brothers and the Islamic Liberation Party of old were propagated among Israeli Arabs. Conversely, Israeli Muslims who attended Islamic institutions of higher learning in the territories went back to their communities in Israel imbued with the new Islamic revivalist spirit. These processes had an immediate impact on the Muslims in Israel: a massive return to Islam among the young in tandem with a similar trend in the West Bank and Gaza.

The Islamic movement among the Muslims in Israel has grown by leaps and bounds since the 1980s, and has by now imposed its presence not only culturally but also politically, both in intra-Arab and in Israeli national politics. Prior to the local elections of November 1998, the Islamic movement split between the southern faction headed by Sheikh Abdallah Darwish, the founder of the movement, who has opted for joining Israeli national politics, and the more radical northern faction led by Sheikh Ra'id Salah, the Mayor of Umm al-Fahm, who has chosen the course of isolating his constituents in Islamic enclaves within Israel and remains adamant in his support of Hamas and other fundamentalist Muslim movements. It is the northern faction which engendered the recent acts of terror, but one fears that the general atmosphere of violence created by those acts, and the high prestige which the perpetrators enjoy among their peers, might encourage others to join the circle of terror.

The recognized founder and spiritual leader of the movement is Sheikh Abdallah Nimr Darwish of Kafr Qassem. Outwardly, he and his disciples adopted the slogan of activity and change by peaceful means within the framework of law. Sheikh Ra'id Salah of Umm al-Fahm leads the more radical Islamists, who have split from the mainstream which remains under the aegis of Sheikh Abdallah.

A NEW GENERATION OF LEADERS

Umm al-Fahm, the hub of Muslim fundamentalism in Israel, owes its status to Sheikh Ra'id, a local youth who attended the Islamic College in Hebron in 1976, and after graduating in 1979 began roaming the country and preaching a return to Islamic values. An Islamic organization was set up locally, as in other places, complemented by voluntary welfare associations which sought to step into the social and cultural vacuum left by the lack of involvement of the Israeli government in the township. The Islamic message had a tremendous appeal to unskilled laborers who worked in Tel Aviv and other Israeli urban centers, and underwent daily humiliation in their encounter with Israeli prosperity and cultural assertiveness. It also appealed to the youth who were seeking new avenues and new answers, and to professionals who were in search of new channels for their nationalism and new definitions for their identity. The movement also appealed to the rank and file who observed with admiration and pride the welfare, development, and cultural projects undertaken by the Muslim movement, led by Sheikh Ra'id.

Sheikh Abdallah, who appeared to represent the more conciliatory trend towards Israel, came to be upstaged by the younger and more militant sheikhs who now lent much more primacy to the hard-line Islamic position and came dangerously close to the Hamas line of argument, calling to substitute an Islamic state in the entire expanse of Palestine for the existing State of Israel.

No longer confined to the three regional hubs of Umm al-Fahm, Kafr Qassem and Kafr Kanna, the Islamic movement has now also taken root in the mixed cities of Nazareth (with its sizable Christian population), Jaffa, and Acre (with a sizable Arab minority). Most spectacular were the gains of the movement among the Bedouins in the Negev, where an Islamist mayor was elected in Rahat in 1989.

It was precisely the young leaders of the movement, who were dipped in Western principles, studied in Israeli universities, and knew Israeli society, language, and culture well, who became the most radically opposed to it and veered toward an uncompromising Islamic fundamentalism.

In the local elections of 1993, the Islamic movement further consolidated its position. In addition to the six mayorships gained previously by the movement, it added Islamist local councilors in many other villages and towns, including mixed councils where the Muslim population coexisted with non-Muslims.

PARTICIPATION IN ISRAELI NATIONAL ELECTIONS

After the younger leaders were catapulted to power in the elections, they no longer depended for their status and reputation on the backing and confirmation of Abdallah Darwish. Therefore, the young and militant mayors led by Ra'id Salah, who drew their power and popularity directly from their electorate, could afford to bring to the fore their differences with the founder. For example, before the Israeli national elections of 1992, Abdallah advocated participation of the movement in the Knesset race, while Ra'id was strictly opposed. The ideological stakes were enormous. Unlike the local elections, in which the Muslim movement came to take control of several mayoralties, thus contributing to self-reliance and reinforcing the separateness of their communities from the Israeli mainstream, contesting in the national elections entailed three major doctrinal breaches. First, participation in the elections means acknowledging an acceptance of the rule of the non-Muslim majority; second, it entails a respect for the laws of Israel which every elected member of the Knesset swears to uphold in his inaugural oath; and third, it means recognition of Israel's sovereignty.

Furthermore, a Muslim is not supposed to respect and act according to secular laws made by humans, but follow the Shari'a, the law which emanates from Allah himself. Thus, when the Muslim movement in Israel participates in local elections and elects Islamic mayors, they do not need to swear allegiance to the State of Israel. Moreover, under Israeli law, local councils are entitled to adopt bylaws, for example, governing the separation of sexes at school or forbidding the sale and consumption of alcohol. From the fundamentalist point of view, this is not an enactment of law but merely an application of the law of Allah. However, participation in government at the national level would require acceptance of the secular laws of the Jewish state and behaving in accordance with them instead of cultivating a separate patrimony in isolation and segregation. Despite these convictions that are shared by all fundamentalists as a matter of principle, pragmatists like Sheikh Abdallah Darwish and some of his followers argued consistently for participation in national elections as the only way to bring pressure to bear on Israeli governments to respond to their particular needs.

This issue came to the fore on the eve of the national elections of 1996 and, coupled with personal ambition and other matters of contention, contributed to the split within the Islamic movement when the organs of the organization, controlled by Sheikh Abdallah, overwhelmingly supported the resolution to run for the Knesset. Sheikh Ra'id, and his fellow radical Sheikh Kamal Khatib from Kafr Kanna, rejected the resolution and, taking advantage of Abdallah's absence abroad, published a communique stating that the resolution did not apply to them. Many attempts to reconcile between the parties were made, but all in vain. Then, Sheikh Ra'id gathered his forces and declared the establishment of his own "Islamic movement," with an identical name as the mother-movement but evidently much more radical. Or is it?

THE QUESTION OF COEXISTENCE

The segregated environment that the fundamentalists have been creating around them in Israel is, by definition, a temporary step. With regard to the long-term solution to their plight, the Islamic movement entertains in its midst various points of view, some of which translated into a rift and then a schism. Some of these expressed views are ambiguous and sometimes they even consist of explicit statements of coexistence with and within the Jewish state. Others amount to veiled or even open threats of revolt and visions of establishing a Muslim state over all of Palestine.

To the pragmatists, coexistence permits the movement to organize, participate in the elections (local and national), inculcate their norms into their constituencies, champion Islamic causes, and at the same time maintain their segregation. By exploiting the means afforded to them by Israeli society, they are willing to play by the rules of democracy as long as this serves their purposes. Ultimately, at some undefined point in the future, they entertain the hope to replace the existing system with a new Islamic order. Those among them who speak about an "Islamic state in Palestine" seldom specify its boundaries, leaving open the possibility that it might encompass the entire territory, including Israel.

The pragmatists, who specifically prescribe a "Palestinian state alongside Israel," claim that in such a case they would prefer to continue to dwell in Israel as a Muslim minority. This has been, incidentally, the prevailing position among most Arabs in Israel, and it is not surprising that it should be so.

For both the pragmatists and the radicals, and for that matter for all Israeli Arabs, the realization prevails that they are much freer in the Jewish state to express their views and implement them than in any neighboring Arab country. In most Arab countries, indeed, including "moderate" and "liberal" Egypt and Jordan, Islamic parties as such cannot run for elections while in Israel they can and do. At any rate, an element of Palestinian-Muslim nationalism is implicitly enmeshed in the demand for a Palestinian state, although both currents officially negate nationalism as a matter of principle and view the ultimate solution in merging into the future revived caliphate of the universal Muslim *umma* (the community of all Muslims). In the real world, however, like Hamas and other Muslim fundamentalists elsewhere, the Islamic movement in Israel has also been tinged with nationalist tendencies, except that in Israel, "nationalism" for the Arab minority does not mean Israeli nationalism but Arab nationalism, thereby raising the unresolved contradictions discussed above.

The radicals among the fundamentalists have little patience to wait in indolence, and they prefer to embrace the road of militant activism which, they believe, might hasten the attainment of those goals.

DEMOGRAPHY OF THE ISLAMIC MOVEMENT

Sheikh Abdallah, who has recently distanced himself from the daily management of the Islamic movement but continues to command the respect of his followers as the supreme spiritual guide, enjoys the support of his own town, Kafr Qassem, whose mayor, Ibrahim Sarsur, is the spokesman for the movement; the neighboring village of Kafr Bara, with Mayor Kamal Rayan who began the political revolution of local Islamic rule in Israel; the Bedouins of Rahat in the Negev; the towns of Jaljulya and Kafr Qara; and the Islamists of the mixed cities of Lod, Ramle, Jaffa, Nazareth, and Acre. When this group ran in the national elections in 1996, it counted among its leadership two Knesset members- abd-al-Malek Dahamsheh of Kafr Kanna and Tawfiq Khatib of Jaljulya- who were reelected in 1999. To this group of leaders also belong Tayasir

Masri, the mayor of Kafr Qara'; Jum'a Qasasi, a former mayor of Rahat; and Suleyman abu-Ahmad, a member of the Nazareth city council.

The more radical group, founded and headed by Sheikh Ra'id, consists primarily of Umm al-Fahm, the largest Muslim town in Israel (with a population of some 30,000 as of 1997), some satellite villages around that town, and part of Kafr Kama under the leadership of Sheikh Kamal Khatib.

Nothing is more indicative of the thinking and ambitions of the two groups than their respective modus operandi. Abdallah Darwish focuses on parliamentary activity via the movement's Knesset members, and tirelessly labors for a rapprochement between Arabs and Jews in Israel. He also mediates in local conflicts and rifts between Israeli Arabs and has gained prestige in doing so as a man of peace and conciliation.

Yet the schism within the movement deprived Abdallah of the hub of Umm al-Fahm, where the printing house, the editorial offices of the weekly *Sawt al-Haqq wal-Huriyya*, the Islamic College, the Islamic Sports Association, the Islamic Association, and the Zakat welfare committees are located. He had to set up his own parallel organizations to make up for the lost ones, and founded a new journal, *Al-Mithaq* (the Covenant), which reflects his outlook.

TARGETS OF ISLAMIC ACTIVISM

Ra'id's group, which took command of all the institutions in Umm al-Fahm, has turned to activism of another sort, which can be summed up in two main domains: First, they undertook to rehabilitate physically and restore to Islamic control old *waqf* and Muslim holy sites, especially the destroyed mosques and cemeteries in the multitude of Arab villages that had been ravaged and abandoned during the 1948 war. This was particularly significant as part of the mood in which Israeli Arabs recognized the fiftieth anniversary of Israeli independence as commemorating the *nakbah*, the disaster of the loss of Palestine to the Israelis. Their signal was clear: while other Arabs were commemorating, parading, and demonstrating, they were rehabilitating, reconstructing, and taking the lead in recovering their lost patrimony. They scan and monitor all national construction projects in order to oppose and raise the level of awareness among the Arabs of Israel toward any attempt by the Israelis to desecrate or destroy what they consider to be a religious site.

One prominent example of this is the Istiqlal cemetery near Haifa where Izz a-Din al-Qassam is buried. The memory of this Islamic hero of the 1930s who had fought against both the British and the Zionists until he was killed in battle in 1935 was revived by Hamas, and his name adopted by the military arm of the movement. When the Nesher municipality planned to widen the highway at the expense of the cemetery, the Islamists posted a round-the-clock guard at the newly renovated tomb and warned the authorities against touching the spot. The movement also strives to restore to Islamic control old mosques which had either been destroyed or turned into entertainment and tourist sites. They demand that the revenues from the property be put under their exclusive control.

A second major target of activism involves Arab claims in Jerusalem. Although most Israeli Arabs toe the PLO and Hamas line that eastern Jerusalem should be under Palestinian rule, no element has committed itself more deeply and acted upon its commitment more insistently than the Ra'id group. Sheikh Ra'id has become the chief bearer of the banner of the struggle for Jerusalem. He warns against the "impending menace to al-Aqsa" mosque, and attempts to mobilize local and world Islamic public opinion to his side in order to "rescue the mosque." He virulently condemns the Israeli archeological digs near the Temple Mount and invites delegations of Muslims from Israel and other Islamic countries to come and see for them the works which, he claims, are calculated to undermine the foundations of the Holy Shrine of Aqsa in the Haram a-Sharif compound.

To counter the perceived Israeli threat, Ra'id initiated the takeover and refurbishing of the underground floor of the Aqsa mosque, known to Israelis as "Solomon's Stables," and by Muslims as "al-Musallah and Marwani" (the Prayer Grounds of Marwan, one of the Umayyad Caliphs), thus adding more praying space during the peak flow of worshippers during Muslim holidays. He also organized a meeting of Muslim Brothers in which he lamented the state of affairs of the Jewish occupation of a holy Islamic site, and ran a Jerusalem festival for the same purpose, which attracted some 40,000 believers. All this frenzy of activity, which followed the controversial opening by Israel of an exit to the Hasmonean tunnel next to Temple Mount, has won Sheikh Ra'id support from the Muslim Brothers everywhere. He is perceived as a man of action with an unswerving commitment to the Islamic cause, as he had shown back in 1992 when he mobilized assistance and whipped up support for the 415 Hamas leaders who had been deported by Israel to southern Lebanon.

Sheikh Ra'id travels often to Islamic countries, especially to Egypt and Turkey, which was at the top of his preoccupations and hopes during the brief tenure of the Erbakan government in the mid-1990s, which championed world Islamic causes in the name of the ruling fundamentalist Welfare Party in Ankara. At the time he even sought recognition for his Islamic College by Turkish Muslim authorities. Ra'id has also maintained close relationships with the political branch of Hamas. When Hamas spiritual leader Sheikh Yasin was jailed in Israel, Ra'id built up a close partnership with Dr. al-Zahar, one of the top leaders of the movement in Gaza, and after Yasin was released in late 1997, Ra'id inched closer to him. His activities in support of Hamas, which have apparently included material aid to the families of suicide bombers and subventions to the needy, have won him much scorn from Israeli authorities and public opinion.

When Sheikh Yasin was released from Israeli captivity following the failed Israeli Mossad attempt against the life of the Hamas leader Mash'al in Jordan, Ra'id headed a delegation to Amman to welcome the venerated Hamas hero. The Jordanian authorities, who had become wary of the zealous young sheikh who had attempted to intercede in favor of the Muslim candidates in Jordan's parliamentary elections, had to yield to popular demand and allow him in for the occasion. When Yasin arrived in Gaza, Ra'id and his crowd were there to greet him, and the contacts between the two have not abated despite Yasin's continued incitement against Israel.

Abdallah Darwish, by contrast, has refrained from all these gestures, and his stature among Hamas supporters has greatly declined as a consequence.

Ra'id and his group neither sympathize with nor are supported by the Palestinian Authority. The distribution of *Sawt al-Haqq* has been prohibited in the territory of the PA. In turn, Ra'id and his supporters do not hide their criticism of the Oslo process in which, they claim, the Palestinians have been short-changed. This did not prevent Ra'id from trying to organize a meeting between the Israeli Chief Rabbi and Sheikh Yasin, something that did not materialize due to Yasin's venomous stand against Israel, but a discussion did take place in Gaza with Israeli Rabbi Menachem Fruman of Tekoa. Ra'id's strategy is crystal-clear: he tries to circumvent the political establishments in both Israel and the Palestinian Authority and channel the contacts into religious matters so as to short-circuit the intergovernmental Oslo mechanism.

When the Persian Gulf crisis was rekindled in April 1998, both factions of the Islamic movement like the rest of the Arab and Islamic world, condemned American interference and sided with the Iraqi people. Ra'id's group in particular abhors the godless Saddam, and so does Abdallah; therefore, they refrained from showing any sympathy to him personally or to his rule. If they had, they might also have endangered the generous support received from the Muslim Brothers and other Muslim fundamentalists disbursed by Saudi Arabia and Kuwait.

THE FUNDAMENTALISTS AND ISRAEL

The two splinter groups of the Islamic movement in Israel have become so deeply entrenched in the landscape of the country that they are likely to maintain their separate institutions, their mutual bickering, and ideological differences, which are mainly a question of nuances and tactics, not of doctrine or long-term strategy. Abdallah's group may grow on the national level due to its participation in national politics through its Knesset members and the likelihood of its providing a better and more updated leadership than the defunct communists. Ra'id's faction, which is stronger at the local level, may pursue its policy of capitalizing on the frustrations of the young Arabs in Israel who cannot identify with the Israeli establishment, though they continue to tap its grants and services, and who are happy with the growing segregation of their Islamic enclaves from the Israeli mainstream. Both factions have enough cadres, vested interests, institutions, leaders, and popular support to last. Within a general atmosphere of dissatisfaction with and alienation from the Israeli polity, which has so far failed to reconcile the contradictions between its nature as a Jewish-Zionist state and its democratic aspirations for equal rights and duties for all its citizenry, the prognosis cannot be optimistic.

Admittedly, the processes that the Arab population in Israel has been undergoing are complicated and diverse, and no blanket statements can justly apply to all. For while Israelization is proceeding apace in the internalization of values of democracy, human rights, and freedom of speech; higher standards of living; high-technology education; and the substitution of meritocracy and personal politics for the old machinations of the traditional patriarchal hierarchies, elements of alienation and nationalism are also noticeable. Viewed merely through the focus of the general success story of Islamic fundamentalism in the world today, it is conceivable that many more Muslims in Israel will regroup around their religio-cultural heritage in the years to come. If they do so, and regardless of the Islamic faction they will elect to follow (if by then the two groups have not merged), their common doctrinal and cultural heritage, and the joint ideological infrastructure they have cultivated over the years, will provide them with a common denominator to rally around. This common denominator is made up of two components: one negative regarding the Jews, and the other positive, reflecting the vision of an Islamic state.

The Muslim movement in Israel, especially Sheikh Ra'id's faction, has been professing institutional and political self-reliance in their own enclaves within Israel, much like the Arabs in Israel in general who have also been vying for their own institutional and cultural autonomy. The difference is that

Ra'id's supporters often voice the dream of an Islamic state that might replace Israel, while Abdallah's group has not come that close to denying the existence of Israel. Nevertheless, even during its period of unity under Sheikh Abdallah, the Islamic movement did not mince words, recognizing the *intifada* as a *jihad* (holy war) against Israel and openly urging the Palestinians to raise the banner in order to "die for Allah."

Since the Oslo process began in late 1993, a tone of pragmatic realism seems to have struck Muslim fundamentalists in Israel. The radicals still pursue their rhetoric as in the past, but the mainstream pragmatists seem to have adopted a more realistic approach to their status and dreams, especially since they participated in the national elections and sent their representatives to the Knesset. During the local elections of 1998, the balance of forces between the two groups remained basically unchanged, while permitting the parties to sharpen their messages and to crystallize and update their views. Sheikh Ra'id, for example, has opposed the Wye Plantation accords due to the concessions extracted from the Palestinians there, and strongly objected to the subsequent abrogation of the Palestinian National Charter, while Sheikh Abdallah is on record as supporting both. The end result is that, in fact, the two rival Islamic groups have aligned themselves along the Hamas-Palestinian Authority rift.

There are observers in Israel who regard the process of moderation of the Islamic movement in Israel as irreversible, and they predict that even the radicals will ultimately come around. They find indications of this trend in the fact that the mainstream has joined the fray of Israeli politics and has made itself not much different from prevailing views of Israeli Arabs, something that was manifested in the alliance of the Islamists with the Arab Democratic Party to run together in the 1996 national elections, and thereafter to operate in the Knesset as one faction.

The line-up of the two groups following the 1998 local elections showed mixed results. Sheikh Ra'id ran for the third time for mayor in Umm al-Fahm, received 70 percent of the vote, and took 7 out of the 11 seats on the council. In Nazareth,

Salman abu-Ahmed, who was identified with the Abdallah Darwish faction, lost the mayoral elections but his group won 10 of the 19 seats on the city council.

Yet, as is the case in Israel in general, these results show that municipal politics shun ideologies, and that worthy men and able administrators are valued over ideologues and preachers. This explains the recurring victory of Sheikh Ra'id as well as the failure of some of his supporters in other places. Conversely, many of Abdallah's candidates did win in their villages, something which will certainly prop up the prestige of that group. Ra'id's more radical group may have to moderate its conduct if it wishes to retain its constituency, when it recognizes the gains of its rivals made through moderation and joining in national politics. What happens between Israel and the Palestinians, which naturally relates to what happens between Hamas and the Palestinian Authority, will also either facilitate or obstruct that metamorphosis.

3

Islam and Arabs, Iran and Iraq

ISLAM AND ARABS

INTRODUCTION

Most of the focus on Arab-Israeli relations over the last two decades has centered on the situation of the Arabs in the administered territories, to the neglect of the Arabs in Israel. Yet the intifada has triggered scattered acts of violence by Israel's Arabs as well, mandating a new look at this community.

It would be wonderful to believe that the future of Arab-Jewish relations within Israel will follow the lead of the many Israeli-Arab friendship associations which have been at work for decades to foster greater understanding between the two peoples. Their work stems from a perspective which holds that basically people are good and therefore all we have to do is create an atmosphere of brotherhood in which we can embrace each other, talk to each other, understand each other, and then everything will fall into place. Unfortunately, I believe this is an exercise in futility and is not the way to approach the problem. The problem is soluble, but only via a political solution.

FROM AN ETHNO-RELIGIOUS TO A NATIONAL MINORITY

After forty years of such attempts, relations between Arabs and Jews in Israel have not seriously improved. If anything, they have grown worse from the Israeli point of view. It can be plainly observed that the Arabs in Israel no longer talk about being merely a religious, cultural, ethnic or linguistic minority, as we used to hear. Today they speak about themselves as a national minority, with all that involves.

EQUAL BUT NOT FULLY EQUAL

At the time of the establishment of the State of Israel, Israeli Arabs numbered about 110,000, living under the administration of a military government and numbering 11 percent of the total Israeli population. There were times when this percentage rose and fell, depending upon the rate of Jewish immigration to Israel. In the 1950s and 1960s when there was mass aliya to Israel, it dwindled to as low as 10 percent. There were times when it went up to 15 or 16 percent. Now, partly because Israel annexed East Jerusalem and the Arabs of East Jerusalem are considered Israeli residents, the total number of Israeli Arabs is rapidly approaching 750,000, nearly 18 percent of the total Israeli population, and in about twenty years or less will reach one million, a number which cannot be dismissed as insignificant.

There have been countless declarations about how the Arab citizens of Israel are equal members of Israeli society. It is undeniable that Israel has absorbed the Arabs into many facets of its society- into a democratic political system with a plurality of political parties which does not exist anywhere else in the Arab world. Israeli Arabs have a higher degree of education, a higher degree of medical care, a higher standard of living than Arabs anywhere else. The life expectancy of the Arabs in Israel has grown over the past forty years from about 52 years to over 70 years and is just slightly below that of the Jewish population.

Yet they cannot be fully equal, not only because Israel is in a state of war with the Arab world but because they are, and increasingly so, identifying themselves as a national minority. For example, to the Arabs of Israel, the symbols of the state mean little or nothing. For example, on Independence Day, the most important date in the Israeli calendar, Jews dance in the streets of Jerusalem. For the Arabs it is a day of mourning. It is the date they call Naqba, meaning the holocaust or disaster.

That is the day they lost their land, from their point of view. At best they will sit in their villages and mourn their own fate. At worst they will burn the Israeli flag or other things of this sort. So the cleavage is there and it runs very deep. If Jews cannot even share their national holiday with their Arab fellow-citizens, then what do they have in common?

Therefore it is becoming more and more difficult for them to be fully equal because the basic beliefs, basic systems of values, norms and aspirations of Jews and Arabs are simply contradictory to theirs. They are on a collision course. Therefore all the thinking about the Arabs in Israel becoming good Israelis no longer holds true, especially since 1967. It is becoming more and more of a contradiction in terms to say "Israeli" Arabs; they may have an Israeli passport but they hardly identify with the State of Israel.

Perhaps paradoxically, precisely because they have reached this material standard, a new set of needs has come to the fore. One Israeli Arab member of the Knesset put it very poignantly when he said, "Precisely because our stomachs are full, it is now time for us to satisfy our spiritual needs." This is the contradiction of the "Israeli" identity of the Arabs in Israel. Yet we have never confronted it or attempted to resolve it and have opted to plaster it over and pretend it is not there.

ISRAELI IDENTITY

The Arabs living in Israel today have a mix of four identities- Israeli, Palestinian, Arab, and Moslem. The surging new identity of the Arabs in Israel may be viewed in terms of four concentric circles. They are concentric because many of these identities cut across, coincide, and often overlap with each other, and therefore they are inseparable.

The first circle of identity is the Israeli circle. During the first twenty years, Israeli Arabs came to consider themselves increasingly as part of Israeli society, not because they liked it but because they were cut off from the rest of the Arab world and felt they had no option but to try to assimilate into the Israeli environment. During those years, in my opinion, successive Israeli governments committed the mistake of maintaining a cleavage between Arab society and Jewish society. For example, there was no integrated system of education. It is true that the Arabs wanted to have their own system of education in Arabic, to put an emphasis on Arab history, Arabic language and Islamic religion, all of which is understandable from their point of view. However, if they teach their own heritage, their own patrimony, their own culture as separate from the culture of the state in which they live, then they can be expected to acquire a separate identity which is not likely to tie them to the State of Israel as loyal citizens.

PALESTINIAN IDENTITY

The second circle of Arab identity is the Palestinian one. After 1967 when the so-called "green line" was erased, the Arabs in Israel discovered that they were part of a much larger and much more politically conscious Palestinian people. With the rise of the PLO in the late 1960s and 1970s, its recognition by the UN, the various acts of what we call terrorism and what they call heroic acts against Israel all contributed to an increase in Palestinian consciousness.

Go to any village in the Galilee and ask the people who they are. In 60-70 percent of the cases they will tell you that first of all they are Palestinian. Then they will add Arab, Israeli, or Moslem. This is to be expected because every nation, every people, want to be identified nationally. The Jewish people in the diaspora, even though few have any intention of coming and settling in Israel, consider themselves not only part of a faith but also part of a people, with some kind of national or pseudo-national focus of identity.

As the difficulties grew for Israel both in the territories and among the Israeli Arabs, the growing links across the "green line" could be seen. For example, Land Day is a primary day for demonstrations by Israeli Arabs, commemorating the first Land Day in 1976, during which four Israeli Arabs were killed when they protested against Israeli expropriation of land in the Galilee. Yet Land Day is also commemorated by Arabs in Judea, Samaria and Gaza in identification with their Palestinian brethren in Israel. When the PLO outside the territories refers to Land Day, it speaks about "the resilience of our oppressed Palestinian people on both sides of the 'green line.'" From their point of view there is no difference between the Palestinian Arabs in the territories and in Israel.

This very real, genuine, authentic Palestinian identity has in some ways complicated the lives of the Arabs in Israel because on the one hand they clamor for Palestinian identity, but on the other they claim their Israeli rights. When they say "rights," it always means something they want to receive. You never see a group of Arabs demonstrating in Tel Aviv for the right to serve in the army or perform other national service. Clamoring for rights means demanding more money for Arab education, an education which is not only separate from our own but in many ways cultivates the anti-Israeli currents in their midst.

ARAB IDENTITY

The third identity of Israeli Arabs is their Arab identity. The Palestinians claim not only the right to bring about the Palestinian revolution, which will in turn bring about Palestinian self-determination and nationhood, but they also claim to be the vanguard of revolution in the Arab world. Once the Palestinian revolution succeeds, they expect that revolution to be transplanted to other Arab countries to get rid of reactionary monarchies, and it is obvious whom they mean. So the Arabs in Israel not only feel they are Palestinian but also part of that great revolution which is coming about in the Arab world.

In the meantime they train themselves and cultivate their youth to meet that future challenge. The Arab history they learn in school can only strengthen their Arab identity, their feeling of being a part of the greater Arab world around them. They say that as long as the Arabs are in a state of war with Israel and there are no signs of peace between Israel and all the Arab countries, then it is natural that they should be on the Arab side in their hearts. They used to say in a very impressive way that, "we are torn between our country and our people," their country being Israel. However, today they are less and less torn and increasingly identify with one side of that equation.

ISLAMIC IDENTITY

The fourth circle of identity is the Islamic one. The last twenty years have witnessed an Islamic revival all over the Moslem world from Morocco to Indonesia. (See Rafi Israeli, "The Impact of Islamic Fundamentalism on the Arab-Israeli Conflict," Survey of Arab Affairs, No. 13 [15 August 1988].) As can be seen throughout the Moslem world, in places where conflict is rife, there is always some element which will lean on Islam and use its symbols in order to bring forward its political message.

These are very strong signals. One recent survey reported that more mosques were built in the territories and Israel in the last seven years than in the previous seventy. There are more young men growing a beard, which is the hallmark of the Moslem Brotherhood, in both Israel and the territories. There is a growing alternative Islamic leadership which in some ways has become more authoritative and has a more devoted following than the traditional or political leadership of the past.

We should remember that there is an environmental impact to the rise of Islamic fundamentalism. When the Islamic revolution succeeded in Iran, Moslem fundamentalists all over the world saw that a Moslem regime could finally stand up against imperialism. After being occupied, trampled on and taken advantage of for over three centuries by the West, a Moslem leader had finally emerged who could declare an Islamic revolution, stand up to the West and even take American hostages with impunity. In other words, even if other Moslems may not agree with Khomeini ideologically, he has become a model to follow because he was successful. On Land Day in the Galilee, young people have been heard to shout, "Khomeini, Khomeini."

These sentiments are further aggravated by the fact that Arabs feel they are living in a land that is holy to them too. This is the land which contains Jerusalem, a holy city in Islam. The Mufti of Jerusalem, their religious leader, continually calls upon the people to show resilience, and everybody knows what that means. The former Mufti of Jerusalem, Sheikh al-Saih, has been president of the Palestine National Council, which adds to the symbolic dominance of Islam in Palestinian affairs.

There are about 100,000 Christians among the Israeli Arab population, some of whom are as afraid of Islamic fundamentalism as the Jews are and are quite happy to have some kind of Israeli protection. Yet there are other Christians who are much more extreme in their anti-Israel views than the central stream within the PLO, the most prominent of them being George Habash.

To conclude, over the past two decades the "Israeli" component of Arab identity has been greatly reduced, while the Palestinian component has increased to the point where their surging new identity today is that of a national minority. The recognition of this fact and the formulation of a policy by the Israeli leadership to deal with it is long overdue. Such a policy must lump together Israeli Arabs, who are Palestinians for all intents and purposes, with the rest of the Palestinian people under Israeli rule.

ISLAM AND IRAN

INTRODUCTION

The Constitution of the Islamic Republic of Iran advances the cultural, social, political, and economic institutions of Iranian society based on Islamic principles and norms, which represent an honest aspiration of the Islamic Ummah. This aspiration was exemplified by the nature of the great Islamic Revolution of Iran, and by the course of the Muslim people's struggle, from its beginning until victory, as reflected in the decisive and forceful calls raised by all segments of the populations. Now, at the threshold of this great victory, our nation, with all its beings, seeks its fulfillment.

The basic characteristic of this revolution, which distinguishes it from other movements that have taken place in Iran during the past hundred years, is its ideological and Islamic nature. After experiencing the anti-despotic constitutional movement and the anti-colonialist movement centered on the nationalization of the oil industry, the Muslim people of Iran learned from this costly experience that the obvious and fundamental reason for the failure of those movements was their lack of an ideological basis. Although the Islamic line of thought and the direction provided by militant religious leaders played an essential role in the recent movements, nonetheless, the struggles waged in the course of those movements quickly fell into stagnation due to departure from genuine Islamic positions. Thus it was that the awakened conscience of the nation, under the leadership of Imam Khumayni, came to perceive the necessity of pursuing a genuinely Islamic and ideological line in its struggles. And this time, the militant 'ulama' of the country, who had always been in the forefront of popular movements, together with the committed writers and intellectuals, found new impetus by following his leadership.

THE DAWN OF THE MOVEMENT

The devastating protest of Imam Khumayni against the American conspiracy known as the "White Revolution," which was a step intended to stabilize the foundations of despotic rule and to reinforce the political, cultural, and economic dependence of Iran on world imperialism, brought into being a united movement of the people and, immediately afterwards, a momentous revolution of the Muslim nation in June 1963. Although this revolution was drowned in blood, in reality it heralded the beginning of the blossoming of a glorious and massive uprising, which confirmed the central role of Imam Khumayni as an Islamic leader. Despite his exile from Iran after his protest against the humiliating law of capitulation (which provided legal immunity for American advisers), the firm bond between the Imam and the people endured, and the Muslim nation, particularly committed intellectuals and militant 'ulama', continued their struggle in the face of banishment and imprisonment, torture and execution.

Throughout this time, the conscious and responsible segment of society was bringing enlightenment to the people from the strongholds of the mosques, centers of religious teaching, and universities. Drawing inspiration from the revolutionary and fertile teachings of Islam, they began the unrelenting yet fruitful struggle of raising the level of ideological awareness and revolutionary consciousness of the Muslim people. The despotic regime which had begun the suppression of the Islamic movement with barbaric attacks on the Faydiyyah Madrasah, Tehran University, and all other active centers of revolution, in an effort to evade the revolutionary anger of the people, resorted to the most savage and brutal measures. And in these circumstances, execution by firing squads, endurance of medieval tortures, and long terms of imprisonment were the price our Muslim nation had to pay to prove its firm resolve to continue the struggle. The Islamic Revolution of Iran was nurtured by the blood of hundreds of young men and women, infused with faith, which raised their cries of "Allahu Akbar" at daybreak in execution yards, or were gunned down by the enemy in streets and marketplaces. Meanwhile, the continuing declarations and messages of the Imam that were issued on various occasions extended and deepened the consciousness and determination of the Muslim nation to the utmost.

ISLAMIC GOVERNMENT

The plan of the Islamic government as proposed by Imam Khumayni at the height of the period of repression and strangulation practiced by the despotic regime, produced a new specific, and streamline motive for the Muslim people, opening up before them the true path of Islamic ideological struggle, and giving greater intensity to the struggle of militant and committed Muslims both within the country and abroad.

The movement continued on this course until finally popular dissatisfaction and intense rage of the public caused by the constantly increasing repression at home, and the projection of the struggle at the international level after exposure of the regime by the 'ulama' and militant students, shook the foundations of the regime violently. The regime and its sponsors were compelled to decrease the intensity of repression and to "liberalize" the political atmosphere of the country. This, they imagined, would serve as a safety valve, which would prevent their eventual downfall. But the people, aroused, conscious, and resolute under the decisive and unfaltering leadership of the Imam, embarked on a triumphant, unified, comprehensive, and countrywide uprising.

THE WRATH OF THE PEOPLE

The publication of an outrageous article meant to malign the revered 'ulama' and in particular Imam Khumayni on 7 Jan 1978 by the ruling regime accelerated the revolutionary movement and caused an outburst of popular outrage across the country. The regime attempted to quiet the heat of the people's anger by drowning the protest and uprising in blood, but the bloodshed only quickened the pulse rate of the Revolution. The seventh-day and fortieth-day commemorations of the martyrs of the Revolution, like a series of steady heartbeats, gave greater vitality, intensity, vigor, and solidarity to this movement all over the country. In the course of this popular movement, the employees of all government establishments took an active part in the effort to overthrow the tyrannical regime by calling a general strike and participating in street demonstrations. The widespread solidarity of men and women of all segments of society and of all political and religious factions played a clearly determining role in the struggle. Especially the women were actively and massively present in a most conspicuous manner at all stages of this great struggle. The common sight of mothers with infants in their arms rushing towards the scene of battle and in front of the barrels of machine-guns indicated the essential and decisive role played by this major segment of society in the struggle.

THE PRICE THE NATION PAID

After slightly more than a year of continuous and

unrelenting struggle, the sapling of the evolution, watered by the blood of more than 60,000 martyrs and 100,000 wounded and disabled, not to mention property damage, came to bear fruit amidst the cries of "Independence! Freedom! Islamic Government!" This great movement, which attained victory through reliance upon faith, unity, and the decisiveness of its leadership at every critical and sensitive juncture, as well as the self-sacrificing spirit of the people, succeeded in upsetting all the calculations of imperialism and destroying all its connections and institutions, thereby opening a new chapter in the history of all-embracing popular revolutions of the world.

On 12 and 13 Feb 1979, the world witnessed the collapse of the monarchical regime. Domestic tyranny and foreign domination, both of which were based upon it, were shattered. This great success proved to be the vanguard of Islamic government- a long-cherished desire of the Muslim people and brought with it the glad tidings of final victory.

Unanimously, the Iranian people declared their final and firm decision, in the referendum on the Islamic Republic, to bring about a new political system, that of the Islamic Republic. A majority of 98.2% of the people voted for this system. The Constitution of the Islamic Republic of Iran, setting forth as it does the political, social, cultural, and economic institutions and their relations that are to exist in society, must now provide for the consolidation of the foundations of Islamic government, and propose the plan of a new system of government to be erected on the ruins of the previous order.

THE FORM OF GOVERNMENT IN ISLAM

In the view of Islam, government does not derive from the interests of a class, nor does it serve the domination of an individual or a group. Rather, it represents the fulfillment of the political ideal of a people who bear a common faith and common outlook, taking an organized form in order to initiate the process of intellectual and ideological evolution towards the final goal, i.e., movement towards Allah. Our nation, in the course of its revolutionary developments, has cleansed itself of the dust and impurities that accumulated during the past and purged it of foreign ideological influences, returning to authentic intellectual standpoints and world-view of Islam. It now intends to establish an ideal and model society on the basis of Islamic norms. The mission of the Constitution is to realize the ideological objectives of the movement and to create conditions conducive to the development of man in accordance with the noble and universal values of Islam.

With due attention to the Islamic content of the Iranian Revolution, the Constitution provides the necessary basis for ensuring the continuation of the Revolution at home and abroad. In particular, in the development of international relations, the Constitution will strive with other Islamic and popular movements to prepare the way for the formation of a single world community (in accordance with the Koranic verse "This your community is a single community, and I am your Lord, so worship Me" [21:92]), and to assure the continuation of the struggle for the liberation of all deprived and oppressed peoples in the world.

With due attention to the essential character of this great movement, the Constitution guarantees the rejection of all forms of intellectual and social tyranny and economic monopoly, and aims at entrusting the destinies of the people to the people themselves in order to break completely with the system of oppression. (This is in accordance with the Koranic verse "He removes from them their burdens and the fetters that were upon them" [7:157]).

In creating, on the basis of ideological outlook, the political infrastructures and institutions that are the foundation of society, the righteous will assume the responsibility of governing and adMinistering the country (in accordance with the Koranic verse "Verily My righteous servants shall inherit the earth" [21:105]). Legislation setting forth regulations for the administration of society will revolve around the Koran and the Sunnah. Accordingly, the exercise of meticulous and earnest supervision by just, pious, and committed scholars of Islam is an absolute necessity. In addition, the aim of government is to foster the growth of man in such a way that he progresses towards the establishment of a Divine order (in accordance with the Koranic phrase "And toward God is the journeying" [3 : 28]); and to create favorable conditions for the emergence and blossoming of man's innate capacities, so that the theomorphic dimensions of the human being are manifested (in accordance with the injunction of the Prophet (S) "Mould yourselves according to the Divine morality"); this goal cannot be attained without the active and broad participation of all segments of society in the process of social development.

With due attention to this goal, the Constitution provides the basis of such participation by all members of society at all stages of the political decision-making process on which the destiny of the country depends. In this way during the course of human development towards perfection, each individual will himself be involved in, and responsible for the growth, advancement, and leadership of society. Precisely in this lies the realization of the holy government upon earth (in accordance with the Koranic verse "And we wish to show favor to those who have been oppressed upon earth, and to make them leaders and the inheritors." [28:5]).

The Principles of Governance of the Just Holy Person In keeping with the principles of governance and the perpetual necessity of leadership, the Constitution provides for the establishment of leadership by a holy person possessing the necessary qualifications and recognized as leader by the people (this is in accordance with the saying "The direction of affairs is in the hands of those who are learned concerning God and are trustworthy in matters pertaining to what He permits and forbids"). Such leadership will prevent any deviation by the various organs of State from their essential Islamic duties.

THE ECONOMY IS A MEANS, NOT AN END

In strengthening the foundations of the economy, the fundamental consideration will be fulfillment of the material needs of man in the course of his overall growth and development. This principle contrasts with other economic systems, where the aim is concentration and accumulation of wealth and maximization of profit. In materialist schools of thought, the economy represents an end in itself, so that it comes to be a subversive and corrupting factor in the course of man's development. In Islam, the economy is a means, and all that is required of a means is that it should be an efficient factor contributing to the attainment of the ultimate goal.

From this viewpoint, the economic program of Islam consists of providing the means needed for the emergence of the various creative capacities of the human being. Accordingly, it is the duty of the Islamic government to furnish all citizens with equal and appropriate opportunities, to provide them with work, and to satisfy their essential needs, so that the course of their progress may be assured.

WOMAN IN THE CONSTITUTION

Through the creation of Islamic social infrastructures, all the elements of humanity that served the multifaceted foreign exploitation shall regain their true identity and human rights. As a part of this process, it is only natural that women should benefit from a particularly large augmentation of their rights, because of the greater oppression that they suffered under the old regime.

The family is the fundamental unit of society and the main center for the growth and edification of human being. Compatibility with respect to belief and ideal, which provides the primary basis for man's development and growth, is the main consideration in the establishment of a family. It is the duty of the Islamic government to provide the necessary facilities for the attainment of this goal. This view of the family unit delivers woman from being regarded as an object or instrument in the service of promoting consumerism and exploitation. Not only does woman recover thereby her momentous and precious function of motherhood, rearing of ideologically committed human beings, she also assumes a pioneering social role and becomes the fellow struggler of man in all vital areas of life. Given the weighty responsibilities that woman thus assumes, she is accorded in Islam great value and nobility.

AN IDEOLOGICAL ARMY

In the formation and equipping of the country's defence forces, due attention must be paid to faith and ideology as the basic criteria. Accordingly, the Army of the Islamic Republic of Iran and the Islamic Revolutionary Guards Corps are to be organized in conformity with this goal, and they will be responsible not only for guarding and preserving the frontiers of the country, but also for fulfilling the ideological mission of jihad in God's way; that is, extending the sovereignty of God's law throughout the world (this is in accordance with the Koranic verse "Prepare against them whatever force you are able to muster, and strings of horses, striking fear into the enemy of God and your enemy, and others besides them" [8:60]).

THE JUDICIARY IN THE CONSTITUTION

The judiciary is of vital importance in the context of safeguarding the rights of the people in accordance with the line followed by the Islamic movement, and the prevention of deviations within the Islamic nation. Provision has therefore been made for the creation of a judicial system based on Islamic justice and operated by just judges with meticulous knowledge of the Islamic laws. This system, because of its essentially sensitive nature and the need for full ideological conformity, must be free from every kind of unhealthy relation and connection (this is in accordance with the Koranic verse "When you judge among the people, judge with justice" [4:58]).

EXECUTIVE POWER

Considering the particular importance of the executive power in implementing the laws and ordinances of Islam for the sake of establishing the rule of just relations over society, and considering, too, its vital role in paving the way for the attainment of the ultimate goal of life, the executive power must work toward the creation of an Islamic society. Consequently, the confinement of the executive power within any kind of complex and inhibiting system that delays or impedes the attainment of this goal is rejected by Islam. Therefore, the system of bureaucracy, the result and product of old forms of government, will be firmly cast away, so that an executive system that functions efficiently and swiftly in the fulfillment of its administrative commitments comes into existence.

MASS COMMUNICATION MEDIA

The mass communication media, radio and television, must serve the diffusion of Islamic culture in pursuit of the evolutionary course of the Islamic Revolution. To this end, the media should be used as a forum for healthy encounter of different ideas, but they must strictly refrain from diffusion and propagation of destructive and anti-Islamic practices.

It is incumbent on all to adhere to the principles of this Constitution, for it regards as its highest aim the freedom and dignity of the human race and provides for the growth and development of the human being. It is also necessary that the Muslim people should participate actively in the construction of Islamic society by selecting competent and believing officials and keeping close and constant watch on their performance. They may then hope for success in building an ideal Islamic society that can be a model for all people of the world and a witness to its perfection (in accordance with the Koranic verse "Thus We made you a median community, that you might be witnesses to men" [2:143]).

ISLAM IN IRAQ

INRODUCTION

What will be the nature of Islamist politics in Iraq after Saddam Hussein? We are moving into quite uncharted waters in examining this question. The ruthless character of the Baath Party dictatorship absolutely dominated decades of Iraqi politics, canceling out the "normal" workings of Iraqi politics, especially among Islamist groups, and forcing their activities, if any, underground. Movements still represented today in other Arab countries such as communists, liberals, and Islamists were barely in evidence in Iraq. But most of these obscured forces are now re-emerging into the light of day. This report focuses upon Islamic (or Islamist) politics as they are likely to emerge and develop in the new post-Hussein period of openness, even while Iraq lies under a U.S.-led occupation administration.

This report makes one major assumption: with the end of Baathist repression and new political openings there are no grounds for believing that newly emerging Iraqi politics will dramatically depart from the many familiar pattens of general politics in the Arab world. To be sure, every country is unique, and Iraq has had its own quite special experience over the past five decades. History, geography, and geopolitics furthermore put their distinctive stamp on any country. Nonetheless, there are some general patterns of politics and aspirations across the Arab world to which a freer Iraq will not likely be a stranger. One of these major characteristics is that in most of the Arab world Islamist movements constitute the most important, if not the sole, segment of opposition to existing regimes. Political Islam will thus strongly emerge in post-Hussein Iraq-indeed, there are clear indications that they already have. But an important qualification is essential here: Islamist parties also benefit immensely from the absence of other rivals-as repressive states close down all opposition groups. In today's Iraq, some degree of political competition will be present that will set some limits to any Islamist monopoly on politics. But what forms will these trends take and how will they interact with other forces in the country?

This report examines three major Islamist trends that operate within Iraq's three major sectarian/ethnic communities: the majority Shia Arabs, the Sunni Arabs, and the Kurds. It is significant in itself that we need to examine each one of these in its own independent right, since it clearly demonstrates that political Islam in its existing organizational forms has not managed to seriously cross sectarian/ethnic lines, at least so far. That conceivably could change in the future but more likely will not. This divide is due not primarily to theological differences, but rather to social and communal issues. The two Arab communities have experienced 1400 years of separation in many respects.

It is true, as Yitzhak Nakash points out in his article on "The Shiites and the Future of Iraq" (*Foreign Affairs,* July 2003) that Sunni and Shia Arabs mostly stem from similar tribal backgrounds with some degree of shared world outlook.

Nonetheless, today Shiism is not just a theological vision, but also a psychology and a cultural way of life for Shia around the world. Much of Iraqi Shiite culture has become urbanized and partially influenced by Iranian cultural tradition as well-even while retaining strong Arab consciousness and characteristics. Over time the Shia and Sunni communities of Iraq have thus each grown distinct in many respects and these differences have gradually become embedded in the political and social order. Of course, the borderlines between the two communities are often crossed on the personal, political, and social level, particularly in less troubled times. But today, as a result of years of brutal sectarianism and political violence in Iraq, the Islamist movements of the two communities each operate as independent and separate vehicles for the interests of each community-and are to some extent political rivals. This need not be a permanent condition, but it will take a long period of shakedown and normalcy in Iraqi political and social life before these differences can be overcome-as is true with ethnic differences as well.

THE IRAQI SHIA

The present phase of Iraqi politics is a watershed for the Iraqi Shia, a turning point for a group that after many hundreds of years as a marginalized political group under the Ottomans, British, and Baath can now look to the prospect of becoming the dominant power in Iraqi politics. Their hopes had been raised at the time of the establishment of an independent Iraq that introduced a modicum of democratic process into its Parliament, until it largely came to an end with the 1958 revolution and especially after the 1968 Baath coup. With the fall of Saddam Hussein, the revolutionary new opportunities have galvanized the Shiite community and sparked an extraordinary and rapid wave of identity politics and political activism that was not anticipated by American policymakers or even by most Iraqi Sunnis. The significance of this political turning point cannot be overestimated, either for Iraq or for the region.

In effect, the Shia are now aware that only the U.S. occupation stands between them and the final attainment of political power so long denied. It is this realization that will increasingly be a key source of tension between the Shia community and the U.S. presence in Iraq.

Analysis of Islamic politics today among the Shia is considerably easier than that of the Sunnis. The Shiite Islamists operate far more publicly in Iraq and have been openly active on the political scene, especially from abroad, for a long period of time. Some of its leaders, such as Sayyid Baqir al-Hakim, the leader of the Supreme Council for the Islamic Revolution in Iraq (SCIRI) have been in regular touch with U.S. policymakers for nearly a decade regarding future regime change in Iraq. The names of the movements, their leadership, and their aspirations are somewhat familiar.

To a major extent, Shiite politics is religious politics. Politics among the Shia in the Muslim world is typically characterized by the central role of the clergy. The dilemma of secular Shia is the reality that religion itself is what mainly distinguishes the Shiite community from other communities. The difference is not merely or even primarily theological. The cultural characteristics of the Shiite community over centuries have created distinctive social practices and its own community psychology that figure decisively in the self-perception of the Shiite community. To be "Shiite" outside of a religious context is difficult since it is primarily religion that makes an individual Shiite. Mere adherence to the culture and community aspects of Shiism is enough to mark one as Shia. In this sense it is hard to be a "secular" Shia. Indeed, "secular" Shia have a problem in entering politics: if they ignore their Shiite background and community as part of their identity they win little favor with other Shia, yet if they actively identify themselves as Shia they brand themselves with that sectarian category to non-Shia. Consequently most Shia tend not to seek a "secular identity" that would imply any break with their own community. Interestingly, it was the search for a non-sectarian political identity that drove a considerable number of Shia to join the Iraqi communist party over the years-one of the few political parties in which sectarian or ethnic background was irrelevant to membership.

AYATOLLAH 'ALI AL-SISTANI AND THE QUIETISTS

The most important traditional group is the "quietist" tradition currently represented by Grand Ayatollah `Ali al-Sistani, who follows in the tradition established by the towering figure Sayyid Abu al-Qasim al-Khoei (al-Khu'i), who died in 1992. Sistani is of Iranian origin, but has resided in Najaf for most of his professional life. Among Iraqi clerics he probably has the largest number of followers, both inside and outside of Iraq. Maintaining a quietist approach to politics was nearly a survival requirement in Iraq ever since the Baath party came to power. Shia clerics who did not were jailed, tortured, and killed.

Quietism-a conscious distancing of oneself from politics-represents a mainstream Shiite tradition in which the clergy remains aloof from participation in routine politics but reserves for itself the role of observer and critic of political and social events, speaking out forcefully only on special occasions of national and social crisis. Indeed, Ayatollah Khomeini's introduction in Iran of the quite radical concept of *Wilayat al-Faqih* (Rule of the Jurisprudent), represented a marked departure from mainstream Shiite tradition-a fateful decision with which large numbers of clerics were not in agreement. Sistani's choice to operate in the quietist tradition in Iraq clearly put him at odds with the ruling ideology of the Iranian regime. This helped protect him from dangerous confrontation with the Saddam Hussein regime as well.

Now that Saddam Hussein and Baath rule are gone, however, the concept and appropriateness of quietism may come under greater scrutiny. Quietism does not mean eschewing politics altogether, but it suggests a fairly constrained approach toward offering opinions or involvement on daily political issues. Given the new freedom of politics in Iraq at the intellectual and activist level, the need for restraint from politics as a means of survival has diminished. More important, the urgent need to make important political and social decisions has grown as Iraq embarks on building a totally new political edifice. Clerical leadership or guidance may be more sought after than ever before among those many Shia who look to their *maraji' al-taqlid* or "sources of emulation" for guidance. Thus Sistani will find his position more keenly rivaled in this new period of intense political activism that seeks a dominant role for Shia in Iraqi politics.

The murder in April 2003 of Sayyid Abdul Majid al-Khoei, the eldest son of Sayyid Abu al-Qasim al-Khoei, upon his return to Iraq from exile in London, was a significant blow to the forces representing quietism. It may be that this major wing will find itself eclipsed by more activist elements among the Shia clergy, leading to a decline in Sistani's influence.

THE AL-SADR FACTION

A second major clerical force is represented by the Sadrists, currently represented by Muqtada al-Sadr, the youthful son of Sayyid Muhammad Sadiq al-Sadr who was assassinated by the Hussein regime in 1999, and relative of the great Iraqi jurist Ayatollah Muhammad Baqir al-Sadr (executed by the regime in 1980). Muqtada al-Sadr formed the Jama'at al-Sadr al-Thani (Association of the Second al-Sadr) as the key organization of the Sadrists. Muqtada al-Sadr is a shadowy figure, often reported as headstrong, inexperienced, and clearly lacking any clerical credentials except as inheritor of family name. He has furthermore issued statements insisting on the validity of his father's political rulings that, as Juan Cole points out, according to mainstream (Usuli) Shiite theology, should have lost its legal force upon the death of the issuer. Muqtada al-Sadr verbally attacked Sistani in April 2003 and for a brief period issued threats that Sistani as well as two other leading clerics-Baqir al-Hakim and Muhammad Ishaq al -Fayyad-should leave the country, a call denounced by other leading Shiite clerics. There were press reports that Muqtada al-Sadr might have been behind the murder of 'Abd-al-Majid al-Khoei in the mob confrontation in April 2003 but this has never been established. Meanwhile, the Sadrists maintain dominance among the large Shiite community in Baghdad's massive "Sadr City" (the former "Saddam City").

Al-Sadr has been the key figure to raise the issue of "foreign origin" of several key Shiite clerics in Iraq, including Sistani (Iranian origin), Muhammad Ishaq Fayyad (Afghan), and Bashir Najafi (Pakistani). These charges are significant in that they represent a major effort to promote a "nativist" approach to Shiite politics in Iraq that casts doubts on the appropriateness of religious leaders not of Iraqi blood. Yet, given the cultural intermixing between Iran and Iraq over history, it is hard to find "pure Iraqis."

More important, however, an insistence upon nativist Shiism directly militates against Iranian influence over any future Shiite politics in Iraq-a potentially major turning point in the relations between Iran and Iraq. If the nativist trend in Iraqi Shiite politics grows, it almost certainly guarantees the emergence of a major rivalry between Iran and Iraq for influence over other Arab Shia in the Gulf, Syria, and Lebanon, or among Shia east toward the Indian subcontinent.

Al-Sadr would seem to be pitted against both the al-Hakim and Sistani circles and the latter two grants him no recognition of standing. As an activist he is directly opposed to the quietist faction of Sistani, and would be a direct rival for power with the activist Hakim faction that is supported by Iran. His lack of religious credentials may be offset by the backing he receives from Iraqi Ayatollah Kadhim Hussayni al-Ha'iri in Tehran. He is staking out an anti-Iranian position that could have some resonance. But Iran will be pragmatic in seeking to maintain good relations with any Iraqi Shiite faction that seems likely to emerge on top.

SUPREME COUNCIL FOR THE ISLAMIC REVOLUTION IN IRAQ

Ayatollah Muhammad Baqir al-Hakim is the leader of the Supreme Council for the Islamic Revolution in Iraq, founded in 1982 and based in Tehran. It enjoys the support of the Iranian government that aided him in establishing the Badr Brigade of some 10,000-man Iraqi exile militia forces. Al-Hakim's greatest strengths are his consistent support from the Iranian regime in terms of financing and materiel;

Washington's acquiescence during two successive administrations to his prominence among the Shiite opposition; SCIRI's membership on the exile Iraqi National Council or INC (which enjoyed Washington's support for many years before Saddam Hussein's overthrow) as a key representative of the Iraqi Shia; his leadership of the Badr Brigade; and his lineage from a major Iraqi Shiite family. He reportedly accepts the concept of pluralism in any future Iraqi government.

Al-Hakim's drawbacks include that same close association with the Iranian government from the past, and his siding with Iran during the Iran-Iraq War, which many Iraqis perceived as traitorous. While resident in Tehran, he developed something of a negative reputation among Iraqi exiles in Iran who believed he did not show much sympathy or concern for their plight. He is one of several Shiite figures who remained in exile rather than struggling against Saddam Hussein from within Iraq. He is politically astute as a result of his dealings with both Washington and Tehran over the years and his involvement in the INC, which represented all major political trends within Iraq. He is unlikely to adopt a position of outright confrontation, especially not military, with the United States, unless Washington moves to destroy his movement. While al-Hakim's association with Iran would suggest a preference for the Iranian ideological position of support for clerical rule, conditions in Iraq will lead him to be pragmatic on this issue and Iran itself will be more interested in having direct ties to a major figure of influence in Iran than in his specific ideological stance. Washington, while deeply suspicious of his Iranian ties, also needs his support as an influential Shiite figure.

THE DAWA PARTY

The Dawa (Call to Islam) Party is probably the oldest Shiite Islamist movement in Iraq, going back, according to Amatzia Baram, to 1957, when it was founded by Sayyid Muhammad Baqir al-Sadr and others (communication with the author). The movement early on called for the establishment of an Islamic state and, according to R. K. Ramazani reportedly sought cooperation at the time with the Sunni Muslim Brotherhood, a surprisingly open gesture in that period (*Revolutionary Iran*, Baltimore: Johns Hopkins University Press, 1986). The development of the radical political agenda of Dawa was a revolutionary turning point in the highly conservative Najaf environment at the time and even preceded Khomeini's 1964 arrival in Najaf (Abdul-Halim al-Ruhaimi, "The Dawa Islamic Party," in Faleh Abdul-Jabar, ed., *Ayatollahs, Sufis, and Ideologues*, London, Saqi Books, 2002).

Dawa rapidly achieved prominence through its use of violence against the Saddam regime starting in the 1970s and was ruthlessly repressed. Its boldness in attacking the regime and the price it paid in blood for this resistance earned Dawa a great deal of respect and legitimacy among Iraqi Shia. Dawa joined in the founding of the SCIRI Council in Tehran in 1982 but a key faction broke with both the Dawa leadership and SCIRI two years later in opposition to the principle of clerical rule-the guiding principle of Khomeini-and against Iranian efforts to control the Dawa Party. Since then Dawa has remained split between a faction in Iran that is part of SCIRI and calls itself Islamic Dawa (Ruhaimi) and a more independent London-based branch that is more "Iraqi" in character. Both branches of the party have remained pragmatic about dealing with the realities of U.S. power for the moment, but that tolerance may be short-lived as more Shia come to view the U.S. presence as the chief barrier to assumption of greater national power by the Shia. In my view, the future role of Dawa is still uncertain since its earlier popularity and legitimacy may have diminished with time and new circumstances. It could, however, bid to be the major contender for a "nativist" Iraqi Shiite movement and thus may join forces with the Sadrists, especially given the role of the al-Sadr family in the movement in the past. The inclusion of Dawa in the governing council of Iraq under the U.S.-led occupation could lead it in more moderate directions, compared to the excluded al-Sadr movement, but Dawa remains a key unknown force for the future.

OTHER GROUPS

The Islamic Action Organization (Jam'iyyat al-'Amal al-Islami) is a smaller Shiite organization whose founding goes back to the early 1980s under Tehran's wing. It reportedly had links with SCIRI in that period when it conducted numerous attacks against Iraqi installations inside Iraq (Ramazani, *Revolutionary Iran*). It is currently headed by Muhammad Taqi al-Mudarrisi and remains linked with SCIRI. There is also a less-known Shia Hezbollah Organization led by Abu-Hatim al-Muhammadawi that claimed responsibility for the first Shiite opposition group attacks against Saddam Hussein's forces after the U.S. military operation began (William Samii, Radio Free Europe commentary, April 9, 2003).

IMPLICATIONS FOR THE INTERNATIONAL SHIITE COMMUNITY

The evolution of Shiite Islamic politics promises to have major geopolitical impact across the Arab world and outside. The watershed event is the transformation of a once downtrodden and marginalized community into a vibrant Shiite political community bidding for power in Iraq. Shia everywhere is taking note of this event and will strengthen their own claims to civil liberties and democratic representation. The state first and foremost affected by this process is Bahrain.

The Shia of Bahrain constitutes some two-thirds of the population, but, as in Iraq, has been much excluded from political power by a ruling Sunni elite minority. Recent reforms have introduced some greater measure of representation into the parliament, but Shia are still heavily disadvantaged when it comes to real power. The emergence of the Shia as the major political force in Iraq will be certain to hasten the Bahraini Shia's drive to gain greater voice in the political order and is likely to increase tensions on the island. In a positive sense it could also help bring about greater regime reforms, but the Sunni ruling class in Bahrain is unlikely to yield power in the foreseeable future.

The Shia of Saudi Arabia represents only some 5-10 percent of the population-the figures are much disputed. But they have been the object of both *de facto* and even *de jure* discrimination for years by a Wahhabi political order that considers the Shia to be in effect non-believers (*kuffar*) and the legitimate object of discrimination. (The Wahhabi sect of Islam, based in Saudi Arabia, promotes a narrow, literalistic, and intolerant form of Islam that rejects all other Islamic schools.) Since the fall of Saddam Hussein and the emergence of Shiite political forces in Iraq, the Saudi Shia have themselves become emboldened to call for greater cultural rights within the Saudi system. The intimate family links between the Shia of Bahrain and those just across the causeway in the al-Hasa region of Saudi Arabia means that Shiite politics between the two regions will be highly interactive. The Saudi regime will soon be required to either lessen discrimination against Shia in the kingdom, or else crack down even more harshly, if it is to avoid increased security problems in the area.

In Syria, the heterodox Shiite 'Alawi minority rules over a Sunni majority while the 'Alawis are not part of the mainstream Twelver tradition of Iran and Iraq, the Iranian republic after the revolution took the political decision to recognize the 'Alawis as Shia. Will there be future interaction between the Iraqi Shia and the 'Alawi rulers of Damascus in the years ahead? Amatzia Baram points out that both Dawa and SCIRI have had a presence in Damascus since the early 1980s, working with Syrian support against the Hussein regime (communication with the author). Given the close political ties between Tehran and Damascus, it is quite logical that the new Shiite political forces in Iraq will maintain these same ties. Under these circumstances, might the Sunni Islamists of both countries then seek cooperation against the Shia of both countries?

The renaissance of the Shia in *Lebanon*-the single largest sectarian group in the country-goes directly back to Iranian clerical links between the two communities in the 1960s. Today Iran continues to support Hezbollah, the more radical of the two Shiite political organizations in Lebanon. It is assisted in this by Syria, which finds Hezbollah a useful tool of pressure against Israel. We can easily speculate on a future rivalry between Iran and Iraq for influence among Lebanon's Shia. Shaykh Muhammad Husayn Fadhlallah, the leading Shiite clerical voice in Lebanon, voiced similar thoughts in April 2003 in suggesting that, with Saddam Hussein's fall, Najaf may now emerge as a more important Shiite center than Iran (Azadeh Moaveni, "Fall of Hussein Could Lead to a Shift in Center, Focus of Shiite Muslims," *Los Angeles Times*, April 17, 2003). Significantly, Fadhlallah received his theological training in Najaf.

Outside Iraq, the Shiite minorities in *Afghanistan*, *Pakistan*, and *India* will likely also develop renewed interest in Najaf as a theological center, further strengthening it as a rival to Iran in these areas.

Rivalry between Shiite leaderships in Iran and Iraq over these external relations will affect the power of the radical clerical line in Iran itself. If Iraqi Shiite leadership should reject the concept of *Wilayat al-Faqih*, or clerical rule, then the concept would come under much pressure in Iran itself, where the policy has been controversial from the outset. Indeed, Ahmed Montazeri, the son of Grand Ayatollah Hossein Ali Montazeri who was a candidate to replace Khomeini in the 1980s, acknowledged recently that open religious debate in Najaf would "definitely question the legitimacy of absolute rule by the clergy."

It is hard to predict how Iraqi Shia will react to the rival clerical groups contending for leadership. Rivalries among clerical leaders are not new in Iraqi history. The degree of popular support the public accords to any leader will be based on diverse factors including the individual outlook of each Iraqi citizen. Sistani might evoke the most respect as a purely religious authority among Shia both inside and outside Iraq, but Hakim may be best positioned due to his strong support from Iran and his past recognition by Washington as a significant Shiite opposition figure. Iran's logistical support can do much to help promote Hakim in ways that cannot be easily circumvented by Washington. Regional and tribal affiliations also matter since some figures are stronger in certain cities than others.

The financial resources commanded by each group play a powerful role in its ability to provide social services to the public, which facilitates the winning of adherents. Here Iranian support could be very important. Iran indeed is likely to be pragmatic and lend support to any group that will work to accelerate the U.S. departure from Iraq-Tehran's top priority. The ability of a given Iraqi leader to tithe his followers in Shiite tradition also clearly affects the financial strength of any contender. Acceptability among Sunnis as potential partners for joint governance in the future could also be a factor. Furthermore, ideological positions assumed by each of these movements will also be affected by the tactical positions taken by other groups, that is, a moderate position taken by one group may help impel a rival organization toward a more radical position.

Popular discontent with the U.S. occupation could also force moderate Shiite leaders to move away from current partial cooperation with Washington toward a more uncompromising stand. Indeed, views toward Washington could even become the primary ideological touchstone as hardline Iraqi Shiite clerics consider making common cause with Iranian hardliners. And finally, the aggressiveness of the organizing power of each movement within the country will matter.

In short, the ultimate leadership of the Iraqi Shia is up for grabs and inclined to think that the "nativists" may ultimately be the stronger force, but their actions may not necessarily be more reassuring to Washington even if they are more distant from Tehran. Indeed, no clear-cut leader may emerge from among clerical contenders, requiring cooperation among several contending forces, each with its own constituency.

Ultimately, however, it is important to remember that the Shia of Iraq is hardly monolithic; typically they are most united when under the greatest pressure and discrimination. Otherwise, they, like all communities, are also divided into various political trends-communist, nationalist, Islamist, liberal-with differing class, tribal, and regional interests as well. Even if they attain dominant power, they will not speak with one voice, and various factions will inevitably find political allies within other, non-Shia communities.

THE SUNNI ISLAMISTS

Unlike Shiite Islamism, Sunni Islamism has been largely out of sight and underground for nearly 30 years. Various trends are quickly re-emerging, but there are far fewer indicators available to outside observers about their leaderships, views, plans, and following.

The leading Sunni Islamist force in Iraq from the outset has been the Muslim Brotherhood or MB (al-Ikhwan al-Muslimun), the most important Sunni mainstream Islamist movement in the Arab world, with branches in most Arab countries. The first Iraqi branch of the MB was founded in Iraq in 1948 in the form of the Society for the Salvation of Palestine (Jam'iyyat Inqadh Filastin). Its membership was drawn largely from among Iraqis who had been influenced by Brotherhood writings from Egypt. While Palestine was a central concern of all Arabs even at that time, the Brotherhood also propagated its basic message that the fundamental ills of the Muslim society are due to deviation from the teachings of Islam and that Muslim society can only be cured by a return to those principles. While the Brotherhood regularly excoriated the West for its imperialist policies, a key leader of the movement, Basim al-'Azami, states that it was actually the strong communist movement in Iraq in the 1940s that achieved first rank as the chief ideological enemy of the Brotherhood ("The Muslim Brotherhood: Genesis and Development," in Abdul-Jabar, ed., *Ayatollahs, Sufis, and Ideologues*).

In 1951 a formal Iraqi branch of the Muslim Brotherhood was established. This period was a heyday for political movements in Iraq since politics had not yet fallen subject to nearly five decades of authoritarian suppression that began in 1958 with the coup of 'Abd al-Karim Qasim. In the 1950s the Brotherhood was the primary and largest Sunni Islamist movement. Its platform emphasized education and *Dawa* (propagation of the faith or "call to Islam"); it rejected "sectarianism" among the four major schools of Sunni Islam, as well as "westernization," Marxism, secularism, and nationalism, and believed that its role as a political and social movement transcended operation as a political party. It strongly supported Muslim causes of national liberation in the Palestinian struggle and the Algerian struggle against the French.

'Azami reports that by 1960 the Brotherhood decided that political action was a "religious and national duty" and hence established the Iraqi Islamic Party, a name the Brotherhood still retains. Its party manifesto emphasized the same points as noted above augmented by the following principles:

1. Muslims and non-Muslims must enjoy the same "political, public, and individual rights."
2. A democratic order is required in which non-Muslims have the right to elect their own representatives and to vote for a (Muslim) president.
3. The legal system should be neither Islamic nor positivist, but society should be ruled according to Sharia law.
4. State land should go to the peasants.
5. Women have the right to work.
6. Trade unions should be established.
7. National resources belong to the people.
8. National unity must be upheld on the basis of common citizenship.
9. National unity is the nucleus of a higher stage of Arab unity that in turn is the nucleus of overall Muslim unity.

In global terms "the people of all nations are seen as integral parts of a united whole -humanity- irrespective of ethnic origin or religion."

The Brotherhood leadership called for joint Sunni-Shia membership within the Iraqi Islamic Party. Sayyid Muhsin al-

Hakim, the ranking Shia cleric, declined and forbad cooperation of Shia with the party.

After the July 1968 Baath coup, 'Azami reports, Islamists were deeply opposed to the new secularist Baath power. Very soon Islamist activists were arrested, jailed, and tortured and many fled the country. The Brotherhood believed that the Baath Party had seized power from the pro-communist Qasim regime with CIA backing and concluded that the Brotherhood would not be capable of overcoming Baath power.

The leadership of the Brotherhood remained in exile thereafter. In 1991 with the first Gulf War against Saddam Hussein's regime the Brotherhood decided to revive the party, based in the United Kingdom under its old name of the Iraqi Islamic Party. Even in 1991 the Brotherhood was skeptical about any hopes that the United States would truly eliminate Hussein since it had once been instrumental in his rise. The leadership revived the old platform and publicized four of its leader's names: Usama al-Tikriti, Ayad al-Samarra'i, Faruq al-'Ani, and Basim al-Adhami, and began publication of its periodical, *Dar al-Salaam*.

Interestingly, even in 1991 one of the stated aims of the party was to save Iraq from succumbing to a "U.S.-led western conspiracy which was plotting to destroy it in the interests of Israel and ensuring oil supplies to the western world" (`Azami, "Muslim Brotherhood"), a commentary with disturbingly current relevance. These same themes were to be broadly cited in 2003 not only by Islamists in Egypt and Jordan but by large numbers of those around the world who opposed the U.S. invasion of Iraq.

The Iraqi Islamic Party's pronouncements additionally emphasized the suffering of the Iraqi people under UN sanctions. The party continued to call for an Islamic state, particularly since Iraq would then draw more sympathy and support from other Muslim states than it would if it struck out in a nationalist direction. The party recognized that any Islamic program could only be implemented gradually after so many years of "deviation" from any kind of Islamic life in the country. It eschewed support for any school of Islam and instead emphasized that all jurisprudential judgments had to be broadly based, transcending the traditional schools of jurisprudence and based on interpretation (*ijtihad*) from all confessions. The party continued to support pluralism, but within the context of respect for Islam and its precepts. It supported democracy, but perceived "flaws in the western implementation" of it that often turns "freedom into anarchy, plurality into a sellout of the nation's interests, and the ballot box into an instrument to legalize what is forbidden, which is religiously impermissible." The party eschewed political violence and promoted peaceful electoral practices (`Azami, "Muslim Brotherhood").

While Saddam Hussein's Baath party ruthlessly persecuted the Muslim Brotherhood for the first 20 years of his rule, Hussein's severely weakened status after his huge setback in 1991 led him to publicly embrace Islam as a means of strengthening his legitimacy, a step he had initiated even before the Gulf War in order to draw maximum international support. He opened hundreds of new mosques in the country and established a major new theological school called Saddam University that taught only the Sunni version of Islamic theology but included many of the writings of classic Islamists, enabling its graduates to gain some understanding of contemporary Islamist thinking. Saddam Hussein himself sought to exhibit personal piety at public prayer, and even emblazoned the Islamic invocation "there is no god but God" on a new version of the Iraqi national flag. In his new emphasis on public observation of Islam, he also closed down dancing clubs, casinos, and bars. Twelve tame Islamic scholars were appointed to the Iraqi rubber-stamp Parliament. Public observation of Islam, however, rigorously excluded any hint of political activity or of Islamist activity (Syed Saleem Shahzad, "A Third Force Awaits U.S. in Iraq," *Asia Times*, March 1, 2003).

This same observer reports that in the six month run-up to the U.S. attack on Iraq in 2003, Saddam Hussein began to ease off on persecution of known members of the Brotherhood, ostensibly out of fear that the movement had deep roots in Iraqi society and should not be gratuitously alienated at a time of regime crisis, particularly among his core source of support, the Sunni Arabs.

It is of course, notoriously difficult to judge the level and depth of Brotherhood supporters within Iraq during this period of harsh regime crackdown on all political opposition. Any such activity was underground and known best only to the security organs of the regime itself. Nonetheless, given the strength of the Brotherhood in other Arab states-Syria, Jordan, Egypt, and in the Gulf-it is highly likely that the nucleus of an underground Brotherhood remained in place-now free to emerge.

"The Islamic Party believes that:

An enlightened Islamic project is the most ideal for ending the suffering and oppression of our people.

Coming to power is not an end in itself but rather a means for establishing justice, lifting oppression, and realization of the interests of humanity;

Open freedom and brotherhood are the best means for realization of sound rule;

It is in the interests of Iraq and its security that all parties and organizations work to develop the practice of peaceful elections so that they become deeply rooted custom, and to reject political violence and terrorist operations;

Islam is the source of strength and genuine progress and is the sole factor that unites the sons of Iraq in all their various ethnic and sectarian forms."

In a two-hour interview from London on May 14, 2003 with al-Jazeera TV, the current head of the Brotherhood, Dr. Usama al-Tikriti, noted the intense persecution of the movement under Saddam Hussein but he gave the Brotherhood partial credit for the maintenance of a Muslim environment in Iraq that pushed Saddam Hussein from an outspoken "non-believer" to one of a "hypocritical believer." He acknowledged that the party still faced numerous problems, among them sorting out the relationship between the external leadership-so essential to the movement's survival during the Hussein years- and the internal leadership that can now emerge. He acknowledged that the Sunnis in general were less well organized than the Shia and that the Brotherhood is only slowly returning to the political scene. He claimed that the party has 90 branches around Iraq and that it was attracting "enthusiastic youth" into the party.

Other Sunni Islamist groups also exist in Iraq but it is very difficult to gain information about them or gauge their strength. None have anything like the size, importance, international connections, or historical legitimacy of the Muslim Brotherhood.

According to Phebe Marr, the theologically radical but non-violent Hizb al-Tahrir (Liberation Party), originally founded in Jerusalem, had a branch in Iraq in 1960 that unsuccessfully applied for a legal license to form a political party (*The Modern History of Iraq*, Boulder, Westview, 1985). Information about whether it maintains any significant presence in Iraq today, however, is hard to come by.

Other Islamic/Islamist organizations include the Iraqi Islamic Patriotic Front led by Shaykh Muhammad Nadim Al-Taee. This moderate Muslim grouping reportedly met in Washington with U.S. officials prior to the U.S. invasion of Iraq.

Because the Muslim Brotherhood is the most important and largest Sunni Islamist movement across the Arab world, it takes on special importance in regional terms with overt ties among all its organizations. These organizations will almost certainly have some influence upon the Iraqi Brotherhood. The Egyptian Brotherhood, headquarters of the movement, opposed the American invasion of Iraq in 2003, not because of any love for Saddam Hussein-they universally detested him but because they oppose western and particularly American intervention in the Arab world, particularly if it results in a stronger American presence in the region at the cost of local power. The Jordanian Brotherhood took the same position, as did the Palestinian and Syrian branches.

The Syrian Brotherhood is worthy of special attention here due to its close ties with the Iraqi branch, especially since both have been oppressed by Baathist parties in their respective capitals. Saddam Hussein, however, had at one point supported the underground Syrian Brotherhood, at a time when his relations with Syria were hostile. The Syrian Brotherhood had many years of bloody confrontations with the Syrian Baath Party ever since the Brotherhood was banned in Syria in 1963 after the Syrian Baath Party took power. In recent years, however, the Brotherhood has called for an end to violence against the Syrian regime. The most moderate branch of the Syrian Brotherhood, based in London, remains a key opposition force in Syria, and is undoubtedly delighted at the fall of Saddam Hussein, an event that opens the door to Brotherhood participation in Iraqi politics. These party ties will bear close watch. The probable emergence of a strong Brotherhood movement in Iraq will almost certainly threaten the Asad regime in Syria, since it suggests the possibility of Iraqi Brotherhood support to the Syrian Brotherhood from a neighboring country.

A yet more complex factor is the view of the Syrian and Iraqi Brotherhoods toward the Shia in their respective countries. It will be important to watch the nature of future connections between Iraqi and Iranian Shia and the ruling minority of 'Alawis (a heterodox form of Shiism) in Syria. Will the Iraqi Shia show sympathy for the ruling Syrian 'Alawis? And if so, will we witness heightened tension between the Iraqi and Syrian Shia on the one hand, versus the Iraqi and Syrian Sunni Brotherhood on the other? A growth of such ties may greatly elevate tensions between Syria and Iraq in the coming years.

SUNNI RESISTANCE

Sunni Islamists have not been idle during the sudden surge of Shiite power in Iraq following Saddam's fall, and there are initial indications that some Arab states may be supporting a bolstering of Sunni power.

According to the *Washington Post*, on April 18, 2003 Shaykh Ahmad al-Kubaysi, a leading Iraqi Sunni, a former professor of Islamic studies at Baghdad University who had been in exile in Dubai for six years, delivered a fiery Friday sermon in a Sunni mosque in Baghdad and unleashed a Sunni demonstration of tens of thousands of Sunnis protesting against American occupation. "We fear that sectarianism will be exploited by our enemies," Kubaysi said. "Both Sunnis and Shiites should work for unity. We are all Muslims."

Adel Darwish reported in the *Daily Telegraph* that al-Kubaysi was urged by the United Arab Emirates to return to Baghdad to rally Sunni support in the face of rising Shiite power, and reportedly had the blessings of U.S. authorities to do so ("Returned Exile Rallies Sunnis," April 22, 2003). Al-Kubaysi's affiliation is unclear, but he was a prominent cleric before his exile and almost certainly is affiliated with the Brotherhood.

What is abundantly clear is that Sunni Islamic leaders are calling for Islamic unity to face the American occupation, both to strengthen the Islamist movement and to preempt any Shiite call to expel the U.S. presence. Indeed, the Sunnis have everything to lose in a Sunni-Shia religious competition, while the Shia undoubtedly perceives that they have the demographic power to act unilaterally. There are some indications that the Sunni Islamists for the moment have found tactical common ground with Iraqi Sunni nationalists and even some Baathists, in arguing for expelling the U.S. presence, despite their deep ideological antipathies. Furthermore, there is no apparent indication that Sunni Islamists were involved in working with Washington prior to the invasion, unlike several key Shiite figures.

On the other hand, it is almost certain that both the international Muslim Brotherhood itself, and many Arab states, have been working to develop a Sunni "alternative" in the Islamic field as well. Certainly the Brotherhood is working to bring back Brotherhood leaders to Iraq from abroad. Gulf States, as suggested by the news report on al-Kubaysi above, also seem interested in helping assert Sunni Islamic power. Saudi Arabia, which has much to fear from a recrudescence of Shiite power in Iraq, almost certainly will be active in trying to strengthen

Wahhabi forces within Iraq, and to protect its own interests in Iraq. (The kingdom broke rather dramatically with the Brotherhood in late 2002 when it accused the Brotherhood, and not Wahhabi Islam, of being the chief force behind international Islamic terrorism.) While the kingdom may not seek to use violence against the United States in Iraq, uncontrolled Wahhabi elements in Iraq will almost certainly gravitate to violence against the U.S. presence.

The extent of potential support for Wahhabi views in Iraq is almost impossible to gauge. One can hypothesize that support for Wahhabi views grows with the growth of dissatisfaction with conditions and the intensity of anti-American attitudes. Wahhabism serves more as a vehicle for these feelings than as the cause. Islamist movements also directly profit from the absence of alternative political vehicles for political opposition. Thus Wahhabi views might well have lurked beneath the surface of Iraqi Sunni Islamist life under Hussein, in the absence of other opposition forces. The United States would not, however, have been perceived as the primary enemy by Islamists under Hussein. It is only with the U.S. occupation that anti-U.S. feelings have some initial grounds to emerge, especially if that occupation is prolonged. One can hypothesize that some degree of Wahhabi influence is certainly emerging in Iraq as a natural part of the Islamic spectrum.

Finally, throughout all this analysis that there is some kind of zero sum game between Sunni and Shia forces in Iraq. For many decades considerable social interaction and even some degree of intermarriage has existed between the communities. Furthermore, neither community is monolithic. There are leftists, Islamists, nationalists, and liberals on both sides who may find grounds other than sectarianism on which to agree in developing a new national agenda. Regrettably, since the fall of Saddam Hussein the lines between the two communities have been hardening and is becoming the primary fault-line in the country today, affecting secularists as well as Islamists on both sides.

IRAQI KURDS

The Kurds had their own tradition of Islamist movements

long before the creation of the modern Iraqi state, reflecting their ties with the Ottoman Empire. As noted by Sami Shourush, the Kurdish nationalist movement in the 19th century came to be led by Kurdish shaykhs, including an armed movement against both Iranian and Ottoman power led by a Naqshbandi shaykh. While the Muslim Brotherhood began to influence the Kurds of Iraq in the 1950s, by the 1980s when the Baath repressions against the Kurds reached new intensity, the Kurds felt that the Brotherhood had failed them in not devoting attention to the Kurdish issue and in not supporting an armed struggle against Saddam Hussein ("Islamist Fundamentalist Movements Among the Kurds," in Abdul-Jabar, ed., *Ayatollahs, Sufis, and Ideologues*). As a consequence, the Kurds have tended to form their own Islamist movements that are better designed to meet their own national needs.

This fact is significant in that it suggests that political Islam has not been able to bridge the fault-lines dividing the three major ethnic-religious groups in Iraq. (This same situation exists between Kurds and Turks in Turkey to some degree.) There is no reason why political Islam should not be able to bridge the ethnic gap, especially since Islam and Islamists speak out against any division of the *umma* (community) along ethnic lines. Nonetheless, the reality of Iraqi politics, at least today, demonstrates that the ethnic gap is still meaningful in organizational terms.

The Kurds also produced their own Kurdish jihadist movement, the Ansar, who were linked with the jihadist constellations around al Qaeda, although the movement was dispersed and possibly destroyed-at least for now-by U.S. forces during the February 2003 war that overthrew Saddam Hussein. The U.S. occupation will not permit its return if at all possible.

It is unlikely that we will see a serious merging of Kurdish and Sunni Arab Islamist movements in the foreseeable future as long as Kurdish aspirations have not been met and a distinct "nationalist cause" remains among the Kurds. This does not rule out possible cooperation as distinct organizations on selected issues within Iraqi politics, including in all likelihood, a call for an early end to the U.S. occupation.

According to Shoroush, the largest Kurdish Islamist movement today is the (Sunni) Islamic Movement of Iraqi Kurdistan, which has been part of the umbrella Kurdistan Front and has run in several elections, placing well behind the two dominant Kurdish political parties, the Kurdish Democratic Party and the Patriotic Union of Kurdistan. It has established good working relations with other Islamist movements in other countries but is not anti-western. A very small Kurdish Shiite movement (among so-called Fayli Kurds) exists, primarily in exile, and is not a factor on the Kurdish political scene in Kurdistan. A point of speculation is the possibility of Kurdish Islamists in both Turkey and Iraq joining forces in some meaningful way in the future. Such a development would produce immense anxiety in Ankara and Tehran. What is a near certainty is that Kurdish Islamists will have little reason to adopt anti-western positions as long as the West is perceived as supportive of Kurdish aspirations for autonomy.

A number of key issues emerge in this overview of the future prospects for Islamist parties in the new Iraq:

Islamism, as a basic feature of Muslim and especially Arab politics, is destined to play a major role in the future of Iraqi politics, now liberated from the Saddam Hussein strait-jacket. While Iraq has had a long secular tradition, the Baath regime has created immense resentments within Iraqi society that will seek expression. More important, in the wake of the brutal and corrupt Baath regime, a huge moral and ideological vacuum has emerged in Iraq, and Islam is tailor-made to provide a new moral compass to the people.

There has already been a resurgence of Islamic norms in dress and public decorum that functions at a societal level entirely outside the purview of the U.S.-led occupation administration and its policies.

Neighboring states are, predictably, already moving quickly where possible to establish centers of influence within

Iraq to prepare for the day when U.S. power departs. Iran will support Islamist movements among the Shia while Saudi Arabia and the Gulf states will seek to bolster Sunni forces in Iraq-most likely through the vehicle of Sunni Islamists.

Sunni Islamism in Iraq will be dominated by the Muslim Brotherhood. Wahhabi influence from abroad will also be present, although largely as a result of foreign funding, primarily from the Gulf by those who wish to bolster Sunni power in Iraq. The growth of Wahhabi power in Iraq will most likely stem from any growing hostility to the U.S. occupation and they will probably take the lead in armed opposition to the U.S. presence. It will be difficult for the Brotherhood to remain outside this resistance to occupation, even if they are otherwise non-violent.

The emergence of Shiite power in Iraq, rather than giving Iran a major hold over the new Iraq, is more likely to lead to rivalry with Iran over time and pose a basic ideological threat to Iranian hardliners who champion clerical rule. While the Shia in particular rejoiced at the overthrow of Saddam Hussein, it is now the United States, in their view, that stands between them and the attainment of national power. This will render them more impatient than any other Iraqi group with a prolonged American occupation.

Divisions between Sunni and Shia communities are regrettably hardening among both secularists and Islamists on each side. Nativist trends among the Shia may emerge strongly, reflecting elements of Iraqi nationalism even within religious circles. In that case, the Sadr group, possibly augmented by the independent Dawa group, might emerge as the most powerful forces, and possibly as the most hostile to the United States. Both Iranian and U.S. policies could weaken the Sadr group's bid for power, but that would leave the United States working with elements close to Iran.

It is hard to foresee the emergence of any "secular" Shiite movement to rival clerical influence, even though individual Shia may indeed opt for a secular government, oppose religiously linked movements, and work in cooperation with liberal

Sunnis. Iraqi Shia are much less likely than Iranian Shia to accept clerical rule, even while possibly supporting some kind of Islamic state in which clerics do not dominate.

Saudi Arabia and Bahrain have the most to lose from resurgent Shiite power in Iraq.

The Islamists-Shia and Sunni-are not automatically hostile to the U.S. presence, especially since both gained from the overthrow of Saddam Hussein. But they are determined to retain the "Muslim character" of Iraq, especially in the face of non-Muslim occupation. They will pursue a policy of opposition to the U.S. presence, building a consensus against any cultural changes in Iraqi society. Both Sunni and Shiite Islamists are strongly nationalist in outlook and will cooperate fully with secular nationalist forces to speed the end of the occupation. At what point non-violent opposition to the occupation might transform into violent opposition is unknowable, but such a transition seems almost a certainty the longer the occupation is maintained, with all its inevitable stresses and shortcomings.

Sunni Islamists among the Muslim Brotherhood will likely be more open to cooperation with the Shia than the converse. Iraqi Sunnis lost heavily with the fall of Saddam Hussein and need cooperation with the ascendant Shia power to maintain a voice. However, the demographic strength of the Shia makes it easy for them to ignore cooperation with Sunni groups.The Wahhabis are not likely to cooperate with the Shia.

Islamist power inside Iraq will be diminished to the extent there is freedom enjoyed by other political and religious parties within the country to rival the Islamists. As nearly everywhere, repression of political pluralism invariably works to the benefit of the Islamists.

Any U.S. administrative presence in Iraq will have to reckon with the abiding force of Iraqi geopolitics that can be temporarily suppressed, but never eliminated. Iraq as a state will almost certainly continue to see itself as a leader of the Arab world. It will see itself as the "natural" protector of the Gulf against Iranian power, and possessed of a mission to change what it perceives as the dated, corrupt, pampered, and pro-western character of Gulf regimes. It will continue to have sympathy for the Palestinian cause. Islamists and secularists alike will support these goals.

4

Islamic Revolutions in Iran and Radical Politics in Turkey

REVOLUTION IN IRAN: AN INTRODUCTION

The intensity of the Iranian Revolution of 1979 and the suddenness with which it appeared "out of the blue" surprised many people both in Iran itself and in the rest of the world. There were, of course, many and varied factors and we are probably still too close to the event to be able to make any meaningful assessment of their relative importance.

There is undoubtedly an important economic background to the Revolution. The large amount of money flowing into the country following the oil price rise led to a boom, which eventually rebounded with ensuing hyper-inflation and unemployment. The results included much corruption in the upper echelons of society and a sense of disappointment and frustration among the people at the non-appearance of the prosperity that had been promised them. The suppression of protest and even of political discussion in the country, the activities of foreign powers within the country, and the organization of the opposition forces are among factors that should be looked at in any full analysis of the background of the 1979 Revolution. We can detect it occurring in all parts of the Muslim world (and elsewhere also). Therefore it must represent a response to factors that are affecting a wider area than just Iran. There appears to be a widespread perception that the adoption of the practices and standards of Western civilization has not only failed to bring about improvement, it has led to a deterioration in moral standards, causing a loss of sexual morality and a rise in the taking of alcohol and drugs. In Islamic societies, there is also the humiliation of seeing the Muslim world subservient, economically and militarily, to the countries of the West, together with the associated factor of the creation of the state of Israel. These may be considered to be the general religious and cultural factors contributing to the Revolution.

A. The Role of the Ulama in Society

The active role of the Shi'i religious scholars (the ulama) in the Revolution has been noted by almost everyone who has commented on this episode. How then did it come about that the ulama, which in the rest of the Islamic world tend to maintain a low profile in social and political matters, were able to take such a prominent part in the 1979 Iranian Revolution?

The early history of Shi'i Islam was that of being a persecuted minority within the Islamic community. Since those in authority were inimical to the Shi'is, it was only natural that the leadership of the Shi'i community fell to their religious scholars. It is therefore part of Shi'ism's history and ethos that the ulama have been seen as leaders, spokesmen of and intercessors for the Shi'i community. When Shi'i states did eventually arise, the role of the ulama nevertheless continued as upholders of individual and community rights in the face of any tyranny from the authorities.

The theoretical basis for this role of the ulama was through the evolution of the *na'ib al-'amm* (collective or general vicegerency) concept. The history of this concept goes back to the earliest period of Twelver Shi'i history. With the occultation of the Imam, all of his functions, including the giving of judgements on points of religious law, the collection of religious taxes, the leading of the Friday prayers, etc. were at first considered to have lapsed. However, as time went by and the Imam did not reappear, the theoretical absence of all religious authority became a doctrine that was increasingly difficult to maintain. Therefore the *ulama* began gradually to argue that they, as a body, had been designated the deputy of the Imam. The basis of this assertion was the existence of a number of traditions that appear to give the *ulama* the authority to act on behalf of the Imam. These traditions relate to specific circumstances, and not all of them are considered reliable; but those who wished to advance the scope of the activities of the *ulama* argued that these traditions gave them the authority to act as the deputies of the Hidden Imam. Using this argument, the *ulama* began gradually to assume more and more of the functions of the Imam in the religious sphere: the giving of judgements on religious law, the collection of religious taxes, the leading of the Friday prayers, etc.

There was, however in Shi'i history, an ongoing tension between those who pressed forward the social role of the ulama and those who held back. There have been at various times in Shi'i history different issues over which this unresolved tension has played out. In the earliest period, Shi'i ulama such as Kulayni (d. 940 C.E.) and Ibn Babuya (d. 991 C.E.), felt themselves to be primarily transmitters of the Traditions (*hadith*) of the Imams. They decried the Sunni used of analogical reasoning (*qiyas*) and innovative exegesis (*ijtihad*). In the later Buyid period, the balance swung towards those ulama, such as Shaykhu't-Ta'ifa al-Tusi (d. 1067 C.E.) who wanted to be able to give judgements in an increasingly wide range of social matters. This was accompanied by a move towards Mu'tazilite rationality and increased social involvement of the ulama in directing the affairs of the community. The same conflict between different attitudes of the ulama can be seen in the conflict between the Akhbari and Usuli schools of jurisprudence. This disagreement, which had undoubtedly been brewing for some centuries, emerged during the Safavid era (16th- 17^{th}century C.E.). The Akhbaris were conservative in giving legal judgements. They confined themselves to those areas in which they felt there was clear, unambiguous guidance from the Qur'an and Traditions and were content to leave other matters to secular courts. They tended towards piety, mysticism and mystical philosophy. The Usulis were prepared to use the tool of *ijtihad* to deliver legal judgements (*fatwas*) on almost any social or personal issue. They were therefore able to extend the social role of the ulama. This conflict was eventually won by the Usulis at the beginning of the eighteenth century.

The Usulis were faced with two major challenges in the 19th Century. The first was the Shaykhi movement, which through its emphasis on piety and mysticism, was again an attempt to move Shi'ism away from its social involvement. The ulama moved against the Shaykhis and succeeded in eliminating this threat. A more significant threat emerged in the form of the Babi movement in the middle of the 19th century. The Bab claimed to be the author of a new revelation, superceding Islam; he claimed his message was a new teaching from God and his writings a new holy book, superceding the Qur'an. This claim, together with the denunciations of the ulama that the Bab made, was a direct challenge to the ulama. While they had succeeded in dealing with the challenge of the Akhbaris and Shaykhis largely through debate, they were not successful in halting the Babi movement in this way. Eventually they resorted to violence and succeeded in inciting the Iranian government to launch a campaign which succeeded in driving the Babis underground. Eventually the Babi movement transformed into the Baha'i movement and has gone on to become a world-wide religion. But its persecution in Iran has always prevented it from being a threat to the position of the ulama.

Although in formal terms the Usulis won over their adversaries, the tension between greater and lesser degrees of involvement of the ulama in social affairs has remained. In general one can say that three courses of action have been open to the ulama in their social and political role:

1. **Political Aloofness-** This attitude stems from the belief that the *ulama* should concern themselves only with the *shari'a.* The secular authorities have the obligation to ensure that conditions are suitable for the carrying out of the *shari'a.*

As long as they do this, then the *ulama* do not concern themselves with political matters. This has traditionally been the attitude of the majority of the leading *ulama* from the time of the Qajar dynasty until recent years. Many of the most important figures in Shi'ism from this period exemplifies this attitude, for example: Shaykh Murtada al-Ansari (d. 1864) and Ayatollah Burujirdi (d. 1962).

2. **Support for the Government-** Those that advocated this position argued that the *shari'a* can only be promulgated in conditions of political stability and social order. Therefore it is the duty of the *ulama* to support the Government in the execution of its duties. This view seems to have predominated during the Safavid period when the interests of the *ulama* the state were more or less identical. The foremost *ulama* of the period- such figures as Shaykh Baha' al-Din Amili (Shaykh-i Baha'i, d. 1622 or 1623) and Muhammad Baqir Majlisi (d. 1699 or 1700)- accepted state positions (both of them held the post of Shaykh al-Islam in Isfahan), and were incorporated into the state apparatus. During the Qajar period, a few of the *ulama* remained supporters of the state. Not surprisingly, the majority of these were those whose positions depended on state appointment, for example the successive Imam-Jum'ihs of Tehran.
3. **Opposition to the Government-** This position was buttressed by the theoretical illegitimacy of all temporal authority in the absence of the Hidden Imam. In practice this position was adopted whenever the *ulama* felt their position threatened either directly, through secularizing reforms, or indirectly, when their main financial supporters, the merchants of the bazaar, were threatened. Some of the *ulama* were more prone to adopt this position than others, for example Shaykh Mahdi al-Khalisi (d. 1925) in Iraq, and Sayyid Abul-Qasim Kashani (d. 1962) in Iran.

It should not be imagined, however, that these three positions represent three different schools of political thought, and that Shi'is would choose one position to follow. Rather they represent three options to be exercised by Shi'is according to circumstances. Thus it is common to find individual *ulama* who moved backwards and forwards between these three positions, according to circumstances. For example Mirza Hasan Shirazi (Mirza-yi Shirazi, d. 1895), the leading Shi'i scholar of the late nineteenth century, is usually remembered by most historians as the person who issued a *fatwa* forbidding the consumption of tobacco, and thus brought about the collapse of the Tobacco Regie in 1891. He is therefore usually thought of as having been a revolutionary figure. In fact, for almost all of his life, following the example of his teacher Shaykh Murtada al-Ansari, he studiously avoided any interference in political affairs. Then in the matter of the Tobacco Regie he decided to abandon this policy and become actively involved. A few months later, when the issue was over, he reverted to his former position. Conversely, Shaykh Muhammad Husayn Na'ini was politically active for some twenty years, at first opposing the Shah as one of the most active supporters of the Constitutionalists, and later opposing British rule in Iraq. And yet after he was expelled from Iraq in 1923 for his political agitation, he played no further political role even though he returned to Iraq in 1924 and lived until 1936.

The majority of the *ulama* were flexible in their social and political attitudes, being fully able to vary their approach according to what they perceived to be their best interests. Prior to Khomeini, we can find almost no figure in Shi'i history who was opposed to the existing government in the sense that he advocated its complete overthrow and replacement with a clerical government.

The most that Shi'i *ulama* have demanded in the past has been that the government of the day make its policies conform more closely to the *shari'a,* which in practical terms has meant that the government should make its policies conform with what the *ulama* perceived to be their own best interests. It is really only with Khomeini, and then only in his later years, that opposition to the Government became a fixed and unnegotiable position based on a political theory that made the very existence of the government illegitimate.

One factor that has helped the ulama whenever they have wished to take an active social role is the fact that, in contrast to the Sunni ulama, they have a financial base that is independent of the state. Shi'i law states that the religious taxes of *khums* and *zakat* should be paid to the Imam. In the absence of the Imam, the ulama have asserted that they were the rightful recipients of these taxes. The income derived therefrom gives the ulama an independent financial base which makes it much easier for them to oppose the government if they should choose to do so.

As economic conditions in Iran in the 1970s deteriorated, political repression became more pronounced, and Western influence increasingly penetrated Iranian society, the people increasingly turned to the ulama in their traditional role as the spokesmen of and intercessors for the masses. While most of the ulama contented themselves with their traditional aloof attitude towards social and political questions, a few under the leadership of Khomeini began to take a more active stance.

B. Political Authority in Twelver Shi'ism

Among the questions that must be asked is: how did a sect that at its outset in early Islamic history was regarded as the most least aggressive and most accommodating of the Shi'i sects become transformed into a revolutionary force that was able to sweep away what had been regarded as one of the most stable regimes in the Middle East?

Shi'ism was, of course, the expression of support for the claims of Ali, the cousin and son-in-law of Muhammad, and his descendants to leadership of the Islamic community. Three main sects of Shi'ism have survived from the earliest period of Islam to the present day. Historically, the first of these to come to prominence was Zaydi Shi'ism. Politically, this sect believed that authority belonged to any descendent of Ali who rose to claim it, and was able to achieve it. A large number of revolts during the Ummayad and early Abbasid periods were Zaydi in origin, but apart from some limited success in Yemen and Tabaristan in Iran, the Zaydis were never able to achieve much political power. The second of these Shi'i sects to come to prominence was Isma'ili Shi'ism. It held that political authority belonged to its line of Imams, who were descendants of Ali. This Shi'i grouping arose in revolt in North Africa, and was able to establish its line of Imams as the Fatimid caliphate in Egypt from 909 to 1171 C.E. However, these two sects today represent only a minority of the world's Shi'is.

By far the largest grouping of Shi'is today are the Ithna-'Asharis (Twelvers), which is the group that we are concerned with in this presentation. They believe in a succession of twelve infallible religious leaders called Imams, the first of whom was Ali, the cousin and son-in-law of the Prophet, and the twelfth of whom is believed to have gone into occultation in 874 C.E. Since Twelver Shi'ism cannot be said to have come into existence until this latter date, it was the last of these three Shi'i sects to be established. But it differed from the other two Shi'i sects in a radical way. Zaydi and Isma'ili Shi'ism were revolutionary, and never really succeeded in establishing themselves in any appreciable numbers in the Islamic heartlands, where their revolts were crushed and they were persecuted relentlessly. They were always a phenomenon of the fringes of the Islamic world. The Twelvers on the other hand, from the very start, existed primarily in the Islamic heartlands. Their main centre was for many years in the Abbasid capital at Kufa and, later, Baghdad. Many of their most prominent figures were leading statesmen in the Abbasid power structure; the al-Furat and Nawbakhti families, for example who held the highest positions in the Abbasid administration.

For these Shi'is at the centre of Abbasid power, the Shi'i tradition of revolt and opposition was clearly undesirable and unwanted, as it made them suspect in the eyes of their Abbasid patrons. The resolution to this problem was found among the influential circle in Baghdad that included the Nawbakhti family. Politically this involved the declaration that the Imam had gone into hiding (occultation). This mystic removal of the Imam from the eyes of men served two purposes. Firstly, it effectively removed the Imam from being a focal point for opposition. For no-one could raise a rebellion in favour of an

Imam who was not there. The second consequence of the occultation was that, since the Imam was still alive, although occulted, no one else could claim to be the Imam (and there had been numerous claimants to the Imamate in Shi'i history). The Imamate, which for the other Shi'i sects was a political institution, a rival for the caliphate, had been depoliticized by the Twelvers and transformed into a focus for theological elaboration and eschatological expectation. It was no longer a threat to the political establishment and so the Twelvers could be seen as loyal citizens within the Abbasid power structure.

It may be thought that if the Twelver Shi'is were not militant and revolutionary in their early history, then this tendency arose within the sect prior to the Safavid conquest of Iran in 1501 and the establishment of Twelver Shi'ism as the state religion. But in fact, the Safavid assumption of power in Iran had little to do with Shi'i militancy. The Safavids were primarily a Sufi order that became increasingly militaristic and Shi'i in orientation. This Shi'ism was not however of the Twelver kind, but of the kind that is generally referred to as *ghulat* (extremist). This designation refers to various doctrines held by these groups which were considered, by orthodox Shi'is and Sunnis alike, to make them heretics and outside the pale of Islam. Thus, for example, Isma'il the first Safavid ruler of Iran, wrote poetry in which he equated himself with the Divinity. It was this mixture of 'extremist' Shi'ism and militaristic Sufism that gave the Safavid order the fervour and dynamism to rise against the established order in Iran, and take over the country in a very short period of time. However, once the conquest was achieved and the new state established, Isma'il proclaimed Twelver Shi'ism as the state religion. Part of his thinking was no doubt that Twelver Shi'ism would be a more quietist, and therefore more stable, religious basis for the new state than the extremist Shi'i/Sufi admixture of his Safavid supporters. Once again, we find Twelver Shi'ism being identified with stability and quietism, rather than with revolution and militancy.

There was, however, at the heart of Twelver Shi'ism a certain tension. Over against this history of quietism and political accommodation, there was the doctrine that all political and religious authority belonged by right to the Hidden Twelfth Imam and anyone who held power was therefore a usurper of the rights of the Imam. There was thus a contradiction between what the Shi'i texts said and what in practice the Shi'is themselves did. The difference was bridged, in part, through the doctrine of *taqiyya,* the Shi'i doctrine of pious dissimulation. This doctrine held that a Shi'i could deny their faith or assert a different position from that which the Shi'is believe in order to protect themselves from danger. The difference was also in part accounted for by other teachings which stated that since it was necessary for there to be social order for the Shari'a to be implemented, it was necessary to obey a just ruler.

It cannot be said that Shi'ism in its early history developed any coherent political theory, in the same way that Sunni Islam did. With a Hidden Imam, all political questions were frozen. No-one had the authority to replace the Imam, but equally no Shi'i could claim religious authority for trying to overthrow the existing regime. Those Shi'i writers of the early period who do mention the question of opposition and rebellion were of the opinion that revolt and rebellion against the established ruler, even if he be unjust, were not permissible as the overthrowing of oppression and wrong, and the establishment of justice, constituted one of the tasks that the Hidden Imam would perform on his return.

Typical of early Shi'i expressions of opinion is the following passage from the Buyid scholar, al-Shaykh al-Mufid. Writing about the return of the Hidden Imam, he states:

> 'His fathers [i.e. the preceding Imams] on the other hand allowed [their followers] to practise dissimulation before their enemies, engage in social intercourse with them and be present at their assemblies. In fact they forbade [their followers] to draw the sword against them and warned against inciting anyone to do so.'

Very few of the Shi'i *ulama* have written political treatises. Those that have been written date mainly from Qajar times up to the present. Several treatises were written in the early Qajar period by eminent *ulama* who were supporters of the state. The Qajars, having established them by force and not having a supposed descent from the Imams which the Safavids claimed, were in need of a basis of legitimacy to act as a buttress for their authority. In these treatises, the principle was enunciated that the political rulers were the agents of God, and of the Hidden Imam, in establishing social order and thus promoting the Holy Law.

In a later period, some of the *ulama* wrote treatises in favour of the Constitutional Movement. Although modern scholars have sought out and brought these political treatises into prominence, in their own time they were not held to be of any great importance, and were among the more obscure of the writings of their authors.

When Imam Ruhullah Khomeini (1902-1989) began to write on political matters, therefore, he was going outside the tradition of the major Shi'i *ulama*. In order to understand the revolution in Shi'i political thought that he brought about, it is necessary to review briefly the background of the basis of the authority of the *ulama*. The authority of the Sunni *ulama* is based on their appointment to a particular office by the State. Thus the authority on the basis of which a Mufti gives judgement is by virtue of his appointment as Mufti. The theoretical basis for the authority of the *ulama* in Shi'i Islam is quite different. Their authority is based on the concept that they are collectively the deputies of the Hidden Imam *(na'ib al-Imam al-'amm,* see above). Thus, according to the most authoritative texts, even if they are appointed by the government to a position such as judge in a court, their authority to give judgements is still by virtue of the *na'ib al-'amm* concept.

Until the advent of Khomeini, however, none of the leading *ulama* formally laid claim to the right to deputize for the political authority of the Imam. This political authority was either held to have lapsed with the occultation of the Imam or, as described above, the *ulama* would sometimes advance arguments to justify the interim derivative legitimacy of the secular political authorities.

Khomeini was the first to outline a theoretical position which involved an uncompromising assertion that only a government by experts in religious jurisprudence *(vilayat-i faqih)* is an acceptable form of Islamic government. This was not always Khomeini's position. His earliest writings only insisted that the Shah's government should conform to Islamic norms as defined by him. It was only after his exile to Iraq in 1964 that he began, in his lectures to the religious students at Najaf, to call for the *vilayat-i faqih*. His position was that an Islamic ruler needs to rule in accordance with the Holy Law (the *shari'a)*, and only an Islamic scholar, an expert in jurisprudence (the *faqih)*, can have a sufficient knowledge of the *shari'a*. Therefore leadership in an Islamic country belongs by right only to a *faqih*.

There is however nothing illogical in Khomeini's extension of the *na'ib al-'amm* concept to include the political authority of the Hidden Imam. The distinction between church and state which exists in the West is meaningless in Islam. Islam is not just a religion, but a religio-political entity in which all religious and social matters come under the purview of the *shari'a*. And if the *ulama* are the general vicegerents of the Hidden Imam in all religious matters, why not in the political sphere also?

Although Imam Khomeini's concept of the *ulama's* right to supervise political affairs *(vilayat-i faqih)* can thus be seen as a logical extension of the *na'ib al-'amm* concept, it is nevertheless a radical break with the Shi'i tradition that the leading *ulama* concern themselves in political matters only very rarely; and then only when issues of major importance arise. This had certainly been the attitude of the major *ulama* right up to and including Ayatollah Burujirdi (d. 1962), the last Ayatollah who could claim to be sole *marja al-taqlid*. Even now, despite Khomeini's prestige, the concept is not universally accepted among Shi'is. In Iran itself, opposition to the *vilayat-i faqih* concept was led by a group calling itself the Hujjatiyyih. Outside Iran, the major *marja al-taqlid*, several important ayatollahs have voiced reservations about it (in particular the late Ayatollah Khu'i).

C. The Karbala Paradigm

Much of the power and intensity of the 1979 Revolution came from the willingness of ordinary people to go out onto the streets and court death by confronting armed troops. What was it that inspired ordinary people to risk their lives, to move from a pattern of ordinary every-day life into the mould of heroism and self-sacrifice?

In traditional societies (and even in modern societies to large extent), people are inspired by and try to live their lives in accordance with certain mythic paradigms. In the telling and retelling of the myths of the society, the psychological and ethical norms of the society are built up, the role models by which people live their lives are inculcated and the general ethos of a society is created.

In Shi'i Islam, as indeed with most religions, popular religious activities play a major role in the life of the individual by creating the myths by which the individual lives. In Shi'i Islam, centre place in popular religion is taken by the various re-enactments of the Karbala episode. From early childhood, most Shi'is have been immersed in a culture in which the martyrdom of the Imam Husayn plays a very prominent role. The martyrdom of the third of the Shi'i Imams, Husayn, at the hands of the Umayyad armies of the caliph Yazid at Karbala in AD 680, is undoubtedly one of the most important and emotive episodes in Shi'i history. The first ten days of the month of Muharram are completely given over to commemorating the martyrdom, culminating on the tenth day, *'Ashura*, the day of the martyrdom of the Imam. This forms the most important religious event of the year, far outweighing any of the commemorations associated with the Prophet Muhammad, or any other of the Imams. The commemorations take the form of orations recounting the episode, plays depicting the events, and ritualized processions of mourning at which it is usual to see people whipping themselves, and cutting themselves in a state of frenzied mourning for the martyred Imam. For the rest of the year also, it is not uncommon to hold meetings at which narrations of the Karbala episode are given, and at which expressions of grief abound. Thus the Karbala episode is not an event in distant history, but rather a powerful symbol kept alive among the Shi'i masses by frequent emotive rituals and ceremonies.

In the rest of the year, there are numerous commemorations of the other Shi'i Imams who were persecuted and martyred by their enemies in the first three centuries of the history of Islam. The other ten Imams of Twelver Shi'ism did not, however, rise up in rebellion to assert the leadership that they believed had wrongfully been taken from them. They lived quiet lives of prayer and piety, restraining their followers from any active opposition to the Sunni caliphate and ordering them to practice *taqiyya.*

Here again we can observe some degree of polarity and tension between two opposite paradigms. The Husayn/Karbala paradigm of *qiyamat* (uprising) is one of taking an active role, rising up against injustice and tyranny; its opposite paradigm, *mazlumiyyat* (patient endurance of tyranny) is one of political quietism and was espoused by the other Shi'i Imams. Both are available to Shi'is. Both can inspire paths of social and political action.

Three themes that are specific to Shi'i Islam- the leadership role of the Shi'i ulama, the question of political authority in Shi'ism and the role of the Karbala paradigm in the popular religion have shown how each of these three themes had their origins in the earliest days of Islam and how they culminated by playing a major role in the 1979 Revolution. But each of these three powerful motivating impulses for the Iranian Revolution were in fact only one pole of opposing tensions within Shi'i Islam: the tension within the leadership role of the ulama between political activism and quietism; the tension within Shi'i political theory between obedience to the government and the concept that all government is an unjust usurpation of the authority of the Hidden Imam; and the tension between the *qiyamat*paradigm of Husayn rising up against tyranny and the *mazlumiyyat* paradigm of the other Imams patiently enduring the tyranny of others.

In the history of Shi'ism and Iran, these tensions within Shi'ism have at times pulled in one direction and at other times in the other, particular in the last two centuries. It was perhaps the misfortune of the late Shah of Iran to experience the effects of a point in time when all three factors were moving powerfully in the direction of social action and against his government.

RADICAL ISLAMIC POLITICS IN TURKEY

RADICAL POLITICS: AN INTRODUCTION

It focuses on the most radical groups within the framework of overall Islamic activity in Turkey and argues that radical Islamic terrorist organizations active in Turkey during the 1990s have striven to establish an Islamic Sharia'-based state on the Iranian example, profited from deeper social and political trends in Turkish society, and at the same time strengthened these trends by their violence. These groups enjoyed wide Iranian support and often acted on behalf of Iranian local and regional, political and strategic interests. The reaction of Turkish authorities in the past to Islamic terrorist activity was limited and thus encouraged leaders of these groups and their sponsors to continue escalating violence hoping it will bring down the secular democratic regime in Turkey.

Most observers in Turkey and abroad have viewed the Kurdish Workers' Party (PKK) as the main threat to the Turkish state's national unity and defense. Despite recent interest in the Islamic fundamentalist Welfare Party (Refah Partisi, RP) growth, hardly any research examines the even more radical, violent Islamic movements in Turkey. These most extreme groups are largely ignored because of their small size and apparently limited threat.

It has been argued that the marginality of violent Islamist groups in Turkey in contrast to the vigorous armed opposition in Egypt or Algeria is due to the Turkish political system's pluralism and the RP's full integration into this system. But the leaders and sponsors of these extremist organizations think that by violence against the secular symbols of the Turkish state, leading secular intellectuals and journalists, and representatives of "Imperialism and Zionism," they will indeed help install an Islamic state. The limited reaction by the authorities up to 1996 and the RP's electoral victories seemed to provide reasons for this hope.

POLITICAL AND STRATEGIC BACKGROUND

The military coup of 1980 was intended to end a long period of widespread terrorism and violence throughout the country perpetrated by extremist left-wing and right-wing organizations, and also to hold back the threat of radical Islam embodied in the National Salvation Party led by Necmettin Erbakan. But while military rule between 1980-1983 did break up the extreme left and right, the Islamic movement survived and even grew in importance during the 1980s.

A new ideological concept was developed by a group of right-wing intellectuals (Intellectuals' Hearth-Aidinlar Ocagi) and adopted by the military, "The Turkish-Islamic Synthesis" which, on its pragmatic side, represented an attempt to integrate Islamists and the nationalists. The main idea was that the Islamist influence in the system would contribute to the territorial integrity of the Turkish nation-state and counter revolutionary sentiments, especially among Kurdish youth. The Islamists offered an attractive alternative even for ex-communists after the collapse of communism in the Soviet bloc.

On the foreign front, the Turkish-Islamic synthesis was supposed to help contain Soviet expansion southward and to combat the radical Iranian brand of Islam by constructing a coalition of U.S.-backed moderate Islamic states. This policy favored closer relations with Saudi Arabia to gain big loans for the needy Turkish economy. The Cold War's end, USSR's disintegration, the birth of new republics mostly inhabited by peoples of Turk origin, the Gulf war's result and the Bosnian crisis created at the beginning of the 1990s a new international environment which put Turkey in a key position, sometimes in direct competition with Iran for regional strategic influence and economic assets.

THE HISTORY OF THE ISLAMIC MOVEMENT IN TURKEY

The Islamic subversive and terrorist activity in Turkey began in the 1960s. As early as 1967 and 1973 the leaders of

Hizb-al-Tahrir (Islamic Liberation Party) were imprisoned for attempting "to bring the Islamic State Constitution to Turkey" Islamic Jihad appeared as a real terrorist threat in the 1980s, after a series of assassinations of Jordanian, Saudi and Iraqi diplomats. In October 1991 Islamic Jihad took responsibility for killing an American sergeant and wounding an Egyptian diplomat to protest the Middle East peace conference in Madrid. For many years it was assumed that this group was a Lebanese Shiite terrorist organization, until it was discovered that a Turkish branch existed, engaging in assassinations of secular intellectuals.

As Anat Lapidot correctly notes, defining the Islamic movement is a complex task, since the term is applied to different organizations, with their own ideas and strategies, seeking to establish an Islamic state and society. Citing Sabri Sayari, she distinguishes between traditionalists and radicals, the latter being a minority inspired by the Iranian revolution.

Ismet Imset points to the confusion about these different groups among the general public, researchers, and government circles in Turkey. A report by the Turkish National Intelligence Organization (MIT) and the Security General Directorate of the Police in October 1991 mentioned no less than ten Islamic organizations active in Turkey: Turkish Islamic Liberation Army (IKO), Turkish Islamic Liberation Front (TIK-C), Fighters of the Islamic Revolution (IDAM), Turkish Islamic Liberation Union (TIKB), World Sharia Liberation Army (DSKO), Universal Brotherhood Front-Sharia Revenge Squad (EKC-SIM), Islamic Liberation Party Front (IKP-C), Turkish Fighters of the Universal Islamic War of Liberation (EIK-TM), Turkish Islamic Fighters Army (IMO) and Turkish Sharia Revenge Commandos (TSIK).

In this article, Islamic movement is the term used to describe all the currents in Turkish Islam while Islamic Movement refers to one of the main radical groups.

Imset makes a distinction between western and southeast Turkey. In the West the Islamic Movement (Islami Hareket), called also Islamic Resistance (Islami Direnis), is considered to represent the ideological influence of the original (Iranian) Hezbollah. Both Movement and Resistance were only temporary code names, at least until 1990. In southeast Turkey the movement spread first under the name of Hezbollah, and then was referred as the Hezbol-contra, to address its anti-PKK activity. According to Imset, the concepts of Hezbollah and Islamic Movement are in fact one, representing an umbrella organization of groups acting on behalf of what he calls "The International Islamic Movement."

At the end of the 1970s, under the influence of the coalition between left-wing organizations and Khomeini's followers in Iran, in Turkey was established an alliance of the left, especially Maoists, with radical Islamic elements and together they attacked the nationalist right. The conflict peaked in February 1979 when a young Muslim leader was killed by nationalists (known as "Idealists") in the yard of the Fatih mosque in Istanbul.

The Turkish Islamic Movement, like all other radical organizations, received a serious blow during the September 1980 military coup. But, as the regime encouraged the general Islamic trend as a solution to political polarization and as both Marxists and nationalists lost their influence, Islamic activists were afforded ample space to strengthen their position. The "Hezbollah Muslims" appeared for the first time publicly in 1984 and, as the original Hezbollah, proclaimed support for the Iranian revolution and the defense not of nations or sects, but of "Allah's way."

According to Imset, Kalim Siddiqui, a Pakistani active at the Muslim Institute in London, had a key role in unifying Turkey's radical Islamic Movement. Thus, the first Hezbollahi appeared in Turkey as the "followers of Siddiki." A pro-Hezbollah magazine published in November 1987 "The guidelines of the Islamic Movement," which included the acceptance of the Islamic State as the center of religious belief, the leadership of Muslim scholars, the spread of the mentality of martyrdom and the leadership of the Islamic revolution in Iran.

A significant development occurred in the middle of the 1980s, with the conversion of some members of the right-wing Nationalist Movement (MHP) to Islam. The death of one of their leaders in prison in 1984 and the tortures suffered by many others convinced a group of extreme nationalist activists (called also Ulkucus)"to turn to Allah" and condemn the "darkness of nationalism." They were heavily influenced by the Egyptian Muslim Brotherhood, but later concluded that Sayyd Kutub's death forced the Egyptian Islamists into a nationalist position and that true Islam could not tolerate nationalism. These militants were already professionals in the field of terrorism and street fighting and represented significant operational support for the Islamic Movement.

In southeast Turkey, Islamic radicalism emerged in poor towns and villages with a large Kurdish population (Dyarbakir, Silvan, Cizre, Kiziltepe and others), especially among the young and unemployed. They followed the teachings of local Muslim scholars or sheiks and often organized themselves around extremist Islamic publications such as Tevhid, Yeryuzu and Objektif. Their activity became more visible at the beginning of the 1990s, influenced more and more by Khomeini's teachings, and they were identified by the local public as Hezbollah, although they considered themselves as belonging to the Islamic Movement.

THE IDEOLOGY OF THE TURKISH ISLAMIC MOVEMENT

There are few sources for research on the Turkish Islamic organizations, although they have their own publications and manifestoes distributed quite freely even when they threaten future victims of terrorist attacks. All the material is in Turkish and has neither been collected nor translated. The only other source consists of interviews given by anonymous leaders and activists to Turkish journalists.

In one such interview, published in February 1993, a militant declared: "We are fighters of the Islamic Liberation Movement, the sword against Satan, blasphemy, Zionism and Imperialism. We have begun taking action only recently in Turkey and our move is based on pain, suffering and patience.

We do not pursue a tribal case; our objective is to establish a state for the Muslims." Asked whether he belonged to Hezbollah, the militant replied that the press gave that name to the organization and that they will adopt it only when the movement will be worthy of it. Meanwhile it has not reached "that level of perfection"

In speaking about the special relationship of the Movement with Iran, the same militant seemed careful not to confirm "the lies of the Turkish state" about such links. Iran is seen as an example and a guide but the instructions are "from the Koran" and not from Iran, "the land of Dar-ul Islam where blasphemy has been crushed." The Movement needs no instructions from any country because the Koran is the program and shows the strategies and the tactics to be adopted.

A report prepared by the Turkish security authorities for the National Security Council at the beginning of 1997 outlined the objectives of the radical religious movements and stressed that their strategy consists of three stages.

The first stage is the message (teblig), and calls for an effort by the radicals to persuade the people to adopt the Islamic religion, establish an Islamic state and administration, live in accordance with Islamic rules and struggle to safeguard the Islamic way of life.

The second stage is the community (cemaat) and calls for the restructuring of communities in accordance with the requirements of the first stage.

The third stage is the struggle (jihad) and calls for the armed struggle to safeguard the Islamic way of life.

Special mention should be made of a strange organization called The Great Eastern Islamic Fighters Front (IBDA-C) active since the middle of the 1970s but more extremist and aggressive since the beginning of the 1990s. Although an Islamic movement struggling for the constitution of an Islamic state, it uses leftist slogans in its publications and accepts ex-Marxists in its ranks. It is also extremely antisemitic and anti-Christian in its propaganda and terrorist activity as well.

ENEMIES AND STRATEGIC OBJECTIVES

A chronological analysis of terrorist activity of Islamic groups shows that 1990 was probably the starting point for their offensive against the Turkish secular establishment: A professor, journalist, political scientist and writer were assassinated by Islamic Jihad and the Islamic Operation (or Action), the first time this name was used. Muammar Aksoy, a liberal political scientist, was also killed in 1990 and then for the first time the name Islamic Movement appeared.

During 1991, the year of the Gulf War, Islamic radicals seemed to enter a period of reassessment, which ended after the Madrid peace talks between Arab countries and Israel. In October an American soldier was killed and an Egyptian diplomat wounded by Islamic Jihad. The year 1992 represented the turning point in radical Islamic terrorist activity. The objectives attacked during this year being from the exiled Iranian opposition as well as Jews and Israelis.

But the government, security authorities, public and even the press became really aware of and shocked by the Islamic terrorist threat when Ugur Mumcu, one of Turkey's top investigative reporters- who had covered the PKK, the rise of Islamic radicalism, and drug smuggling networks was killed on 24 January 1993 by a car-bomb similar to that used in the assassination of an Israeli diplomat in March 1992 and an American computer specialist in October 1991. Both the Islamic Liberation Organization and IBDA-C took responsibility for the murder.

Several days later an attempt was made on the life of a well- known Turkish businessman and community leader of Jewish origin, Jak Kamhi, by a group of four terrorists who used automatic weapons and even a rocket-launcher. He escaped uninjured. The same month the tortured body of an exiled Iranian dissident- Abbas Gholizadeh, a former officer and the Shah's bodyguard- kidnapped several weeks before, was discovered by the police.

This series of terrorist events provoked a sharp reaction from Turkish public opinion: huge street demonstrations in favor of the secular regime, a strong press campaign, and swift action by security authorities against the perpetrators and their sponsors. For the first time the Islamic Action or Movement and Iran were directly accused of and implicated in acts of terror against the state. The arrests and interrogations of many Turkish members of these organizations unveiled the story behind the killings of Turkish secular intellectuals and anti-Khomeini Iranian exiles in the years 1990-1992.

But the arrest and trial of dozens of Islamic terrorists did not dissuade more extremists from continuing to attack Turkish intellectuals fighting for the secular state and values. In July 1993 they set on fire a hotel where a cultural festival was taking place and 37 intellectuals were burned to death. Aziz Nesin, one of Turkey's leading literary figures, was the main individual target of the fundamentalists. He was accused of intending to publish Salman Rushdie's "Satanic Verses." A trial opened against the suspects of the massacre involved only 20 participants of a much bigger group of those responsible.

The fight of the security authorities against the radicals continued during 1994, when 659 members of Hizballah were caught, some of them responsible for murders of activists in exiled Iranian opposition groups. In January, four members of the Islamic Movement in Istanbul were arrested for their part in the killing of a Mojahedin-e Khalq activist, the Shah's ex-bodyguard and a member of the Kurdish opposition, KDPI. In October, a six-man Hizballah team was arrested while preparing to assassinate, on orders from Iranian intelligence, a woman of Armenian descent guilty of employing "only" Muslim women in her brothel! They were also involved in the assassination of Iranian dissidents.

This same year IBDA-C was responsible for 90 terrorist incidents, including five bombings in various cities. A prominent cinema critic and writer, Onat Kutlar, was killed in December by a bomb attack carried by IBDA-C aimed "at spoiling the colonialist Noel [Christmas] celebrations."

In 1995, attacks continued. IBDA-C may have been responsible for a bomb attack in January on the building of the Ataturk Association and the attempted assassination in June of a prominent Jewish community leader in Ankara.

One of the most controversial terrorist activities of Hizballah in southeast Turkey has been the liquidation of dozens of pro-PKK activists, journalists, intellectuals and politicians beginning in the fall of 1991 and throughout 1992 and 1993. It has been widely assumed that this was the work of some splinter group. The amount of immunity it enjoyed from the security authorities due to its anti-PKK nature, earned it the name "Hezbol-contra."

It must be stressed that its members were mostly of Kurdish origin. The Hizballah regarded the PKK as Islam's enemy and has accused it of "trying to create an atheist community, supporting the communist system, trying to divide the people through chauvinist activities and directing pressure on the Muslim people." An interviewed Hizballah militant in the southeast described the goal of his organization as the establishment of an "Islamic Kurdish state in Turkey."

In March 1993 the PKK signed a "cooperation protocol" with the "Hizballah Kurdish Revolutionary Party" aimed at ending the conflict and finding "methods for a joint struggle against the Turkish state." The agreement was achieved after Hizballah has recognized that it has been exploited by "the colonialists" and that the clashes in no way benefitted the cause of Islam.

A turning point in the Turkish authorities' attitude toward the Islamic terrorist threat occurred in March 1996, with the arrest of one of the leaders of Islamic Action, Irfan Cagarici, and his confessions about the role his organization has played since the early 1990s in the assassination of secular politicians and intellectuals, with direct support and supervision of Iranian intelligence.

The relations between Turkey and Iran reached a new low as a result. But then, in June 1996, the RP achieved power in an alliance with the center-right True Path party (DYP) in the first Islamic government in 73 years of secular Kemalist regimes, with Erbakan as prime minister.

ISLAM'S GROWING POLITICAL POWER AND THE PROBLEM OF TERRORISM

The "Turkish-Islamist Synthesis" was a strategy adopted by the political and military establishment at the beginning of the 1980s to counter revolutionary sentiments-especially among Kurdish youth-with the traditional conservatism of tribal leaders and Islamic scholars. The increase in the influence of Islam seemed a modest price to pay for the territorial integrity of the Turkish state.

Turgut Ozal, the first Prime Minister of a civilian government after 1983, himself had strong connections to the Nakshibandi religious order. He pushed for a relaxation of Kemalist and secularist policies and a public admission of Islam as an essential component of Turkish identity. During the long period of his rule as prime minister and then president of Turkey, Muslim associations, foundations, publications, television and radio stations, flourished and spread the message of Islam. Islamists built strongholds in the Ministry of Education.

The important role played by Islamic radical publications in the recruitment and indoctrination of militants and the designation of objectives to be attacked, cannot be underestimated: Two printing houses, the Istanbul-based Akademi and Objektif, and the monthlies Yeryuzu and Tehvid have been accused of being behind Hizballah.

IBDA-C sent death threats to the head of the Jewish community in Ankara before a bomb was placed in his car, and published a list of Jewish targets in the extreme religious periodical Akinci Yolu. IBDA-C's weekly, Taraf, took responsibility for the bomb attack on the film critic Onat Kutlar in December 1994 and sent "a warning not to play with fire" to TV journalist Ali Kirca, whom it accused of being "anti-Islam."

In this atmosphere, pro-Islamic politicians received important appointments in the sensitive field of security, such as the Ministry of Interior. This happened even before the 1980 coup, while it was under the control of Erbakan's National Salvation party. Under the interior minister at the end of the 1980s, Abdulkadir Aksu, the security apparatus- especially the intelligence and personnel departments- was penetrated by pro-Islamic elements and the slightest resistance to fundamentalism was broken. According to Ismet Imset, during this period there was a general inclination in the Ministry towards the "Saudi and even Iranian Islamism." At the end of 1991, Aksu was replaced as minister and an extensive purge was launched in the ranks of the Police to rid it of fundamentalist officers.

According to Zubaida, 700 of the 1,600 key ministry executives, provincial governors and other functionaries were believed to be RP supporters. Even in April 1994 they permitted the waging of unauthorized mass Islamist demonstrations in Ankara and Istanbul. Ironically, they were reassigned to posts in the southeast where they supported or ignored the attacks of Hizballah against the PKK.

The attitude of the Refah party's leadership regarding the violence and terror on the radical fringes of the Islamic movement is at least ambiguous, if not clearly supportive. Erbakan condemned the violence used in the assassination of journalist Mumcu in March 1993 and declared that it is incompatible with the values of true Islam but at the same time important members of his party accused Israel for killing him.

In November 1993, Erbakan said at his party's parliamentary meeting that only "Islamic fraternity" could combat the PKK, but he did not mention the terrorism of the Islamic groups at all. Hizballah has even been considered as the RP's armed protector.

Despite all the evidence, as late as the end of 1995 the leading Islamic circles denied even the existence of fundamentalist terrorist organizations. The deputy RP leader, Abdullah Gul, declared that no terror movement is compatible with Islam and that the accusation is "being circulated intentionally before the elections" in order to influence them.

According to another leader, most of the crimes in Turkey blamed on the Islamic movement are in fact "international operations" and "plots of the West" against Turkey.

Erbakan's real policy toward the Islamic terrorist groups can be judged by the hosting of representatives of Palestinian Hamas, Egypt's Muslim Brothers and Algeria's FIS at RP's political convention after his ascent to the premiership. Erbakan was not even impressed by President Mubarak's protest against the invitation of Egyptian Muslim Brothers to the party congress, which sparked a diplomatic incident with Egypt. Over the years, he maintained a strange silence about the complicity of neighboring Muslim countries in anti-Turkish terrorism.

THE IRANIAN CONNECTION AND TURKEY'S REACTION

It is quite obvious that there was deep Iranian involvement in the terrorist activities waged by Islamic groups and organizations in Turkey. In several of the most important and sensitive cases of terrorism, this interference in Turkish internal political life was proved in court. In other cases there was ample intelligence information transmitted or leaked to the press by the security authorities. The Turkish Islamic militants indicted for the murder of Mumcu and an Iranian dissident in 1993, and two of those accused of murdering three intellectuals in 1990 and a Jewish businessman in 1993, were connected with Iranian agents, among them diplomats stationed in Turkey. They received military training in Iran, on "pursuit, counter-pursuit, weapons and bombs."

The Iranians began their propaganda and indoctrination work through the numerous Cultural Centers they opened in Turkey. There they recruited and sent to Iran for training sympathizers of Khomeini's doctrine ready to work for their interests.

As noted previously, an abrupt change occurred in the Turkish authorities' attitude after Mumcu's killing. It was only when the murders got out of hand and under growing international criticism that Ankara acknowledged that the Turkish Hizballah truly existed.

For the first time, a Turkish minister of interior declared at a press conference that members of radical Islamic organizations underwent months of military and theoretical training in Iranian security installations, traveled with Iranian real and forged documents, had weapons and explosives of Iranian origin and participated in attacks on Turkish citizens and also Iranian opposition militants.

In spite of these grave revelations, the overall political approach towards Iran was very cautious. The minister of interior concluded that Iran as a state was not behind these actions, that it had no interest in such murders in Turkey, but, however, "The perpetrators had connections in Iran."

A detailed account of the "Iranian Connection" in these cases and the official Turkish ambiguous position was given by Imset. President Ozal remarked that "foreign forces" may be behind provocative incidents and may have supporters in Turkey, without naming them. Prime Minister Demirel called for a "coolheaded" approach to the Iranian link in order not to disrupt bilateral relations unnecessarily. He expressed the belief that the Iranian state was not involved in the murders and that it would cooperate on the issue with the Turkish authorities.

Although Iranian officials denied any involvement in aiding or training Turkish terrorist organizations, the Iranian Foreign Minister, Velayati, had a more subtle reaction. In an interview to Turkish television he excluded even the possibility that any anti-Turkish activity can be conducted on Iran's territory and escape the Iranian state's control. He denied that Iran geared activities or movements against Turkey but at the same time he accused its government of supporting, directly or indirectly, terrorist groups opposed to the regime in Iran.

He proposed then to discuss these "mutual allegations" in the framework of the common security committee. He vaguely denied any ties with anti-secular circles in Turkey but added that if there were groups in Turkey which liked the Iranian model and were inspired by its values, it could not be argued that Iran has created them. A Turkish political commentator noted that Velayati's general behavior during the interview strengthened the conviction that Tehran supports acts of terrorism by radical Turkish supporters and that Iran wanted to use Mumcu's murder to bargain with Turkey.

Turkey has indeed given humanitarian shelter to more than a million Iranians, many of them political refugees from Khomeini's regime. In fact, Iran has never presented any evidence of Turkey's alleged involvement in terrorist activities on its territory. It is known that since the end of the Gulf War, the main opposition violent organization, Mujahedin-e Khalq, has not mounted terrorist operations in Iran, apart from occasional cross-border operations by its "National Liberation Army" from Iraqi soil and with Iraqi assistance.

The relations between Turkey and Iran in the following years continued to be strained with persistent ups and downs. But the main matter of conflict was the issue of Iran's support to the PKK. The PKK intensified its terrorist activity in 1994 and began a campaign of international terrorism inside and outside Turkey. Iran offered a safe-haven to the PKK fighters.

This was also due to successful operations waged by the Turkish security forces against the Islamic groups and the consequent decline in their terrorist activities in 1994 and 1995, compared with 1993. Radical Islamist organizations staged 86 acts of violence in 1995, compared with 464 attacks in 1994. A total of 25 persons died and 21 were wounded in these attacks, staged mainly by Hizballah and IBDA-C. "Ilim," one of Hizballah's two splinter groups (Ilim and Menzil) stopped most of its armed activity, many cadre of the Islamic Movement were arrested and IBDA-C retained its level of activity mostly by acts of bombing and arson.

The assassination in February 1996 in Istanbul of two leading Iranian opposition activists and the arrest in March 1996 of the Islamic Action leader, Irfan Cagarici, and his revelations about the "Iranian Connection" again sparked the political and diplomatic dispute between the two governments. But the accusations were related mainly to the old known terrorist attacks of 1990-1993 and did not seriously affect bilateral relations.

But then in June 1996 the Islamic-lead coalition came to power in Turkey and Erbakan embarked upon an enthusiastic effort to improve relations with Iran. Iran's policy of supporting and inciting Islamic terrorist activity in Turkey in the early 1990s can be understood as its drive to export the Islamic revolution to a key Muslim country, symbol of secularism and a strategic adversary. Its evaluation of the complex Turkish internal situation and the Islamic trend's growing influence probably played an important role in the decision to pursue such an aggressive policy. According to this evaluation, the emergence of Turgut Ozal as leader of Turkey in the 1980s caused a gradual change in the relations between the two countries because he succeeded in reducing the sense of opposition to Islam among the political elite in Turkey, pursued a policy which included attention to Islam and expansion of good relations with its Muslim neighbors. Islamic Iran looked at Ozal's policy on the whole positively and encouraged its continuation.

The Gulf War, the defeat of Ozal's Motherland Party in the elections of early 1990s, stronger critical views of Islamic Iran among the Turkish authorities, and the increasing press attacks against Iran weakened Ozal's "legacy" after his death. Hostility toward Iran reached its peak when a minister openly accused Iran of "creating insecurity" inside Turkey, some border violations occurred and the Ankara authorities were reluctant to curtail the activities of Iranian "counterrevolutionary groups" on its territory. Ironically, Iran considered that its "excessively moderate and reactive behavior" produced the escalation of Ankara's "unfriendly approaches".

But the failure of secular power circles to get closer to Europe and the United States as a solution for Turkey's economic problems, the growth of Islamism resulting in the RP's victory and Erbakan's premiership, and Turkey's need for Iran's support to solve some regional problems, caused a decline in tension between the two countries. According to the Iranian evaluation, President Demirel's inclination to "combine Islam with the particular conditions of Turkey and the more Islamic viewpoints of Premier Erbakan" made possible the improvement of the relations.

THE GOALS OF THE RP

Most scholars agree that although Turkish Islam shares many common features with other Middle East Islamic fundamentalist movements, it has grown and developed in a very different political and social environment shaping its unique nature. As Sami Zubaida points out, Turkey's Islamist ideology is tied up with Turkish nationalism in a unique fashion and challenges the secularist components and European identification of Kemalism, the dominant and official form of Turkish nationalism. At the same time the RP, the Islamic movement's leading political force, has integrated fully in the Turkish pluralist system. This may account, according to Zubaida, for the marginality of the violent Islamic groups. The question remains if the RP can be considered a legitimate democratic party that unconditionally supports the existing system, or if it uses the pluralist system and democratic methods only as a means toward its ultimate goal of installing a religious-based regime in Turkey.

This question is dealt with these days by the Turkish Constitutional Court itself, after it was asked by the State Prosecutor to decide if the RP's policy endangers the secular regime. RP's ambiguous and tortuous policy over the issue of Islamic terrorism in Turkey and Iranian involvement in it during the years 1990-1996 casts some doubts about its genuine acceptance of the democratic values and system. What probably most influenced the RP's moderate and cautious policies over the years has been the need to keep in mind the Turkish army's firmness in defending the Kemalist secular regime and avoiding a direct clash with its secular nationalist core.

This seems to have been also the strategy of the more violent, terrorist groups of the Islamic movement. The Islamic terrorist groups never attacked military or security personnel, although many of their members were killed during the security forces' anti-terrorist campaigns. Only low-level local, mostly Kurdish, politicians have been killed by these organizations but no top secular politicians. This contrasts with Egypt or Algeria, where high-ranking military and police personnel or politicians involved in the fight against the Islamic organizations have been one of their preferred targets. Moreover, Turkish Islamic groups did not attack Western targets or act abroad, like other Islamic groups or the PKK, though they have some infrastructure in Europe.

The main targets attacked were secular intellectuals and media professionals, so important in defending secular values and shaping public opinion's views against the Islamic movement. The elimination of these personalities profited all streams in the Islamic movement and did not seem to provoke a strong reaction against terrorist groups and their political mentors, at least until the assassination of Mumcu. Islamic groups attacked and threatened Jewish personalities, the Jewish community and probably also Israeli diplomats. By these actions they implemented the anti-Jewish, anti-Zionist aspect of the extremist Islamic ideology. In this they were not different from RP, which expressed antisemitic and anti-Israeli views in its propaganda, its official economic platform, or by accusing Israel for murderous attacks against secular personalities perpetrated by the Islamists themselves.

It can thus be hypothesized that even if there was no structural or formal connection between the Islamic movement's political and violent streams, there was an objective ideological alliance and de facto cooperation toward achieving the goal of establishing a Turkish Islamic state. The tolerance shown by part of the security establishment- especially those in the Ministry of Interior and the Police who came to senior positions due to their Islamic views or connections- helped terrorist groups in their formative period. It is quite clear that RP leaders tried to cover up the radicals' violent practices but there is no evidence about the Islamic terrorist organizations' attitude toward the RP's role in advancing and deepening Islam's influence in Turkey and the relations with the main Islamic party.

Iran's radical anti-secular, anti-Zionist ideology explains the close cooperation with the terrorist Islamic groups in Turkey. Commenting on an anti-Turkish demonstration of Turkish Islamists in Tehran, an Iranian daily claimed that the domination of secularism and Zionism are "the two anti-Islamic platforms linked together in the artificial and short history of Turkey" and that the Muslim people of Turkey has the right to protest those who have imposed "these two flimsy and foreign ideas on their fates." According to the commentator, "Zionism's increasing mischief, the inefficiency of the broken arrow of secularism, the growing religious awareness of Muslims and of political Islam in Turkey" permitted RP's anti-alien, anti-Zionist, anti-secularist policies to emerge, for the first time in 73 years, as the main political party.

Riding on the Islamic anti-secular, anti-Zionist wave, the Iranian government also achieved a more immediate tactical bonus by liquidating dozens of Iranian opposition activists. The fact that part of the "dirty work" was done by radical Turkish groups made the attacks more effective and made it easier for the Iranian government to deny involvement in the killings. At the same time, the Turkish terrorist organizations profited materially from Iranian backing in training, logistical support, weapons and explosives and a much-needed safe-haven.

Although Iran claimed Iranian-Turkish relations were optimal during Ozal's government; Iranian support to Turkish terrorist groups began as early as 1987 and peaked in the early 1990s when he served as Turkey's President. It is more realistic to assume that Iran tried to take advantage of the "Turkish-Islamic Synthesis" policy and Ozal's government pro-Islamic tendencies in order to accelerate the radicalization of the Islamic movement.

The pressure on Turkey grew after the Gulf War, when Iran felt stronger regionally, eager to counter-balance Turkey's influence in Central Asia and encouraged by the lack of reaction from the Turkish authorities, at least until 1993.The weakening of the Islamic radicals and the RP's strengthening in the Turkish political arena, reduced Iran's role, though it substantially increased its support to the PKK guerrilla and terrorist activity.

The Islamic fundamentalist movement in Turkey has many common features with movements in many Muslim countries but, as we have seen, it has understood the constraints and dangers of a direct clash with the nationalist Kemalist ideology and, above all, with a military establishment sworn to defend the secular regime and its values at all costs. The use of Islam by the new intellectual and economic elite and military for their own political needs-believing they could tame and transform it to be a pillar of the regime-has been skillfully exploited by the Islamic movement in its bid to achieve power and install an Islamic regime.

This is also true regarding the more radical, violent offshoots of the Islamic movement. Their expansion and relative freedom of action was tolerated on the same grounds until they became a real threat for internal political stability. The RP's parallel growth, electoral success, and its leadership's indulgence toward the Islamists' terror has no doubt encouraged and fed their violence. It is noteworthy that following Refah's biggest electoral success in December 1995 and until the resignation of Erbakan's government in June 1997, no serious terror acts were perpetrated by Islamic groups, except low-level actions waged by IBDA-C, the most independent of these groups.

Despite exposure of its role backing the terrorist activity of Turkish Islamic groups, Iran continues to support the PKK's terrorist activity while paying a very low price for it. Iran also welcomed the RP's rise to power. In exchange, Erbakan did his best to improve bilateral relations and overlook its terrorist dealings. The resignation of Erbakan's government under the army's pressure and the new government's steps to curtail Islamic influence on the education system- or even to try to outlaw the RP- have changed the "rules of the game." The RP's leadership, Islamic radical groups and Iran will have to re-evaluate their strategy. One option open to them could be the use of terrorism. The question is if they will be ready to adopt this strategy when it seems that the military and the secular elite have abandoned the idea of the "Turkish-Islamic Synthesis" and decided on a firm confrontation with the Islamic forces.

5

State, Islam and Opposition in Saudi Arabia

The historical roots of opposition to the monarchy are traced and it is noted that while the monarchy did consolidate its authority and adapt over time, groups critical of the government and its positions have occasionally appeared. Recently, economic leadership and security crises have given rise to a new opposition, unique in its combining Islamic and "modern" concepts. Thus far, as in the past, the regime has dealt with its opponents effectively, although the ultimate impact of this latest opposition surge is not yet determined.

The formation of the Saudi Kingdom-transformation of the rudimentary, tribal Saudi chiefdom into an organized monarchical state in the late 1920s and early 1930s, transformed Islam's role in Saudi society. Until the late 1920s, Islamic principles practiced according to the Wahhabi creed, which dominated the core Saudi society of Najd, were all-embracing. These tenets were the motive for Saudi expansion: expunging unlawful religious practices (bid'a) in the newly occupied territories; propagating a moral code of behavior according to the holy law (Shari'a) to establish an exemplary Islamic polity (Siyasa Shar'iyya); and promoting a unifying ideology beyond tribal and regional identities. With the establishment of state institutions, political centralization and borders, processes that began evolving during the late 1920s, Islamic functions developed in two different forms: a state-controlled religion and the opposition's untamed Islam, which objected to state interests and resisted state control.

The split was reflected in the dispute during this period between the Saudi leader 'Abd al-'Aziz Ibn 'Abd al-Rahman, commonly known as "Ibn Saud", and a collection of tribal groups, the Ikhwan, fiercely loyal to Islam and resisting the Saudi state-building process. Ibn Sa'ud sought to capitalize on their expansionist tendencies, while subjugating them to a centralizing government. There were fierce debates between the two parties, which also included the leading 'Ulama.

In 1930, as Ibn Sa'ud was winning his campaign against the Ikhwan, and afterward, the Saudi king was designating Wahhabi Islam as a state religion. This meant that only the senior 'Ulama, part of the Kingdom's establishment, would wield supreme religious authority. Mandatory religious opinions would only come from them and not arbitrarily by any competent interpreter. It also meant that the senior 'Ulama would not operate independently but in the framework of state-controlled and funded institutions. Moreover, state interest, as defined by the King and the government, would take precedence over any Islamic interests. Wahhabi Islam thus remained a moral code, a unifying factor and ideological motivator of society, but only in accordance with state interests and by legitimizating royal Saudi rule.

The Saudi regime thus implemented several principles and strictures of Islam, mingled with state practices and institutions: the Shari'a served as the main source of law and as a constitution; the Wahhabi code was adopted to govern public behavior; education and intellectual life were mainly shaped by the 'Ulama's preaching and sermons. Yet there was no Wahhabi doctrine for governing. The political order evolved according to state interests. The royal family, government ministers, elite businessmen and regional governors together ran the regime.

In 1929-30, the Ikhwan tribal groups were decisively defeated and their version of how to uphold Islamic principles did not dominate Saudi society. In addition, the Ikhwan's version resisted the incumbent Saudi government hegemony, preferring a different regime. Islamic goals should be supreme over state interests.

However, their convictions remained as a latent, undercover factor serving various opposition groups over the years. Religious authority does not rest, at least not entirely, with the establishment 'Ulama. Even today, other qualified persons may interpret holy law as they understand it, challenge the establishment interpretation and gather followers.

Two conclusions can be reached. First, the vagaries of state formation provoked the opposition's attempt to restore what it regarded as a controlled, just rule. They objected to the sometimes extreme intensification of modernization-evident in a Westernizing lifestyle and of a centralizing, bureaucratic, even absolute, government. Second, both the authorities and their opponents used the language of Islam, accusing each other of breaching holy law, neglecting Islamic goals and deviating from Islamic practices even in administrative, economic and political affairs. Thus, while Saudi Arabia emerged as a state with a puritanical, Islamic-oriented regime, the phases of state formation maded opposition groups accuse the government of unlawful Islamic conduct and to suggest alternatives-even a new government-in the name of Islam.

To be sure, outward tension between an emerging opposition and the government was rare in Saudi Arabia. The Saudi state was a flexible, accommodating institution. Its evolution into an organized state in the 1930s, driving toward economic development and a centralizing government, was balanced by maintaining personalized, informal decision-making at the top, contacts between the rulers and the lower ranks, intermarriage between princes and commoners, and cultivation of senior 'Ulamas.

True, in the late 1950s, during King Sa'ud's reign (1953-1964) an opposition movement developed that questioned the state arrangements and exposed that order's anomalies. In light of initial oil income and the advent of radical pan-

Arabism, the process of unordered decisionmaking and personal, arbitrary conduct of King Sa'ud was deemed obsolete. At that time, the intellectual or even literate community in Saudi Arabia was still limited so an opposition movement emerged chiefly from among young princes, led by Prince Tallal. They advocated a constitutional monarchy, based on liberal and socialist principles. With the exception of Prince Tallal's short period of participation in government in 1960, this movement remained a vocal, non-violent but also ineffective critic. In 1962 Tallal and some of his associates went into exile (to Lebanon and then to Egypt) where they continued their futile calumny of the Saudi regime for some time.

During King Faysal's reign (1964-1975), a new stage of state building emerged; focusing on the reforms he introduced to remedy the shortcomings of the earlier state order. This structure, initiated by Faysal and continued by his successor, King Khalid (1975-82), strove to continue the supreme, unrestricted rule of King and even reinforced his role by an elaborate government and strong bureaucracy. It also rested on an economy based on oil wealth and geared to the development of business, health and education services. From this framework emerged socio-economic stratification and educated groups. Absolute rule, socio-economic and technological change were balanced by maintaining both the Wahhabi moral code and patron-client, tribal and personal contacts among the different groups, notably between princes and commoners, all of which reinforced a traditional, familiar lifestyle. An elaborate welfare system was introduced, guaranteeing free health insurance and free education to Saudi citizens, especially to support those elements that did not benefit from business opportunities and social change.

Faysal's order was sustained for many decades, mainly by satisfying most of Saudi society. Consequently, the opposition movement of November 1979 was an exception to the relative calm and did not portend further challenges. In that instance, several hundred activists, mostly from the former Ikhwan tribe 'Utayba formed their group amilitary service with the National Guard. While some of them were students at the Islamic University of Medina, they were motivated in several ways, as their leader, Juhayman al-'Utaybi, demonstrated in his published letters which explained their anti-establishment religious convictions.

'Utaybi's group violently took over the Grand Mosque in Mecca, the holiest of all Islamic sites, on 20 November 1979. It drew support only from the manual workers and students of tribal origin, of the lower classes and foreign laborers (from Egypt, Yemen and Pakistan). The vast majority of Saudi society regarded them as a marginal group whose elimination by security forces was fully justified. A fatwa of 30 leading 'Ulama, dated 24 November, depicting them as rebels and troublemakers, added to the negative image. In addition, 'Utaybi's demand that oil should not be sold to the United States and that state wealth should not be squandered but used only to meet society's needs, had little appeal against a regime using considerable funds to raise its subjects' living standards.

'Utaybi's group was reacting, in an extreme fashion, to the sudden affluence and Western lifestyle which had begun to emerge in the Kingdom. He attempted to delegitimize Saudi rule in the tradition of the Ikhwan: Ibn Sa'ud deceived the Ikhwan by failing to lead them in a Jihad against neighboring states, instead forming an alliance with the "Christians". A good Muslim's duty, contended 'Utaybi, was to fight the West and reject the socio-technological "progress" of Saudi society. Further, he argued, the authority of the main 'Ulama was false. They were aligned with the Saudi family in a bond of corruption. Like the Ikhwan, Juhayman's movement rejected the state's Islamic authority and monopoly of interpreting Wahhabi Islam with a call to overthrow the Saudi family, and combat the West and the senior 'Ulama. However, in 1979, there were no obvious and widely agreed reasons in Saudi society to do so. Most Saudis were basically satisfied with Faysal's order.

A challenge from a different source, Saudi Arabia's Shi'i minority living in the Gulf region of al-Hassa, erupted shortly after the Grand Mosque takeover. Demonstrations on the Shi'i 'Ashura festival on 28 November 1979 and 1 February 1980, deteriorated into riots against the authorities. While the Shi'i suffered discrimination in jobs and welfare, the protests were kindled mainly by Iranian provocation, among Khomeini's efforts to export a newly victorious Iranian revolution. The regime harsly suppressed the riots (with 21 dead in the two incidents) as well as improving economic conditions and developing their home areas. The Shi'i outburst was not repeated and did not demonstrate a well- organized opposition movement.

The Decline of Faysal's State Order

Only in the 1990s did a more sustained radical Islamic opposition movement emerged. Like its predecessors it questioned the existing state order and gave its own interpretation of Wahhabi Islam. This development was sparked by a decline of some of the state order's underpinning and inherent balances, partly catalyzed by the 1990-91 Gulf War which exposed deep structural problems in Saudi society. Saudi leaders, who should have been the primary force in the ongoing process of state building, were both aging and losing prestige. King Fahd, Crown Prince 'Abdullah and Defense Minister Sultan were all septuagenarians. King Fahd suffered from cardiac and diabetic problems, and in November 1995 had a minor stroke, which compelled him to transfer authority temporarily to 'Abdullah. Their ability to lead the country was thus increasingly doubtful. Moreover, the need to rely on 500,000 foreign soldiers to cope with the Iraqi threat during 1990-91 and the expenditure of around $80 billion from Saudi financial reserves (about $20 billion paid to Iraq during its 1980-88 war with Iran, and $60 billion for Desert Storm) left the Kingdom in an economic recession, and worsend the Saudi people's image of the royal family as charismatic, resourceful and invincible rulers.

The economic well-being which anchored the state was no longer guaranteed. The economy had been in recession since the mid-1980s when oil prices started to decline. In the 1990s, a barrel of oil sold for $18 or less, budget deficits neared

$20 billion, unprofitable investments, a declining GDP per capita from $17,000 in the early 1980s to just over $7,000 in 1995, and growing internal government borrowing meant a relatively poor situation.

In addition, social conditions, proof of the regime's previously successful balancing acts, were also declining. Growing unemployment (about 25% among university graduates) and reduced health and educational services were particularly disturbing in a fast-growing Saudi society with an extremely high birth rate (about 3.6% annually). Building a healthy, well-educated and growing Saudi society became more difficult under new budget constraints.

Changing demographic conditions, a relative economic recession, the rise of a new, educated generation, and the country's aging and somewhat incompetent rulers all shook Faysal's order and exposed its deficiencies in the 1990s. A fundamentalist opposition movement, though not extensive, gained some support since the Kingdom's economic, social and political arrangements were unsatisfactory to a considerable segment of Saudi society. Opposition leaders were able to interpret grievances in an Islamic language which, unlike the 1979 movement, related to current circumstances.

The new fundamentalist opposition's most important characteristic has been its educational and socio-economic base. Its members were neither lower class nor tribally identified. Instead, the common denominator was membership in the new middle class: graduates of higher education graduates working as professionals or administrators. These activists were the product of an affluent era.

As William Ochsenwald has noted, many young Saudis opted to take advantage of higher education opportunities, either in one of the seven Saudi universities or in a Western university. In their studies, young Saudis mixed lay, academic or technical studies with a religious curriculum. A new sort of young 'Ulama also emerged, who mixed traditional tutorials with university education, where they were exposed both to a secular education and currents of thought popular among foreign 'Ulama', the Moslem Brotherhood in Egypt and various Islamic revivalists. In addition, many 'Ulama' embarked on secular careers. So a new mix emerged: lay-educated professionals with religious knowledge, and 'Ulama interacting with wider elements of Saudi society.

The careers and occupations of some of the main activists in the fundamentalist opposition reflect these changes. Safar al- Hawwali, a preacher with his own following, was a lecturer and then head of the religious department at the Islamic University in Medina. Another popular preacher, Salman al-'Awda, studied both natural sciences and law before becoming a lecturer in religious studies at the Imam Muhammad University, Qasim Branch, in the city of Burayda. The main activists of the fundamentalist opposition office in London, the Committee for the Defense of the Legitimate Rights (CDLR) (Lajnat Difa' 'an al-Huquq al-Shar'iyya) were Muhammad al-Mas'ari, a physicist, and Sa'd al-Faqih, a lawyer and former head of the Saudi Board of Grievances. In a recent study, R.H. Dekmejian showed how academics and religious sages mingled: the signatories of two petitions presenting Islamic-fundamentalist demands to King Fahd (52 signed in May 1991 and 107 in September 1992) were backed by a group comprised of about 60% academics and almost 40% holders of religious posts.

The opposition's wide-ranging socio-political critique reflected this combination of "modern" and Islamic education. A "liberal opposition" of academics asked King Fahd in April 1991 to establish a Consultative Council (Majlis Shu), grant more rights and make government appointments based on merit. In the ensuing months, however, the liberals were silenced by government intimidation or promises of change and subsequently disappeared from the political stage. The fundamentalists showed more staying power and used arguments representing a wider range of academic, middle-class public opinion in criticizing the government. They aspired to act, in the words of Sa'd al-Faqih, as an "enlightened fundamentalist trend" which deeply "penetrated the public, and has influence over the middle class and among intellectuals".

The fundamentalist opposition maintained that its resentment of Saudi rule was grounded in the government's violation of moral and efficient administration and economics, and lack of attention to strategic planning. The opposition's beliefs echoed the call for consumer rights and a more just economy they learned on Western campuses. Indeed, among the first middle-class Islamic opposition activists were Saudis studying in the US, who faxed home their complaints about the Saudi leaders' corruption. The September 1992 memorandum, a revision of earlier petitions, articulated these arguments against government practices: ministers and officials should be appointed without favoritism based on kinship, ethnic or regional considerations. Overseas spending should be subject to scrutiny. Luxury construction and wasteful expenditure must cease. In its publications, the CDLR often pointed out the high stipends for princes and the commissions they receive on military transactions, while the average Saudi must pay indirect taxes on telephone, petrol and electricity, risk of unemployment and endure worsening health, educational and postal services.

To be sure, the opposition had a clear Islamic agenda and a definite Islamic purpose. The yardstick for measuring government's policies was how it followed the law. The remedy was full implementation of the Shari'a and Islamic goals. In the 1992 memorandum of 1992 and other CDLR publications, implementation of the Shari'a, as an integral part of the virtues of Islamic equality and morality, constituted a guarantee of untainted appointments, prevention of illegal indirect taxes, and controlled social services. Government ministries would have to operate according to Islamic goals which would ensure their correct, lawful conduct.

DISCREDITING THE INCUMBENT REGIME

The opposition's discrediting campaign sought to delegitimize Saudi rule by destroying its foundations. The opposition did not entirely discredit the role of tribal values in Saudi society; instead it criticized Saudi rulers' use of such values to assure their absolute rule. In one publication, the opposition attacked the hegemony of the House of Sa'ud, as evinced by the name Saudi Arabia. The writer, M.S. Zein Al-Abdin, noted that various people of a variety of tribes (i.e. Qahtan, Mutayr, 'Utayba, Shammar and others) should not really regard themselves as "Saudi citizens." "I do not know how their citizenship can be Saudi while they themselves claim purer nobility and ancestry than the family of Sa'ud?" he asked rhetorically. The Saudi rulers were usurpers, depicted as misusing tribal principles, focusing on personal preferences to further their rule. They were described as using state funds to pay rents to maintain their dynasty's personal wealth, appointing their proteges to the state bureaucracy. According to the opposition, the Saudis also conducted internal relations according to negative tribal principles, notably the encouragement of factions within the royal family. The CDLR thus criticized the Saudi leaders for maintaining the rift between Fahd with his six Sudayri brothers and Crown Prince 'Abdullah. The example which they tendered was Prince Sultan's (Fahd's full brother and Minister of Defense) public announcement in November 1995, describing Fahd's recent health problems as a "slight ailment," thereby trying to dispel the impression that Fahd's handover of power to 'Abdullah was permanent, hinting at Sultan's refusal to acknowledge 'Abdullah as King.

The Islamist opposition also focused on the corrupt, asymmetrical allocation of wealth: the royal family, some cronies, and certain "lucky" regions enjoyed the lion's share of oil wealth, while the middle and lower classes and most of the peripheral regions (bordering Yemen, Jordan and Iraq) were neglected. "Despite these problems, their actions do not suggest that Al-Saud has given the slightest thought to the above questions, since shortsightedness and self-concern guide their activities".

The opposition also pointed out the Saudi rulers' poor human rights' record as demonstrated by the arrest and torture of opposition leaders (notably arrest campaigns such as that launched in 13 September 1994 against Islamist preachers and academics). It was extremely vocal over the regime's attempts to block political freedom and criticism of itself, namely the right to pass on information and hold meetings. The opposition depicted these efforts as proof of the government's weakness; its leaders regarded any criticism as a threat to their existence. Unlike strong, credible regimes, the Saudis could not tolerate criticism. The opposition made public a long list of cases in which their leaders, mostly academics engaged in public preaching against the government's foreign policy, had been warned to stop and taken into custody when they refused to do so.

The Islamists most potent efforts to discredit the regime were directed at the government's outward appearance as a lawful, Islamic regime. The opposition viewed the rulers' association with senior 'Ulama, notably of the Supreme Council of Senior Scholars, as a way to initiate a suitable "fatwa", or religious opinion, to justify policies. Sa'd al-Faqih, the deputy leader of the CDLR, viewed these 'Ulama as fatwa-makers "not out of conviction, but out of fear of the consequences of not doing so". In another opposition publication, the writer, Ehsan Ehsanullah, tried to prove that Saudi rule violated its presumption of upholding Muslim rule within the prescribed limits of the Shari'a, namely (Siyasa Shar'iyya). The Saudis, he declared, had attempted to establish a Mulk, a secular, ruler's estate, rather than an Islamic community (Umma). Their rule over a kingdom was an antithesis to Islam, and their control of the holy places an unlawful practice (bid'a). The Saudi rulers also had not transformed society into a "rightful society" (Umma Wasatan) characterized by law-abiding members of a religious community but rather kept inhabitants content by economic welfare. Saudi rule should thus be regarded as a common power state or sultanate; one CDLR publication referred to the Saudi rulers as "Pharaohs," non-Islamic and idol-preaching rulers.

In the CDLR's view, the regime "can be classified at best as a mix of a mutilated form of Islam combined with tribalism and feudalism. It has even degenerated into a form of Mafia-like family rule". The illegitimacy of the Saudi regime was, in the opposition's view, plain to see, particularly since it had discredited itself in areas where the Saudi rulers hoped to legitimize and solidify their rule: reliance on tribal values, Wahhabi Islam, and economic welfare for the whole Saudi society. These failures stripped them of any meaningful legitimacy. Organizational and Operational Remarks: Where does the threat to the regime lie?

The Sunni Islamist Opposition represents several ideological trends: There are Hijazi neo-Salafi groups, oriented to a strict interpretation of the Shari'a, but these are non-Wahhabi and do not accept the rulings of the Najdi, Wahhabi 'Ulama. In addition, the leading theologians, such as Safar al-Hawwali, Salman al-'Awdah and 'Aid al-Qarni, their students and other "middle-class" followers as well as the CDLR, directed their main effort to discrediting the Saudi rulers. They were all critical of the rulers' interpretation of Shari'a and of the senior 'Ulama's authority. However, they have not (at least until now) established a clear ideological alternative, for a number of reasons:

1. They lack a unifying ideological trend which would define their position within the broader Islamist fundamentalist discourse. The variations among Wahhabi and non-Wahhabi fundamentalist origins, and the need of the Saudi-Wahhabis opposition to appeal and build bridges towards other fundamentalists and Western-educated supporters, led them to draw on Western ideas of good management, Muslim -Brotherhood-related concepts of justice, and Wahhabi responses to unlawful government.
2. They also lack a clear political platform: they preach against Saudi rule and the royal family but do not call clearly for its ousting through revolutionary action or for the Saudi masses to rise up against the regime. They may yet be too unsure of popular support and power to do so. In some major events, such as after the September 1994 arrests, the number of demonstrators may have reached several thousand but in an unorganized, form. Rather they seem to be waiting for the Saudi rule's collapse its own. In the meantime, they would continue efforts to delegitimatize the regime and exacerbate the situation.
3. Despite their main preachers' popular appeal, circulated via cassettes and faxed or printed publications, the opposition had not produced a religious authority of

stature who could match the position of the leading 'Ulama, notably 'Abd al-'Aziz bin Baz. Thus, despite their audacious characterization of the Senior Council of Scholars as a rubber stamp for Saudi rule, they were unable to match its role through an opposition-led body.

In addition, the opposition movement of the 1990s was not reliant on an identified, institutionalized social, tribal, and/or a regionally-based group. The 1990s opposition was also without an established tradition of fighting and violence, typical of tribal groups, thus depriving it of the ability to cultivate an image of bravery and sedition. However, since 1995, a growing readiness to engage in violence has become noticeable. One source for this change might be the thousands of Saudi volunteers (4,000 Mujahidin from Medina alone), sent by the Saudi government to Afghanistan to fight the Soviet armies there. Although there is no clear evidence that Saudi Mujahidin had returned to become an armed opposition in Saudi Arabia, this did happen in Egypt, Algeria, Yemen and elsewhere; the Saudi Mujahidin's acquired skills and access to arms could turn them towards a violent course of action.

Another source of Saudi opposition violence might have emanated from a group led by a Jidda-based businessman, Usama bin Ladin, originally from Hadramawt, who had contacts with the leaders of Sudan's radical Islamist regime. He was expelled from Saudi Arabia and denied his Saudi citizenship in April 1994, due to his involvement in sabotage and anti-government activities in both Saudi Arabia and Egypt. Bin Ladin thereupon focused on publishing anti-Saudi booklets in London, in which his own, and other Saudi opposition factions, were presented as one main body.

In addition, from his place of imprisonment, one of the main Saudi activists, Salman al-'Awda, called on his supporters on 30 April 1995, to stop "studying the law" and embark on an anti- government Jihad. 'Awda did not call for a clear uprising but predicted "events, incidents and happenings" which would kindle clashes between the government and Saudi demonstrators, and pave the way for a broadly-based Jihad against the government.

It is unclear whether these developments led to the car-bomb explosion in a US-staffed communications center of the Saudi internal militia, the National Guard, in November 1995, and the bombing of a US military compound in al-Khubar in June 1996. The perpetrators could also have been Iranian or Iraqi-despatched terrorists.

Despite the gradual increase in violent incidents on the part of the Saudi Islamist opposition, terrorism did not develop into an organized, institutionalized activity. The lack of a violent, anti- government tradition, typical of Islamist opposition activists in other countries, and particularly their tendency to fight the government by religious discourse on the level of moral and religious principles, has so far limited the development of a major terrorist course of action.

The threat posed by the opposition movement will depend on: 1. Its ability to draw supporters from the educated, professional circles. 2. The credibility of its criticism of the government's leadership and administrative incompetence and attack against it on moral and religious grounds. However, the opposition movements did not establish an alternative socio-political order, religious center or prominent ruling figures, to replace the incumbent government.

THE AUTHORITIES' RESPONSE

The governments responded to the opposition in several ways. The Saudi police had initiated arrest campaigns after each outburst of opposition activity, accompanied by restrictions of movement and the banning of preaching cassettes. The activists' movements were also put under surveillance, and meetings dispersed and banned. This type of response reached its peak on 9 and 13 September 1994, with the arrest of two main preachers, Salman al-Awda and Safar al- Hawali together with, according to the CDLR, 1,300 of their followers, in the city of Burayda, Qasim region.

The government also attempted to delegitimize the Opposition by denoting their activities as dissident (bid'a), and unlawful against Saudi leaders and by turning the chief, establishment 'Ulama, against the Opposition. Thus, after the above-mentioned arrests, the Grand Mufti (chief religious authority), and head of the Council of leading 'Ulama, 'Abd al-'Aziz bin Baz, issued a fatwa, that unless the two leading preachers, 'Awda and Hawali, repented their former conduct, they would be banned from lecturing, meetings and cassette-recording. Baz's fatwa justified their arrests, and other leading 'Ulama followed suit. Fahd himself depicted the opposition as unlawfully calling themselves fundamentalists, but in fact being usurpers of the state system and acting against society. However, as in several past cases, there were senior 'Ulama who hesitated to condemn the Opposition, presumably identifying, at least partially, with their preaching.

In October 1994, the King announced the establishment of a Supreme Council of Islamic Affairs (al-Majlis al-A'la lil-Shu'un al-Islamiyya), led by Minister of Defense Sultan, and a few days later the Council for Islamic Call and Guidance (al-Majlis lil- Da'wa wal-Irshad) led by the Minister of Islamic Affairs, Religious Guidance and Endowments, 'Abdullah al-Turki. These two new bodies were made responsible for guidance for Saudis abroad, moral behavior and proper conduct of mosque functionaries, and mosque activities at home. This was a clear attempt to regulate Mosques, over and above the incumbent 'Ulama's authority.

This official response also occured on a political level and the establishment of a sixty-member appointed Consultative Council (Majlis al-Shura), which began operating in Fall, 1992, was a way of placating the professionals who constituted 60% of the Council, with institutionalized advisory rights. However, the Consultative Council was merely a fig-leaf, part of a basic law stressing the King's legislative and executive authority (the judicial bodies being subjected only to the Shari'a) and his responsibility for choosing his Crown Prince from among the Royal family. Another law underlined the position of regional governors, Umara, in the provinces. These laws' main purpose was to reaffirm the Royal family's authority and particularly that of the King, as paramount ruler (Wali al-Amr) over the entire country.

While in many ways the Saudi opposition resembles other such movements in the Middle East, its uniqueness liein roots going back to the Wahhabi opposition school, enabling the opposition to give its own anti-government interpretation to the Shari'a and to thus challenge as unlawful the senior 'Ulama and Saudi government. Moreover, their religious arguments correspond to Western ideas of managerial and administrative misconduct which appeal to educated "middle-class" Saudi professionals and students. Hence, unlike the limited tribal nature of earlier opposition movements, the present movement focuses on a combination of Wahhabi and Western ideas.

Yet except for a few terrorist acts, this movement lacks a clear call for revolution and is not violent. The government has been able to use administrative means and its intelligence system to fight this opposition effectively and reduce the danger to itself. But the opposition's drive to discredit the government's religious and tribal basis may have a long-term corrosive effect.

6

Islam in Lebanon, North Africa and Morocco

ISLAM IN LEBANON

In the last decade, Islamist (fundamentalist) groups in Lebanon have become a significant force not only in that country's politics but throughout the Middle East. Nowhere in the region do such groups have the freedoms they enjoy in Lebanon, giving them a wide cultural influence. In addition, Hizbullah is capable of stopping the Arab-Israeli peace process from advancing by launching Katyusha rockets against Israel and giving Iran an opening to act directly against Israel. Given the great variety and kaleidoscopic changes of Islamist groups in Lebanon, here is an analytical directory of these movements:

MAJOR SHI'I GROUPS

The origins of Shi'i Islamism in Lebanon go back not to Iran, as is commonly thought, but to Iraq in the 1960s where a Shi'i religio-political revival took place in the "circles of learning" (hawzat al-'ilmiya) in Najaf, led by the charismatic Ayatollah Muhammad Baqir as-Sadr. These circles became the epicenter of Shi'i activism and the home base of the Party of Islamic Call (Hizb ad-Da'wa al-Islamiya), which propagated a revivalist message calling for a revolutionary transformation of society among Shi'i communities in Iraq, Iran, the Persian Gulf, and Lebanon. Virtually all of Lebanon's major Shi'i leaders came out of this circle in Najaf.

Although on reaching Lebanon the radical sheikhs established their own circles, they did not develop a revolutionary program patterned after Khomeini's until after two events took place in 1978: the disappearance of the charismatic Imam Musa as-Sadr, an Iranian leader who moved to Lebanon in 1959 and quickly attracted a mass following; and the Khomeini movement in Iran brought Shi'i religious militancy to the cusp of power.

Several factors converged during the 1970s to trigger activism among the Shi'a of Lebanon. They lacked a political role commensurate with their numbers, which made them Lebanon's largest sect; they languished at the bottom of the economy; and the Israeli-Palestinian conflict in south Lebanon led to a massive Shi'i exodus to Beirut's southern suburbs, the breeding grounds of Shi'i militancy in the 1980s and the leaders such as Kamil al-As'ad, 'Adil Usayran, and Sabri Hamada expressed their alienation from the political establishment but it was Musa as-Sadr who permanently changed the Shi'i political role. His influence led to the emergence of two major groups: Amal (meaning "hope," an abbreviation for Afwaj al-Muqawma al-Lubnaniya), 15,000 members.

Sadr launched the Movement of the Deprived (Harakat al-Mahrumin) in 1974, and the next year founded Amal as the Movement of the Deprived's military wing. By about 1976, Amal had become a political organization with an Islamist character. After Sadr's disappearance in August 1978, Amal (first under Husayn al-Husayni and then Nabih Barri) lost its Islamist character. Amal and the Supreme Islamic Shi'a Council (headed by Muhammad Mahdi Shams ad-Din) proposes a democratic pluralism (at-ta'addudiya) based on intersectarian consensus.

Amal has ten seats in Lebanon's parliament. Hizbullah (Party of God), almost 15,000 members. The Israeli invasion of June 1982 then provided the crisis that won Shi'i radicalism a mass constituency. Hizbullah's ideology derives from the political writings of ayatollahs Baqir as-Sadr and Khomeini, plus the experience of the Iranian Revolution. It subscribes to

Khomeini's theory that a religious jurist (wilayat al-faqih) should hold ultimate political power. The authority of this jurist, both spiritual and political, may not be challenged; he must be obeyed. Hizbullah sees itself fulfilling the messianic role of turning Lebanon into a province of Islam. In its "open letter" of February 1985, Hizbullah declared that Muslims must "abide by the orders of the sole wise and just command represented by the supreme jurisconsult, who is presently incarnate in the imam_Ayatollah Khomeini." It also called for a battle with vice, meaning foremost the United States, and for the destruction of Israel to make way for Palestine.

Hizbullah built a powerful presence in Lebanon, so that it now has 5,000 active fighters in its combat organization, the Islamic Resistance (al-Muqawama al-Islamiya). It runs three hospitals, seventeen medical centers, and a commercial network that includes supermarkets, gas stations, department stores, and construction companies. Hizbullah's social welfare activities won it additional members, especially after 1984, when Tehran financed 90 percent of Hizbullah's social program.

None of Lebanon's Shi'i religious leaders has established a Khomeini-like preeminence, but Muhammad Husayn Fadlallah is recognized as Hizbullah's spiritual guide (al-murshid ar-ruhi), though he keeps himself apart from Hizbullah's activities and sees his mission as transcending specific Shi'a groupings to embrace the whole Muslim community if possible. Despite Hizbullah's appeals for Islamic unity and efforts to recruit non-Shi'i Muslims, its membership remains limited to Shi'a. Not just Christians and Druze rejected its declared aim to establish an Islamic order along Iranian lines, but so did most Sunnis.

Amal resisted its goal of establishing an Islamic state and its moves to dominate the south. Hizbullah's militant anti-Israeli stance led to bloody conflict with Amal in the years 1985-89, as the latter feared that Hizbullah would use jihad (sacred war) against Israel as a pretext to undermine its strength. Symbolic of Hizbullah's limited appeal, its representation in the Lebanese parliament amounted to just eight seats in the 1992 parliamentary elections and seven in those of 1996.

MAJOR SUNNI GROUPS

The Islamic Association (al-Jama'a al-Islamiya), 5,000 members: An Islamist group whose origins go back to the height of Gamal Abdel Nasser's efforts at Arab unity in 1964, when members of an older organization established the Islamic Association in Tripoli. Following the Arab defeat in 1967 and the decline of Nasserism, the Islamic Association and other Islamist groups throughout the Arab world gained strength. During the civil war, its militia, called the Mujahidin, fought with the Lebanese National Movement against Christian Maronite forces; in 1982-83 it participated in fighting the Israelis.

The Islamic Association follows the doctrines of militants among the Muslim Brethren in Egypt and Syria. Fathi Yakan, a follower of Sayyid Qutb's radical brand of Islamist thought, is its main ideologue. Yakan joined Sa'id Hawwa of Syria's Muslim Brethren in the wake of the 1967 war to advocate a holy war (jihad al-muqaddas) against the Western and Israeli "crusaders." Later, the Islamic Association tacitly rejected Hizbullah's model of an Islamic state. It believes in achieving an Islamic order based on the Shari'a (Islamic sacred law) through jihad of the heart (spiritual struggle), jihad by word (education and propaganda), and jihad by hand (economic, political and military action). The Islamic Association engages in internecine struggles with the Ahbash and the Tawhid, as well as with the traditional Sunni religious establishment as represented by Juridical Office (Dar al-Ifta') and traditional leaders (the Karamis of Tripoli, the Salams of Beirut, and the newly-emerged Hariris of Sidon), whom it regards as the instruments of foreign interests. Its members tend to live in Lebanon's urban centers with large Sunni concentrations Tripoli, Beirut, and Sidon. It recruits the young via the Muslim Students Association (Rabitat at-Tullab al-Muslimin). The Islamic Association offers social welfare services, though less sophisticated ones than Hizbullah provides, but has not succeeded in attracting many Sunni votes; it won three seats in the 1992 parliamentary elections and just one seat in 1996.

The Islamic Unity Movement (Harakat at-Tawhid al-Islami), almost 1,000 members: Originating in Tripoli during 1982, it was the creation of Sheikh Sa'id Sha'ban, previously a leader of the Islamic Association. Islamic Unity serves as an institutional extension of Sha'ban, one of Lebanon's Islamist movements' few charismatleaders. Its fighters consolidated their control over Tripoli in 1983-1984 by defeating a number of rivals and then, at the height of its power in 1985, splintered, as Khalil 'Akkawi and Kan'an Naji left to organize their own associations. In the fall of 1985 the Syrian army entered Tripoli and crushed Islamic Unity's militia, though it permitted Sha'ban to maintain leadership of his now unarmed movement. This defeat did not prevent the militia's subsequent reemergence in Beirut, Sidon, and south Lebanon. In 1988, the Tawhid forces joined the Islamic Resistance to fight the South Lebanese Army and the Israeli forces in Israel's "security zone." Sha'ban's ideology springs from the radical wing of the Muslim Brotherhood.

Curiously, Sha'ban is said to have come from a Shi'i family of Batroun in North Lebanon and only later became a Sunni. He forged close political ties to Iran during visits to Tehran and through Hizbullah, which considers Sha'ban doctrinally a follower of Ayatollah Khomeini. While accepting the validity of the Iranian Revolution and emphasizing that the path started by Khomeini should be followed by all Muslims, Sha'ban does not call for an Iranian-style order in Lebanon, knowing that this would alienate his Sunni followers. He seeks ways to unite Sunnis and Shi'a, for example by suggesting that the Qur'an and the prophet's biography provide foundations on which all Muslim groups and sects can unite. Instead of arguing about sectarian representation in the parliament, he suggests that Muslims call for Islamic rule based on the Shari'a, without which no government can be legitimate. Sha'ban rejects nationalism, sectarianism and democratic pluralism in favor of an Islamic rule that "absorbs and dissolves all social differences and unites them in one crucible." He laments the Syrian intervention into Lebanon of 1976 to help the Maronites who, he asserts, would have otherwise fled to Cyprus or Latin America. Aside from rare instances of mild criticism, he is careful not to antagonize the Syrian authorities; indeed. he speaks favorably of the Syrian military presence in Lebanon as a framework for unified, armed action against Israel.

The Association of Islamic Charitable Projects (Jami'at al-Mashari' al-Khayriya al-Islamiya), known as Al-Ahbash ("the Ethiopians"), almost 8,000 members: One of the most controversial and interesting of contemporary Islamic groups, due to its origins, its eclectic theological roots, and its teachings, which do not fit the conventional Islamist mold. The Ahbash is a Sufi (or spiritualist) movement that devoutly follows the teachings of Sheikh `Abdallah ibn Muhammad ibn Yusuf al-Hirari ash-Shi'bi al-Abdari, also known as al-Habashi, a religious thinker of Ethiopian origins. It is spiritually Islamist but not politically. By the late 1980s, the Ahbash had become one of Lebanon's largest Islamic movements, having grown during the civil war from a few hundred members to its present size. The Ahbash did not create a militia of its own, nor did it engage in sectarian violence or fight Israel. Proselytizing and recruitment are its main aims, along with a commitment to moderation and political passivity.

The Ahbash became a key player in Lebanese politics by offering a moderate alternative to Islamism, attracting a wide following among the Sunni urban middle class by advocating pluralism and tolerance. Its ideology makes the Ahbash politically significant, including sharp controversies with Islamist movements. While Habashi pays allegiance to the pious ancestors (salaf) and the Shari'a, his emphasis on "the science of hadith" makes him suspect as being a follower of the Kalamiya (literalist) tradition of the Mu'tazila who stressed the superiority of reason over revelation. He rejects such Islamist authorities as Ibn Taymiya, Ibn 'Abd al-Wahhab, and Sayyid Qutb. In contrast to Hizbullah and the Islamic Association, the Ahbash opposes the establishment of an Islamic state on the grounds that this divides Muslims. Instead, it accepts Lebanon's confessional system (which used to give Christians six slots for every five Muslim slots, and now gives them parity). Its foreign policy orientation is equally mild, making no reference to jihad and directing no anger toward the West. To achieve a civilized Islamic society, it recommends that members study Western learning. Also, the Ahbash has established branches in Australia, Canada, Denmark, France, Sweden, Switzerland, the Ukraine, and the United States (with headquarters in Philadelphia). It enjoys excellent relations with most Arab states, particularly Syria. In rivalry with the Islamic Association for dominance of the Sunni community, it entered the parliamentary elections of 1992 and won one seat in Beirut, though it lost it in 1996.

Islamic Amal, almost 500 members: Headed by Husayn al-Musawi, who left the Amal movement in 1982 to protest its secular orientation? Musawi, a former school teacher, made Islamic Amal a devoted follower of Khomeini's ideology, including his theory of the religious jurist and its strong opposition to the West. Principally based in Baalbak, with close ties to the Islamic Revolutionary Guards (an Iranian militia sent to Lebanon in 1982 and mostly withdrawn in late 1991), Islamic Amal appears to be aligned at present with Rafsanjani and the Syrian government. The Islamic Movement (al-Haraka al-Islamiya), almost 200 members: A seemingly independent, semi-clandestine group based in the Bekaa Valley, headed by Sadiq al-Musawi, a cousin of Islamic Amal's Husayn al-Musawi. It follows Khomeini but is independent of Hizbullah and enjoys direct access to Iranian militants. Its militia, Army of the Truth (Jund al-Haqq), has ties with Shi'i minorities in the Arabian Peninsula; in the mid-1980s it targeted Saudi diplomats in revenge for the Saudi execution of Shi'i activists. Though apparently inactive since 1989, the movement may have gone underground. In 1993, Sadiq al-Musawi accused Hizbullah of having deviated from Khomeini's teachings and called for an Islamic Republic in Lebanon.

The Faithful Resistance (al-Muqawma al-Mu'mina), almost 200 members: An Amal splinter group, seemingly independent. It carried out a Katyusha rocket attack on northern Israel in January 1986 (at a time when Shi'i Islamists were accusing Amal of having entered into a secret agreement with Israel).

The Revolutionary Justice Organization (Munazzamat al-'Adala ath-Thawriya) and the Oppressed of the Earth

Organization (Munazzamat al-Mustadafin fi'l-Ard), almost 100 members each: Both served as covers for Hizbullah's militant activities and held Western hostages: the former in December 1986 claimed responsibility of kidnapping four university professors whom it described as spies and the latter claimed responsibility for kidnapping two U.S. citizens and four French television crewmen. Both organizations have been inactive since 1988. The Husayn Suicide Squads (Majmu'at Husayn al-Intihariya), almost 100 members: Obscure except for the name of its leader, Abu Haydar al-Musawi, a relative of the other Musawis. The group surfaced only in 1982 when it claimed responsibility for attacks against the South Lebanese Army to protest its collaboration with Israel.

The Islamic Struggle Movement (al-Haraka al-Islamiya al-Mujahid), almost 100 members: First appeared in 1987 under the direction of Sheikh Abdullah al-Hallaq, a Sunni influenced by Hizbullah and the Islamic Resistance. The movement aims to recruit Sunni and Palestinian fighters in the Sidon area to attack Israel. It failed, however, to organize a Sunni resistance in the south similar to Hizbullah's.

The Islamic Resistance Movement (Harakat al-Muqawama al-Islamiya known by its Arabic acronym, Hamas), roughly 500 members in Lebanon (and many more on the West Bank and in Gaza): Sheikh Ahmad Yasin of Gaza founded the Islamic Assembly (al-Mujamma' al-Islami), an activist offshoot of the Muslim Brotherhood, in 1973 in Gaza. Soon after the onset of the intifada in December 1987, he established Hamas, the leading Palestinian Islamist movement. It also has a presence in thPalestinian camps of south Lebanon, under the leadership of 'Imad al-'Ali. Islamic Jihad Movement in Palestine (Harakat al-Jihad al-Islami fi Filastin), almost 1,000 members: A grouping of small, militant Sunni bands such as the Brigades of Islamic Jihad (Saraya al-Jihad al-Islami) and the 'Izz ad-Din al-Qassam Brigades. Born in the despairing slums of Gaza, Islamic Jihad followed the teachings of Khomeini and Egypt's Jihad Organization (Tanzim al-Jihad) in its use of violence and readiness for martyrdom to achieve an Islamic order. With PLO support; it accelerated guerrilla attacks against

Israeli targets in 1986, thereby helping trigger the intifada. Israel responded in the spring of 1988 by expelling its spiritual guide Abd al-'Aziz 'Awda to Lebanon and arresting scores of his followers. The Islamic Jihad continues its attacks against Israel from Gaza and south Lebanon.

Supporters of the Islamic League (Ansar al-'Usba al-Islamiya), almost 200 members: Headed by Ahmad as-Sa'di (known as Abu Muhjin), formerly of the Islamic Association. The League declares its aim to be the liberation of Palestine and the Muslim community. The League first appeared in August 1995 with the assassination of Nizar al-Halabi, president of the Ahbash. Despite evidence of Abu Muhjin's involvement in the assassination, the Lebanese authorities have not been able to locate him.

The Association of Muslim Clergy (Tajammu' al-Ulama' al-Muslimin), almost 200 members: An umbrella group led by two activist sheikhs, Mahir Hammud (a Sunni) and Zuhayr Kanj (a Shi'a), that seeks to promote Muslim unity. Founded by Sunni and Shi'i leaders in response to the Israeli attack of 1982, the Association represents a coalition of militant clerics who share Khomeini's ideals and a determination to fight Israel and to establish an Islamic order in Lebanon.

The Islamic Front (al-Jabha al-Islamiya), almost 100 members: A second umbrella group, founded in 1985 by Sheikh Mahir Hammud. It brought together sheikhs and lay leaders; its program is generally critical of the West, its Arab allies, and their willingness to make peace with Israel. Party of God Collectivity (Ummat Hizbullah): Despite its name, not a political party but an umbrella organization of some half dozen radical Shi'i groups affiliated with Hizbullah.

Lebanese Islamic Resistance Front (Jabhat al-Muqawama al-Islamiya al-Lubnaniya), almost 500 members: Founded by Sheikh 'Abd al-Hafiz Qassim in the wake of the 1982 Israeli invasion of Beirut. A militia made up of an alliance of the Sunni Muslims and Palestinian guerrillas, it claimed responsibility in 1982-83 for attacks against Israeli troops inside West Beirut. It flirts at Arab unity in 1964, when members of an older organization established the Islamic Association in Tripoli. Following the Arab defeat in 1967 and the decline of Nasserism, the Islamic Association and other Islamist groups throughout the Arab world gained strength. During the civil war, its militia, called the Mujahidin, fought with the Lebanese National Movement against Christian Maronite forces; in 1982-83 it participated in fighting the Israelis.

MINOR GROUPS

In addition to these five major groups, a number of lesser organizations, many clandestine, operate in Lebanon. Many are affiliates and offshoots of Hizbullah.

Islamic Resistance (al-Muqawama al-Islamiya), almost 5,000 members: Established after the Israeli invasion of 1982, when it fought a guerrilla war against Israel and General Lahd's forces. It originally consisted of both Shi'i and Sunni fighters, who represented virtually all Islamic militant groups, but Shi'i fighters played a growing combat role over time. In 1985, the Islamic Resistance became the combat arm of Hizbullah.

Islamic Jihad (al-Jihad al-Islami), almost 200 members: Widely believed to be the twin of the Islamic Resistance, used by Hizbullah for attacking Western interests. The name first appeared in claims of responsibility for the bombing of the U.S. embassy in Beirut in April 1983, followed by the suicide bombing of the Israeli military headquarters in Tyre in October 1985, and the kidnapping of Westerners, mostly Americans, in March 1984. 'Imad Mughniya reportedly controlled the organization. Although no news has been heard about Islamic Jihad since 1988, some reports indicate Mughniya is still active and in charge of Hizbullah's overseas security apparatus (which handles intelligence and conducts overseas terrorist acts).

FUTURE PROSPECTS

Lebanon's Islamic movements enjoyed tremendous growth due to crisis conditions that beset the region in recent years: Arab defeats by Israel, the failure to achieve balanced socioeconomic development, political oppression, gross maldistribution of wealth, and the disorienting impact of Westernization. Other factors contributing to Lebanese instability before the civil war broke out include the sharpening of class differences in a market economy beset by official corruption; strife between Israel and the Palestinians; and the proxy battles fought by Arab states on Lebanese soil. The victory of Islamist forces in Iran further shaped the dynamics of Islamic militancy in Lebanon. But this florescence of Islamism will probably not continue long into the future due to the Islamists' lack of unity, the role of Syria, the decline of Iranian militancy, reconstruction efforts by the Lebanese government, and the possibility of a Syrian-Israeli peace.

Deep doctrinal differences and conflicting objectives make the Islamists more likely to fight each other than work together. Although the large Islamic movements have created a political, social, and economic presence in the Muslim community, their constituencies remain segmented. They developed along geographical and sectarian lines, with Sunnis in some organizations and Shi'is in others. Within each community some ten groups pursue their sometimes contrary interests. The lack of unity among Islamists has made them weaker and prevented any group from capturing political power. Only Hizbullah has managed to increase its constituency, due mostly to its social welfare services; but even it has neither dominated the Shi'a nor attracted Sunni participation.

The Syrian government, which maintains a military presence in Lebanon and makes key decisions in the country, has made it clear that Islamist groups must be disciplined as a prelude either to a war or to a settlement of the conflict with Israel. Damascus has prevented them from expanding by its support of the confessional formula, which is a direct impediment to the establishment of an Islamic order. Instead, Damascus has used the Islamist organizations as a military instrument against Israel. It permits them to exist, in other words, as a means to pressure Israel, not as a threat to Syria's interests.

Iran's strength in Lebanon began to decline soon after 'Ali Akbar Hashemi Rafsanjani became president of the country in 1989. He charted a more pragmatic course, one opposed by militant factions led by Ali Akbar Mohtashemi and Hasan Kharubi. With the radicals' eclipse, the most militant Islamist factions in Lebanon also lost power, which had the effect of forcing them to work within the Lebanese political system.

The Lebanese government of President Ilyas Hirawi and Prime Minister Rafiq al-Hariri has to a certain extent succeeded in accommodating sectarian interests that bring tangible benefits to Lebanon's poor, for example by launching reconstruction projects in public transportation, education, agriculture, state hospitals and by providing housing loans and this somewhat undercuts Hizbullah's social welfare programs.

Finally, a peace agreement between Syria and Israel would very much harm Lebanon's Islamists. The Arab-Israeli conflict did not create Islamist movements in Lebanon (or in other Arab countries) but it undoubtedly helped them win popular support. Conversely, an Arab-Israeli settlement would contribute greatly to the decline of Islamic militancy by automatically leading to a Lebanese-Israeli agreement, ending Hizbu's activities in the south.

ISLAM IN NORTH AFRICA

A proper understanding of the Islamic challenge in Algeria and comparing the Algerian experience to Morocco and Tunisia is urgent. Not only is the Maghrib different than the Mashriq (Arab East), but experience within the Maghrib itself is highly varied.

Algeria's sudden, wholesale adoption of a Western-style political liberalization program in 1989-91 was unprecedented in the Arab world. It included the unqualified legalization of explicitly Islamic political parties. No other Arab regime had dared to make such a move. The consequence was the implosion of the Algerian polity.

Algeria became a place conforming, ironically, to Moroccan

sociologist Fatima Mernissi's definition of the gharb (West): a place where "all terrors are possible." Sweeping victories by the new Front Islamique du Salut (FIS) in municipal and then the first round of parliamentary elections, triggered a military coup in January 1992 which deposed President Chedli Benjedid, canceled elections before the second round of parliamentary voting, and arrested thousands of Islamist activists. The state quickly descended into chaos. Years of brutal warfare between Algeria's military authorities and armed Islamist groups took an estimated 60,000 lives and ripped the already tattered fabric of Algerian society. The current situation is an uneasy, unstable stalemate, though the Zeroual regime clearly maintains an upper hand.

ROOTS OF THE CONTEMPORARY CRISIS

The ideological roots of modern day Islamic fundamentalism are not solely recent: the ideas of the salafiyya current of Islamic reform and purification were present in pre-Protectorate Morocco among both the 'ulama and various sultans, and became widespread in the Maghrib in the era between the two world wars. One can argue that more than in the Mashriq, Islam was one of the core values for Algerian, Moroccan and Tunisian nationalist movements that opposed European domination. In Algeria, the crystallization of a modern national identity between the two world wars was considerably shaped by the Islamic reformist movement led by Shaykh 'Abd al-Hamid Bin Badis. The movement promoted both the purification of Islamic practices from "polytheism" (maraboutic practices) and creation of an educational network that would stress that Islam and the Arabic language, and not French culture, are at the core of modern Algerian identity.

Similarly, salafi activity in Morocco played an important role in shaping the nationalist movement, personified in the 1920s by 'Allal al-Fasi, the religio-nationalist leader of the Istiqlal party. Likewise in Tunisia, Islam "as a component of Tunisian identity and a legitimizing value...suffused the first generation nationalist movement [in the decades prior to World War I] and...persisted even into the age of Bourguibist secularism."

In contrast to the general salafi current, political Islam in North Africa was not a "pan" movement. Nor, again in contrast to the Mashriq, was pan-Arabism a competing ideology. Thus, the legitimacy of the state in North Africa has never been in doubt: "The state appears more as an appropriately adjusted transfer of technology than as an alien institution."

State power grew exponentially during the post-independence generation, intruding decisively into every sphere of society. However, in the words of the Tunisian scholar Abdelbaki Hermassi, by the 1980s, policies once seen favorably as constituting the etatization of society increasingly began to look like the privatization of the state as small numbers of individuals' accumulated great wealth from their privileged positions. This occurred at a time of austerity imposed by international financial institutions. Also, the resources available for development were sharply cut by the post-oil boom economic contraction. The effect was felt across the Arab world, among both petroleum-based economies, including Algeria, and "labor-exporters" like Egypt, Jordan, and Tunisia. What resulted was the obvious inability of Arab regimes, maghribi and mashriqi alike, to deliver the social, economic, political and psychic goods to their expanding, increasingly youthful, urbanized and literate populations. This failure caused a profound sense of crisis (azma) among wide sectors of their populations and endless debate among intellectuals over what should be done (spawning a cottage industry, or azmatology, in the words of Muhammad Guessous, a Moroccan sociologist).

The Maghrib's proximity to Europe rendered its youthful population (two-thirds under 30 years of age) especially vulnerable to psychic dislocation, especially since North Africa had already been widely penetrated by the gharb (primarily France) during the prior 150 years. The proliferation of satellite dishes and powerful television transmitters brought images of Europe's material glitter into people's living rooms, raising expectations and prompting demands that had no chance of being fulfilled, thus opening the way to profound disillusionment. In Mernissi's words, [W]hat strikes me as a sociologist (when visiting a Muslim country) is the strong feeling of bitterness in the people- the intellectuals, the young, and peasants. The bitterness over blocked ambition, over frustrated desires for consumption- of clothes, commodities, and gadgets, but also of cultural products like books and quality films and performances which give meaning to life and reconcile the individual with his environment and his country....In our country (Morocco) what is unbearable, especially when you listen to the young men and women of the poor class, is the awful waste of talent. "Ana daya`" ("My life is a mess") is a leitmotif that one hears constantly.

The crisis, which took root during the 1970s and gathered strength during the 1980s, spawned a new kind of dissent, articulated most forcefully by Islamist movements. They spoke not only on issues or strategies of development but on matters concerned with justice and cultural identity. Given the dual legacy of popular-maraboutic Islamic practice and the Maghrib's penetration by the modern gharb, it is not surprising that Maghribi salafists-fundamentalists often found themselves alienated from their own societies and thus sought guidance and inspiration from outside the Maghrib: e.g., the Egyptian-based Muslim Brotherhood, Iran's Islamic Revolution, and Sudan's Hasan al-Turabi. This interaction marked a departure from pre-modern historical patterns.

Morocco

Despite the strongly similar development patterns of their Islamist movements, the specific socio-political and historical circumstances of the three Maghrib states varied widely. This produced a disparate state-society/regime-opposition dynamic which, in each case, produced very different political outcomes. Consider Morocco: apart from Saudi Arabia, no other Arab regime has so thoroughly draped itself in Islam's mantle. King Hassan II, who has reigned and ruled since 1961, is constitutionally the Amir al- Mu'minin- the Commander of the Faithful- deputized by virtue of his descent from the Prophet Muhammad to lead the Moroccan Islamic Umma in all matters, both temporal and spiritual. His erudition in religious matters, displayed in dialogues with religious scholars on Moroccan television, reinforces this dual role.

One can argue against the oft-made claim that the monarchy is the central religious institution of Moroccan life and that Hassan's longevity rests less on blind obedience and belief in his special sacredness (baraka) than on his astutely wielding the levers of power at his disposal, including repression. As Hasan himself told his biographer, "One doesn't maintain order by wielding croissants." At the same time, it seems reasonable to conclude that the Moroccan regime has been a relatively successful "modernizing monarchy" because it aitself in Moroccan political and socio-cultural traditions. This enabled it to avoid some of the harsher social, political and psychic dislocations of revolutionary Arab regimes.

One of these realities is the institution of the monarchy itself: the ruling Alawite dynasty is almost 350 years old. At the same time, as I. W. Zartman argues, the monarchy under Hasan has evolved through interaction with society. Part of this involved Hasan's modification of religious traditions to reinforce his legitimacy. More prosaic factors promoting relative political stability include a liberal economy and multiparty politics. Hasan has described his political strategy as "homeopathic democracy," a process of controlled, well-managed change that maintains social peace while promoting economic development and the general welfare. His ultimate declared goal is a "bipolarized democracy," in which two parliamentary blocs will alternate in power, with the monarch serving as the ultimate arbiter and source of authority.

The results of this approach have been mixed. The well-established opposition parties, led by the Istiqlal and Union Socialist d'Forces Populaires, scored impressive gains in the 1993 parliamentary elections. However, Hasan failed in his efforts to entice them into a central role in the government, due to their unwillingness to serve alongside the all-powerful Interior Minister Driss Basri as well as their own internal divisions. Hasan clearly hoped the August 1997 parliamentary elections would pave the way for their agreement to take office.

More interesting than the snail-paced change of parliamentary life has been the growth in recent years of authentic "civil society" elements. Labor unions have become increasingly combative; human rights groups have bucked considerable pressure to make their voices heard; women's organizations attained 1 million signatures on a petition to change the mudawanna, Morocco's personal status law, which discriminates against women in many areas. Of related interest has been a significant lowering of the population growth rate from 3% per annum in the early 1970s to just over 2% in 1995, and a corresponding halving in the average family size.

The downside of Hasan's controlled change strategy is that his reliance on existing economic and political elites carries a danger of stagnation, a lack of attention to social and economic distress, and disaffection among the educated classes. The slow pace of change undoubtedly breeds cynicism among the latter and does little to make the urban poor feel empowered. His IMF-directed policies of structural readjustment, involving debt rescheduling, subsidy cuts, liberalizing capital movements and beginning to privatize state firms, have won considerable praise from the Paris Club governments and international and commercial lending agencies. The budget deficit, which in the early 1980s reached 12% of the GDP, was cut to less than 2% in a decade, foreign investment rose fourfold between 1988 and 1992, and annual growth rates were impressive. On the micro-economic level, however, the picture was quite different. Gaps between rich and poor, in a society where the average per capita income is just over $1,000, further widened; urban unemployment is at 20-30%, and two years of severe drought in 1992- 93, followed by the "drought of the century" in the winter of 1994- 95, exacerbated the plight of rural areas and reinforced long-standing trends toward migration to urban areas. The last two years have again demonstrated Morocco's overdependence on climatic vagaries: bountiful rains in the winter of 1995-96 produced a record 11% growth rate in 1996, while the failure of late winter rains in 1997 is expected to curtail this year's growth rate.

Like many Middle East governments, Hassan initially gave budding Islamist movements some freedom of action in order to balance opposition from the radical left. But though he continues to allow non-political activities, since the 1970s he has severely restricted their ability to operate politically while adopting a strategy of manipulation and cooptation. The regime's efforts to control Islamism were made easier by the fact that Moroccan Islamists are not homogenous. One researcher counted no less than 23 politicized religious associations in the early 1980s. However, these are generally grouped into three trends. By summer 1996, three weekly newspapers representing the three main trends had a combined circulation of 40,000.

One of these trends has been explicitly reformist but not overtly political, concentrating on matters of individual piety and righteousness, and criticizing corruption. As such, it has been the least restricted. The leading figure of this trend, before his death in the late 1980s, was an elderly mosque preacher in Tangier, Fqih al-Zamzami. Venerated by peddlers, laborers, and shopkeepers, cassettes of his sermons are sold in most cities. His three sons have tried to follow in his path. At the other extreme was a small group, al-Shabiba al-Islamiyya; (Islamic Youth), drawn mostly from student and high school movements, which advocated the regime's violent overthrow. Its leader, 'Abd al-Karim al-Muti', is in exile somewhere in Europe. Some of the group, led by 'Abdallah Benkirane, chose a non-confrontational, reformist posture similar to that advocated by Zamzami. In recent years, under the banner of the Harakat al-Islah wal-Tajdid bil-Maghrib (HATM; Movement for Reform and Renewal in the Maghreb), they have sought to become overtly involved in the political process, while retaining their pragmatic approach.

The best-known Moroccan Islamist figure is 'Abd al-Salam Yasin, a former Education Ministry school inspector who leads the outlawed al-'Adl wal-Ihsan (Justice and Charity) movement. Yasin's followers are more educated and more radical than Zamzami's. Yasin openly challenged Hasan's legitimacy- and that of any monarch in Islam- back in 1974.

He later admitted to having prepared his burial shroud for the occasion. (Instead, King Hassan felt confident enough not to have him executed and merely kept him under various forms of detention for most of the time since then.) During the Gulf War, 30,000 of Yasin's followers mustered under their own banner as part of a massive anti-war march, providing the only public indication of their strength. In December 1994, the government briefly eased Yasin's house arrest but swiftly reimposed it when Yasin declined to refrain from political sermons. The authorities' effort to coax Yasin into working within the system indicates their recognition of the Islamists' potential strength and the need to defuse it by cooptation. Yasin's cause has been taken up by opposition political parties and human rights groups.

An incident in the summer of 1994 provided evidence that Morocco was not entirely immune to radical, violent Islamic currents of the kind manifesting itself in Algeria and Egypt. On August 24, two Spanish tourists were shot to death in the lobby of a hotel in Maarakesh, the first and so far only violent attack against foreigners. The government immediately blamed the Algerian intelligence services for being behind the perpetrators, precipitating renewed Algerian-Moroccan tensions and the closing of their land frontier.

Two weeks later, four alleged perpetrators of the act were arrested. They turned out to be a group of young French-Moroccan and French-Algerian fundamentalists, possibly connected to the remnants of Muti''s al-Shabiba al-Islamiyya, who in the late 1980s organized themselves into a group to advance the cause of Islamic revolution. Their activities included receiving weapons training in Peshawar, Pakistan near the Afghan frontier, smuggling weapons to Algerian Islamists via Morocco, and a number of robberies in France to support themselves and the cause. Their alleged head, Tariq Fellah, a Moroccan, was arrested in Germany in December 1994 (a diperson, 'Abd al-Ilah Ziyad, also a member of al-Shabiba al-Islamiyya, subsequently claimed he had organized the hotel attack during his trial in France). In January 1995, the group of 4 plus 14 others went on trial in Fez for the shooting plus other violent acts carried out during 1994. Three of the eighteen were sentenced to death (the sentences have not been carried out); the others to sentences ranging from six months to life imprisonment. Official Algerian involvement was never confirmed, and the affair pointed more to the common danger posed by Islamist radicals to both the Moroccan and Algerian regimes.

At the same time, the swift arrest and trial of the group confirmed anew that the Moroccan Islamists current ability to pose a serious challenge to the regime is extremely limited. Nonetheless, Islamist activities, particularly on university campuses where they came to control nearly all the student unions and periodically clashed violently with leftist groups, were publicly acknowledged by at least one government minister as constituting a worrisome development.

Tunisia

Tunisia's Islamists have enjoyed a higher international profile than their Moroccan counterparts but suffer from even greater repression. As in other cases in the Middle East, the Tunisian Islamists' protests can be seen partly as a response to socio-economic dislocations stemming from the complex processes of modernization and development. Also contributing is the existence of a clogged political system. However, the most important factor has been the "psycho-social alienation" that has resulted from the predominant Western liberal model of modernity.

This model has been the objective of President Habib Bourguiba since the state became independent in 1956. Notwithstanding Bourguiba's efforts to legitimize his policies in Islamic modernist terms, his initiatives brought more secularization than in any other Arab country. For example, the Personal Status Code, which guarantees equality between men and women in matters of divorce and forbids polygamy. A second example is the relatively large number of women in managerial and executive positions. President Zayn 'Abidin Ben 'Ali, who assumed power in November 1987, softened some of Bourguiba's strident secularism and put more emphasis on Tunisia's Arab-Islamic heritage. The regime permitted Islamists to run in elections as independents in 1989. Officially, they captured around 14% of the vote, came close to winning a majority in several urban areas. Some have claimed that the real percentage attained by Islamist candidates was 30-32%. The regime quickly took notice and cracked down harshly, banning the newly formed Islamist Nahda (Renaissance) Party and taking advantage of some Islamists' violent acts to imprison thousands of activists. Stern reprimands from international human rights organizations did not deter the regime.

For now, Ben 'Ali rules Tunisia with a firm hand and, unlike in Morocco, guided political pluralism is only in its infancy: all but 19 of the 163 seats in Tunisia's parliament elected in 1994 are held by the ruling Rassemblement Constitutionnel Democratique. This is an improvement, since the previous parliament contained no opposition deputies. Economically, the Tunisians have followed a similar course to Morocco, instituting structural reforms and obtaining good results. Tunisia's small population, reinforced by the lowest rate of population growth in the Arab world, educated middle class, high rate of literacy, relatively high percentage of women in the work force and European orientation make the state a less fertile ground for Islamists than other countries in the region. Nonetheless, the groundswell of support for Islamist movements during the 1970s and 1980s indicates that Tunisia is not immune from region-wide currents.

Like their counterparts elsewhere in North Africa and the Sunni world in general, Tunisia's Islamists have been influenced by Egypt's Muslim Brotherhood and the teachings of Sayyid Qutb and Pakistan's Mawlana Mawdudi. Nonetheless, there was considerable talk during the 1980s within Islamist circles of developing a specific "Tunisian Islam." Part of the rationale was the rejection of the predominant Islamist view that legitimacy is solely divine and instead supporting the idea of popular will as the source of legitimacy. The Islamic notion of shura (consultation), declared Rashid Ghannushi, the movement's leading figure, legitimizes multiparty politics, alternation in power and the protection of human rights. In November 1995, Ghannushi and a group of non-Islamist exiled opposition members, including former prime minister Muhammad Mzali, published a joint communique appealing for democracy in Tunisia via the election of a parliament representing a diversity of views and political parties. The problem, Ghannushi stressed, was the repressive Ben `Ali regime and most Arab governments, for that matter, which rejected all notions of civil society (al-mujtama` al-madani)! Ghannushi's avowed goal to promote a modernist-Islamic synthesis oppoxinb the Tunisian regime's "superficial modernity," makes him one of the more interesting and original of contemporary Islamist thinkers.

To be sure, his views are not entirely congruent with Western liberal values. As he said in one interview, state-building must begin with recognition of the umma's Arab and Islamic identity. Without first agreeing on this central pillar, the "cultural context" of state-society relations, there can be no stable, legitimate authority. Once the identity question is solved, he continued, democracy can be practiced. (He did not address the place in society of those without an Arab-Islamic identity).

Ghannushi frequently speaks from his London exile of the need to open a dialogue (hiwar) with the West, rejecting the "clash of civilizations" notion put forth by both Samuel Huntington and numerous Islamists. At the same time and in contrast with other Tunisian Islamists, his rhetoric has become increasingly radical in recent years. His condemnations of the allegedly perfidious Western domination of the New World Order, praise for Sudan's regime as a state founded on Islamic concepts and efforts to promote the cause of Algeria's FIS have weakened his credibility and appeal to Western governments. In a wide-ranging conversation with the New York Times, he repeatedly placed primary blame for excesses committed by Islamic regimes on Western "rejectionist attitudes," and justified the murder of Arab and Muslim intellectuals who had embraced secularism, referring to several as "the devil's advocate...Pharoah's witches. The educated that put their brains and their talent in the service of an oppressive regime have made their own decisions. They must bear the responsibility for their choice."

Ghannushi has also repeatedly emphasized that Western hostility to Islam is due to the activities of Zionism, which, in order to retain aid and support, is striving to convince the West that following the collapse of communism and the failure of Arab nationalism, Islam is the new evil force in the world. Speaking in closed sessions at radical Islamic conferences, his rhetoric was even fierier: "Zionism does not only target Arabs and Muslims. It targets goodness...the entirety of values that have crystallized in humanity. Every evil in the world, the Zionists are behind it. This is no exaggeration. There are so many evils in the world, and behind which are the Children of Israel."

Speaking in May 1995 at the Royal Institute of International Affairs, Ghannushi expressed the hope that the Algerian crisis would soon be resolved in the Islamists' favor. This would be followed by a "swift end" to the deadlock in Tunisia, "either as a result of an initiative by the regime itself, which we would prefer, or due to a massive popular pressure, which is more likely to happen. H, should Algeria continue to bleed slowly, the political situation in Tunisia will move in the same direction, but slowly too." It seems that Ghannushi may have been overly optimistic. The immediate future for the Islamists in Tunisia does not appear to be a promising one.

Algeria

As for Algeria, nowhere was the azma more acutely felt. The socio-economic dimension is obviously crucial in explaining Algeria's slide into chaos. A generation of misguided, mismanaged "state capitalist" policies, the worldwide slump in the hydro- carbon sector beginning in the mid-1980s, rampant corruption, rapid population growth and high unemployment all fueled the breakdown of the ruling FLN (Front de Liberation Nationale) regime and the Islamists' rise. Taken alone, however, a socio-economic explanation for Algeria's woes is insufficient. From a historical perspective, the sudden, dramatic swing to the Islamist camp and resulting war for Algeria's soul is the latest chapter in a pattern of extreme changes and dislocations marking Algerian history: the general absence in pre-colonial times of a relatively strong central authority and unified political tradition (as compared to Morocco); the colonial power's thoroughgoing destruction of existing elites; the terrible bloodletting during the 1954-1962 war of independence, not just between Algerian Muslims and the Europeans, but within the Muslim community as well. Finally, a mobilizing, revolutionary ideology and authoritarian leadership in the newly independent state left no room for other visions or political activity.

Throughout the post-independence years, the ruling authorities in Algiers, like counterparts elsewhere in the Maghrib and Mashriq, sought to manipulate Islam in the regime's service. Measures taken included were- enactment of a personal status code in 1984 adhering closely to Islamic precepts of banning alcohol in some cities, making Friday the day of rest, promoting religious education in schools and implementing an Arabization program in schools and public institutions. At the same time, the FLN regime, under Houari Boummedienne and then Chedli Benjedid, sought to wed Islam to the governing socialist revolutionary ideology and block any independent Islamic political activity whether urban-reformist or rural-popular. Algerian Islamists had to go to Tunisia, Morocco or Cairo for proper Islamic training because Algeria lacked an Islamic institution of high caliber. It is thus not surprising that Algeria has not produced Islamist theoreticians comparable to Khomeyni, Turabi, or Ghannoushi. Indeed, the "thinness" of Islamist clerics in numbers and learnedness, might make it tougher for Islamists to govern effectively should they gain power. This scenario is quite different from Iran, where the religious classes were able to establish sophisticated networks of power quickly, even down to the neighborhood level book. Notwithstanding the regime's efforts to monopolize and manipulate Islam, signs of an Islamic revival outside of authorized state structures were widespread during the 1970s and 1980s. Violent clashes between leftists and radical Islamists occurred on university campuses; Mustafa Bouyali, an ex-FLN fighter in the war of independence, attempted to promote an armed insurrection in the countryside between 1984-87; and the regime placed hundreds of activists in detention, including a number of the future founders of the FIS. Islamists also expanded their activities in the social welfare sphere at the neighborhood level. Nonetheless, nearly all observers believed that the authorities had matters well in hand. The literature analyzing Algeria during the period is devoid of any reference to `Abbasi Madani, the most prominent personage of the soon to be established FIS, or any sense that the Islamists had reached a critical mass. To be sure, one cannot demand clairvoyance, and the situation did become increasingly more dynamic and fluid after 1988. Nonetheless, it is a fact that scholars and observers, many of them "secular-modern" Algerians, were slow to recognize the budding power of the Islamists.

This tendency continued even following the FIS's successes in the 1990 municipal elections. Many sought to explain away the movement's successes as a mere protest against a discredited and corrupt FLN regime, which to a large extent it was, or as the result of voter apathy or the boycott of municipal elections by other political parties. But what in the end stands out as most salient was the FIS's ability to repeatedly mobilize large-scale support in competitive, highly-charged electoral contests, even after its top echelon was imprisoned in June 1991, and then in its capability to mount a sustained armed uprising beginning in January 1992. The two more moderate, "gradualist" Islamist parties, Hamas, led by Mahfoud Nahnah, and al-Nahda, headed by Shaykh Abdallah Djaballah, were completely overwhelmed by the FIS and won only minimal support in the 1990 and 1991 elections.

One keen observer of Algeria, Hugh Roberts, explains the FIS's appeal in the context of modern Algerian history. In ideological terms, he states, the FIS has developed the Islamic aspect of the FLN's governing vision, rather than repudiating it entirely. In fact, the FIS explicitly claims to be the new bearers of the FLN's torch, and the authentic inheritors of the FLN's legacy. The FIS-FLN connection is further strengthened by the fact that Shaykh 'Abbasi Madani, first among equals of the FIS leadership, was an early member of the FLN, and was even imprisoned for his activities for most of the 1954-62 period. Also like the FLN, the FIS maintains a sort of collective leadership, befitting its status as a "front" and helping it to gather together a number of streams and groups belonging to Algerian Islamism. But what is most important is that the FIS constituted a political body which gave primacy to political action over religious activities.

Its two most prominent figures prior to their imprisonment in June 1991, Madani and Ali Belhadj, epitomize FIS's two faces. Madani, in his mid-60s, has a doctorate from the Institute of Education at the University of London. He has been unswerving in insisting on establishing an Islamic state governed by the Shari'a and on the need to reinstitute allegedly Islamic norms, such as the separation of men and women in the workplace. Nonetheless, his tone prior to imprisonment was relatively benign and his commitment to political pluralism, while ultimately tactical, at least left room for a dialogue with other political forces in Algeria. He told an interviewer that pluralism was absolutely necessary for a just society. "We are not angels...we make mistakes....There were different views and opinions even among the Prophet Muhammad's associates....We'll make Algeria a Hyde Park not only for free expression but also for choice and behavior."

While Madani was talking about Hyde Park, Ali Belhadj, a 28- year-old preacher based in a mosque in the overcrowded Bab el-Oued quarter of Algiers, was exerting a powerful appeal on the masses of deprived, frustrated youth. His militant message was unadorned: combat the "French" (meaning the secular forces in Algeria), transform Algeria into an Islamic state immediately, by elections, if possible, and by force if the authorities reject the peaceful transfer of power, and exact retribution on all those who have committed crimes against the people.

If the FIS's mobilizing capacity in the street and electoral arena was impressive, no less significant has been the Islamists ability to survive a brutal crackdown by the Algerian military authorities since January 1992, and to inflict heavy punishment of their own. One can partially ascribe the Islamists' resilience to its very nature as a "front", attracting not just Ph.D.'s like Madani preachers like Belhadj and intellectuals of the so-called "Algerianizatiocurrent", but also ex-army officers; radical militants who had already served prison terms for violent anti-regime actions in the 1980s as part of the Bouyali group; various jama`at (societies) whose spiritual and military leader, Shaykh `Umar al-`Alami, was killed by the security forces in April 1993; members of the takfir wal-hijra group, modeled after-and perhaps-connected to the Egyptian radicals of the same name; and the so-called "Afghans," Algerian veterans of the Afghanistan war against the Soviet-backed regime in Kabul.

The armed struggle against the regime has been conducted by two loosely organized bodies. The larger is the l'Arme Islamique du Salut (AIS), known until May 1994 as the Mouvement Islamique Arme (MIA), which functions as the FIS's unofficial armed wing. The other, smaller armed Islamist coalition of different armed networks is the Group Islamique Arme (GIA). As the war dragged on, the FIS became increasingly desirous of an alliance with non- Islamist forces and willing to engage in dialogue with the regime. In January 1995, FIS representatives took part in a dialogue of eight opposition parties in Rome and signed on to a joint statement calling for the "progressive return of civil peace," based on the relegalization of the FIS and freeing of jailed FIS activists in return for a gradual end to violence and its rejection as a means to attain power, negotiations for establishing a transitional government to prepare for multi-party elections and formation of an independent commission to investigate abuses of human rights.

By contrast, the GIA is "purist" in its advocacy of unbridled violence and rejects any suggestion of dialogue with the regime. It has been responsible for some of the more shocking acts of murder and terror during the civil war. These have included burning schools, the slitting of "immodestly" dressed women's throats, car bombs in crowded city streets, the hijacking of an Air France jetliner, the systematic killing of journalists and the targeting of other representatives of Western culture such as intellectuals, athletes, scientists and musicians. Their approach may be said to constitute an Islamic version of Frantz Fanon's teachings on the cleansing, purifying properties of violence or, alternatively, of the Khmer Rouge's vision of how to build a new society. The differences in approach between the GIA and the FIS led to sharp disagreements and even open warfare between them in 1995.

Decentralization among the armed groups renders the Islamists more prone to infighting. This was especially so in the case of the so-called "war of the leaders" during 1993, pitting the MIA's `Abelkader Chebouti against the GIA's `Abdelhaq Layada. Following the latter's arrest by Moroccan authorities in the Algerian- Moroccan border area and subsequent handing over to the Algerian authorities, Chebouti gained the advantage. However, one report described this as a double-edged sword, since Layada was likely to repay Chebouti's alleged betrayal in kind. As it happened, Chebouti was subsequently killed by government forces.

Decentralization or even fragmentation may be a weakness for the Islamists. In March 1995, the FIS National Shura (consultative) Council sought to overcome the problems engendered by a lack of military structure by appointing Madani Merzaq, an Afghanistan veteran and former prayer leader, as the AIS "national emir" [commander]. However, the appointment was not accepted easily, causing some defections among GIA field commanders.

At the same time, decentralization is also strength, complicating the authorities' efforts to defeat the Islamists. The number of Islamist fighters may reach 10,000; they clearly have considerable backing within the population, often reinforced by the harsh repressive measures of the authorities.

Questions have been raised about how much control the Islamist civilian leadership exerts over the AIS. One of its leading commanders, Sa'id Makhloufi, for example, was removed from the FIS Higher Council in July 1991, owing to his utter opposition to the democratic process as a way to create an Islamic state. Chebouti, though close to Ali Belhadj, was never a member of the FIS or its Consultative Council. Merzaq also seemed to be positioning himself as a rival to Shaykhs Madani and Belhadj. One of Madani's preconditions for a true dialogue with the regime is that the entire FIS leadership, including the military wing, be pardoned and allowed to engage freely in consultations among themselves. The regime has rejected this demand and consequently, its efforts to conduct a substantive dialogue with Madani have foundered.

As for the GIA, its leaders have been repeatedly killed by security forces, and the GIA's current inner workings remains shrouded in mystery. Further complicating the picture is the widespread belief that the GIA is thoroughly penetrated by the regime's intelligence units. Some have gone so far as to blame those in the regime opposing a dialogue with the Islamists for some of the GIA's violent acts. Another case of Middle Eastern conspiracy theories at play? Perhaps. But there are important components of the regime, both military and civilian, led by chief of staff Mohammed Lamari, Gens. Nezzar and Belkheir, and former PM Redha Malek, who suspect that President Liamine Zeroual's pursuit of dialogue with the Islamist political wing will inevitably lead to an eventual Islamist takeover known as the "eradicators," they advocate a policy of crushing the Islamist threat by whatever means necessary and may well threaten Zeroual's hold on power.

Still another complicating factor is increasing unrest in the Berber stronghold of Kabylia, the only area where the FIS failed to triumph in the 1991 elections. An Islamist triumph, or even a deal between the regime and FIS, is viewed by many Kabylians as threatening their own interests, which center on demands for the recognition of Tamazight as an official language alongside Arabic, the right to promote and develop Tamazight culture, secularism, democracy and perhaps even communal autonomy. Given the current crisis, self-conscious Berber activism increasingly seems like at least a proto-nationalist current. In response, the Zeroual regime has made concessions regarding the recognition and propagation of Berber culture which, however unsatisfactory Berber activists deem them, would have been unthinkable during the 1980s.

By now it should be evident that a successful "reinvention" of the Algerian political community is a long way off. Even if the intermittent efforts at dialogue eventually bear some fruit, ending violence and assembling an interim national pact or power-sharing arrangement are herculean tasks. What is left of the state-the military and security apparatus, bureaucracy, civilian politicians, still possesses considerable coercive power. So do the Islamists. Despite the numerous political parties, the January 1995 Rome declaration does not yet portend the emergence of a democratic "third force" able to occupy the middle ground between a noxious, repressive regime and an equally noxious, radical opposition. Nor do the small, more moderate Islamist alternatives to FIS have any real political following.

Throughout the civil war's first years, most observers continued to believe the Islamists would eventually gain the upper hand. One possible alternative was the partial disintegration of the political system and state structures and the emergence of multiple power centers in different regions, a kind of "warlordism". Up until now, however, the military's ability to survive and maintain power during years of bloodletting vividly contrasts with the Iranian military's disintegration during the Shah's last days. One key variable to watch will undoubtedly be the regime's ability to block any attempts at disrupting the petro- chemical complexes which give it the finances necessary to stay afloat (again the Iranianexperience comes to mind). Another crucial variable will be the position of the Western powers, particularly France. Algerian-French relations have always been brittle, a legacy of their historically tortured relationship. Tensions between the Algerian regime and French government rose anew in December 1994-January 1995, following the hijacking of an Air France jet in Algiers by Muslim militants, subsequent flight to France and eventually it's storming by French commandos.

The event occasioned bitter mutual recriminations by both officials and the media. To the Zeroual government's dismay, the Rome agreement by Algerian opposition groups drew a favorable reaction from French Foreign Minister Alain Juppe.

Both French and American officials hoped that stimulating renewed political dialogue would help to jump-start the process and reduce violence. At the same time, an active policy of support for dialogue could erode the regime's strength. As it happened, French policy since 1995 under Jacques Chirac has been geared to bolster Algeria's authorities, even at the expense of increased Islamist terrorism inside France itself. France continues to perceive the existing regime as the lesser of two evils. Along with Spain and Italy, France fears a massive wave of Algerian emigration across the Mediterranean in the event of an Islamist triumph, a scenario to be avoided at all costs.

ASSESSMENT

An Islamist FIS triumph, should it come, will surely embolden Islamist groups in other countries. At the same time, there is enough evidence of diversity within the Maghrib to avoid a simplistic application of that old domino theory concept. Much will depend on the Islamist leadership's attitudes and behavior after coming to power. Undoubtedly, it would be beset by the enormous task of consolidation and stabilization of power. Such a task, to be sure, did not prevent Islamic Iran from simultaneously looking outward and adopting a revisionist foreign policy. Again, however, the differences in the two sets of circumstances outweigh the similarities. Morocco neither poses the kind of threat nor provides the kind of opportunity for Algeria that Iraq did for Iran. The FIS leadership does not contain anyone with the stature of Khomeini; and Algeria does not possess the geopolitical weight of Iran.

Moroccan-Algerian relations would likely be tense in the event of an Islamist triumph. To be sure, there was never any love lost between Morocco and the FLN regime, and the Moroccans have always expressed confidence that they are immune from the kind of upheaval besetting Algeria. Moreover, Morocco's King Hasan has already hedged some of his bets, suggesting that it would have been preferable had the Algerian electoral process been carried out to its conclusion if only to point out the fundamentalists' inability to fulfill their promises. Nonetheless, Hasan's own combination of Islam, monarchy, and modernity is anathema to Algeria's Islamists. An Islamist government is unlikely to forget Morocco's cooperation with the Algerian authorities in tracking down and extraditing Islamist guerrillas using Morocco as a sanctuary, most notably the GIA's Layada. One can envisage a continuation of the traditional Algerian-Moroccan rivalry for regional preeminence.

Tunisia may be more vulnerable, given its small size, long border with Algeria, dependence on tourism (a target of Islamist extremists in Egypt), and the encouragement which a FIS triumph would give Tunisia's Islamists. Tunisia's vulnerability was demonstrated in a February 1995 cross-border attack by Algerian Islamists in which a number of Tunisian border policemen were killed. Since then, Algerian and Tunisian security forces have cooperated in trying to root out Islamists on both sides of the frontier. Tunisia has eagerly sought support from other Arab regimes in combatting Islamic extremism, particularly in the annual meetings of Arab interior ministers. Even more important, Western countries' support for their traditional Moroccan and Tunisian allies will be vital if they are to stave off Islamist challenges. The regimes in Tunis and Rabat have been made more determined to keep firm grips on power and block Islamist political activism by the Algerian experience.

The level of political stability in North Africa during the next decade will undoubtedly be influenced by the outcome of the Islamist-regime confrontation in Algeria. Still, in retrospect, Algeria has always been sui generis in the Arab world. It had the least distinct historical identity in pre-colonial times of any of the Maghrib's geopolitical units, and indeed perhaps of most of the Arab lands. It experienced the most thorough colonization, the most brutal, violent independence struggle, and the application of the Soviet/Eastern European model of development and political organization, and now, the most comprehensive collapse (excepted Lebanon). Other Arab regimes never imitated Algeria's model of development. Nor did Algeria ever really project power beyond its borders, apart from the vacuum in the Western Sahara. If historical patterns are any guide, perhaps an Islamist triumph in Algeria, if it is to come, will have less of a revolutionary impact in the region, at least initially, than one might expect. One can also expect that its neighbors, together with regimes in the Arab world and Western governments, will seek to contain an Islamic Algeria with a combination of blandishments and inducements.

In any case, the real challenge facing Arab regimes in the Maghrib and beyond will continue to come from within. The degree of mutual aid and succor among the Islamists (more of an Islamic "global village" than an "internationale"), while not negligible, does not represent an irresistible force. Modern states, singly and in alliances, possess considerable capacities of their own.

ISLAM IN MOROCCO

Fundamentalist Islamic movements have become commonplace in most Middle Eastern political systems throughout the second half of this century. They are most readily apparent in those countries where a secular government has been introduced into a historically strong Islamic society. In such cases the fundamentalist movements are able to introduce their sectarian ideals into a governmental system that has chosen to remain neutral in the eyes of God and the society it was meant to govern. The common goal of these fundamentalist movements is to create a leadership to guide the nation of Islam ('umma), and to accomplish this goal these groups seek political power so as to establish an Islamic government and subsequently an Islamic political, social, and religious order. Because the Moroccan political establishment is based on Islamic law and the leadership of the all-powerful ruler, King Hassan II, has been granted his authority under the guise of Allah to be the Commander of the Faithful, the absence of an Islamic leadership that has stimulated the growth of fundamentalist movements in most Middle Eastern countries is non-existent.

Additionally, the original Baraka (religiously inspired charisma) granted to King Hassan II soon after Morocco's independence allowed him to use his position, as the Commander of the Faithful, to prey on the nationalistic and religious sympathies of society while fostering a corrupt governmental structure to progressively enhance the powers of the Monarch and his leadership through coercion and suppression. Thus the extra-constitutional and illicit powers of the King in the late twentieth century have curbed the possibility of fundamentalist or any other political or religious opposition to emerge and forcefully threaten the current political establishment.

MOROCCAN FUNDAMENTALISM

Fundamentalists in Morocco vary a great deal from the general perception Middle Eastern fundamentalists connoting political Islam. Twentieth- century fundamentalists, whatever their religion, typically argue that the ills of the present are due to deviation from the righteous path of virtuous ancestors. God is punishing them for this deviation. As soon as believers once again conform to their sacred scriptures, God or the gods will deliver them from evil. This is, of course, a classical theme in Islam. Although the righteous men of God who defied sultans often argued along these lines, twentieth-century fundamentalists tend to interpret such classical themes differently.

Fundamentalists, although often critical of nationalism as a secular ideology, are usually themselves intensely nationalistic. Iran's Islamic revolution was as much a nationalist revolution against foreign domination as it was a fundamentalist revolution against secularism. The nationalistic dimension of most twentieth-century fundamentalism relates to broader issues. Like countless revivals throughout history, twentieth-century fundamentalism advocates a return to the true form of their religion, but their conception of their religion is always to some extent an invented one.

Late twentieth-century fundamentalism is typically a politicized revival of tradition very different from tradition itself. Fundamentalists usually stress that their religion is an all-encompassing system governing politics and economics as well as what is conventionally thought of as religion. This ideological view of religion is far removed from how traditional believers believe. However, we find considerable deviation from this position in the Moroccan context. Some people who demand a strictly Islamic state are relatively traditional, like the Moroccan fundamentalist leader al-Faqih-al Zamzami. Others are far more ideological, such as 'Abd as-Salam Yasin, who has led the most influential of the fundamentalist movements in Morocco since its independence. Nonetheless, though each varies in his foundations they do not represent a rigid dichotomy, but points on a continuum.

AL-FAQIH AL-ZAMZAMI AND THE SUNNI MOVEMENT

Among the least ideological and most authentically traditional of Morocco's Islamic movements is that exemplified by the late Faqih al-Zamzami of Tangier and his sons. In literary Arabic, the word Faqih means scholar, but in Morocco, a faqih is usually a man who teaches the Quran to children. Al-Zamzami would not be considered a scholar by most Moroccan ulama (religious scholar), though he is viewed as one by his followers who call themselves Sunnis. In Morocco, the term Sunni is widely used to refer to Muslims who advocate a strictly Islamic way of life but are not directly involved in political activities. Al-Zamzami's followers are sometimes also called Wahhabis, the name often given to the puritanical revivalist movement that led to the creation of Saudi Arabia.

Though the few followers of Al-Zamzami revered him and continued to follow his words most Moroccans who new him, or of him, suggested that he was old-fashioned unable and unwilling to stand up to King Hassan II. Some even argued that he may have actually been a government agent in that he aided the government in focusing attention on matters of ritual and dress rather than on the need for a fundamental transformation of Moroccan society. A follower of al-Zamzami, however, while praising the Iranian revolution for having shown "the true face of Islam", states that the Faqih merely wanted to change people rather than overthrow the government.

Al-Zamzami's ideas, like those of similar preachers, have been disseminated through cassette tapes of his sermons and lectures as well by his books and pamphlets with titles like "How to Fulfill the Obligation of Prayer." Some were outright critical of the present social and political order in Morocco. For example, Al-Zamzami's book "The Position of Islam vis-a-vis the Rich and the Poor" which stresses that Islam does not allow people to possess wealth beyond what they need to live on was banned in Morocco. Although he avoided direct criticism of King Hassan II his reference to the rulers and the rich is generally interpreted by Moroccans to be directed at the monarch.

Through his writings and through his relatively peaceful demonstrations of Sunni ways al-Zamzami attempted to influence Moroccan society. In the 1980's he protested the fact that women were being forced to show their hair when photographed for a national identity card. He wrote the Minister of the Interior demanding that this practice be ended. Also, in the 1980's al-Zamzami's sons led a campaign against the way the poor were treated at public hospitals in Tangier, an act indicative of the Sunni's reformist rather than revolutionary nature.

The most influential of al-Zamzami's sons, 'Abd al Bari' bin al-Siddiq, used to preach in a popular mosque in Tangier where in 1983 he delivered a sermon that provoked local authorities to arrest him. He was then detained and forced to remain blindfolded in a house for one month while he was being tortured. Soon after his release, 'Abd al-Bari' began preaching again, but avoided any direct criticism of the King or the government in public. Like those before him he had come to understand the consequences of the sultan's (or the Malik's) wrath, and was careful not to be subjected to it again.

By the late 1980's, nonetheless, the Sunni tendency could be seen in all the cities of Morocco- in terms of clothing, wedding styles, and rhetoric. For most of the people involved, there is nothing explicitly political about all of this. Nor do most of the people who call themselves Sunnis have any organizational link to al-Faqih al-Zamzami or his sons. (Tozy, 154)

Even at the cultural level, the Sunni tendency does not always run very deep. One hears many stories about women who cover their hair and bodies in Sunni fashion simply to avoid being harassed by men in public. There is also talk of men who have sexual relations with women who wear the hijab. Moreover, it would be a mistake to assume that all women wearing Sunni clothes are committed to the goal of an Islamic revolution.

The Sunni movement with which al-Zamzami is identified is actually a diffuse religious and cultural tendency rather than an organized political group. Al-Zamzami often criticized the government in a manner reminiscent of the classical righteous man of God, but he never advocated force or revolution. In fact, it has been suggested that al-Zamzami believed that the very idea of monarchy was contrary to Islam, but he never openly criticized King Hassan II. His fundamentalism was much more traditional and much less ideological than that which has generally appealed to students and other educated young Moroccans.

If al-Zamzami represents the most traditional wing of the Islamic opposition faced by King Hassan II in the late twentieth-century, Abd al-Karim Muti' and his group "Islamic Youth" represents its most radical one. *Al-Shabiba al-Islamiyya* was founded by Muti' who while the inspector of education and an active member of the Union Socialiste des Forces Populaires (USPF) underwent a transformation into an Islamic activist. Under his leadership, *al-Shabiba al-Islamiyya* began to attract supporters in Morocco's high schools and universities in the early 1970's. Although they were able to impact the social and political climate of the country through bold public accusations and criticisms they were quickly diffused and their position undermined by the Moroccan state apparatus. The following passage is taken from an editorial in the first issue of a review published in Belgium by a faction of al-Shabiba:

"Our present and our future are caught between the hammer of American imperialism and the anvil of its agents represented by the corrupt monarchical regime"

"Your review appears in these circumstances to be, God willing, in the vanguard of an authentic Islamic revolution in Morocco; a revolution that enlightens the horizons of this country and liberates its people to bring them back to the Islam of Muhammad and not those of the merchants of oil and the agents of the Americans." (Dhaouadi and Ibrahim 1982, 57)

The merchants of oil in this passage represent the Saudis and the other rulers of the Gulf. These people, like King Hassan II himself, are routinely condemned as agents of the Americans by the more radical fundamentalists. In the same defamatory way the group also published an open letter to the king after he told people not to sacrifice an animal for the feast of sacrifice in the early 1980's, because drought had decimated Morocco's flocks of sheep and goats:

"We have known you ever since you abrogated God's Book in its entirety and became yourself a god who makes laws, forbidding that which is permitted and permitting that which is forbidden; making blood flow and spreading dishonor. The cancellation of the feast of sacrifice only crowns the thirst for Pharaonism and tyranny that controls the core of your vile soul... We say to you: Fear God in his religion and the religion of his prophet before he changes you into a monkey, after having changed you into a drunkard and an opium addict".

"We say to our people, Muslim and believing: Enough humiliation! Enough cowardice and shame! Revolt against this tyrant who wants to turn your country, beloved Muslim Morocco into a land of debauchery and libertinism for the Jews impoverish and starve its inhabitants at leisure. You have in your Quran and the Sunna of your prophet the best support."(Harbi 1991, 159)

It was perhaps this harsh criticism and resentment apparent in the al-Shabiba movement that fostered its demise. While developing antagonistic groups within the movement in the early 1980's *al-Shabiba al-Islamiyya* was being further undermined by the repression and cooptation of the Moroccan government. In 1984, seventy-one members of al-Shabiba received sentences ranging from four years imprisonment to death. Before these events took place a number of activists in the organization had decided that it was too dangerous to challenge the current regime and left al-Shabiba to establish other groups and publications that continued to advocate a strictly Islamic polity but refrained from any direct criticism of the government and, above all the king. The best known of these groups is led by 'Abd al-Ilah Ben Kiran who has made repeated unsuccessful attempts at gaining recognition as a political party. It is worth noting, however, that it is widely understood that Ben Kiran receives a regular stipend from the government to spread his message of nonrevolutionary revivalism.

Al-Shabiba al-Islamiyya effectively ceased to exist during the 1980's, though some of its offshoots remain significant in Morocco's high schools and universities and among Moroccan students in Europe.

'ABD AS-SALAM YASIN AND THE MAINSTREAM ISLAMIC OPPOSITION

Yasin's movement is more radical and ideological than that of al-Zamzami but less so than that of *al-Shabiba al-Islamiyya*, but is the most politically significant of the three. Like the followers of *al-Shabiba al-Islamiyya*, Yasin's followers originally tended to be students. In the 1980's and 1990's, however, Yasin attracted a growing amount of support from young people unable to find work, even some with no more than an elementary school education. He was unable to successfully entertain the support of peasants and the urban poor.

Yasin studied at the traditional Islamic al-Yusifiyya University in Marrakesh and became a teacher of Arabic and then an inspector in the Ministry of Education, a position held until Morocco gained its independence in 1956. He was a devout Muslim in the 1950's praying five times a day and fasting during Ramadan and has suggested that his Islam was relatively gentle and apolitical. At the same time he led a relatively westernized style of life. For example, he sent his children to French schools and allowed them to dress in jeans and other traditionally western clothing.

It was not until 1968 that Yasin had his spiritual crisis, (often cited as a nervous breakdown) which incited him to join the Sufi brotherhood of Butshishiyya, becoming a follower of Shaykh al-Hajj Al-'Abbas. Yasin claims that he was disturbed by the materialism of the brotherhood so he left the order. However, many suggest that Yasin actually left the order in 1971 because he wanted to turn it into a political movement but was unable to do so.

It was at this point that Yasin's attitude toward Islam was politicized after speaking of his realization that Islam is inherently political as opposed to being merely politicized. By 1974 Yasin had decided to write an epistle to King Hassan II entitled al-Islam aw at-Tufan: Risala Maftuha ila Malik al-Maghrib (Islam or the Deluge: an open epistle to the king of Morocco). The epistle, 114 pages long (the number of chapters in the Quran), was a conscious attempt to revive the classical tradition of the Prophet. Yasin begins his open letter to the king by saying: "My epistle to you is not like all epistles for it demands an answer."(p1) He repeatedly addresses the king as "O my beloved one" (ya habibi), terms never used by Moroccans to address King Hassan II.

Yasin contends in his epistle that Hassan II simply camouflages his Western "liberal" ideas with religion when he feels it is politically expedient to do so. He tells the king that his "playing with Islam" has convinced young Moroccans that religion is indeed "the opium of the people and mere trickery by means of which hypocritical rulers exploit the gullibility of the masses and enslave them."

"You do not realize that your senseless and deranged actions are manifest proof of the accuracy of what is claimed by the enemies of God [the Marxists]! How will you face God you so-and-so? Tell me how if you are a believer!"

It is hard to convey a sense of how shocking this language is in the Moroccan context. In the official rhetoric of the government-controlled media, Hassan II is the Commander of the Faithful and the shadow of God on earth. Yet Yasin questions whether he is, in fact Muslim at all.

Yasin says the coups of the early 1970's were warnings from God. He ridiculed the king's claim to have survived these coups thanks to his Baraka. God saved him, not his Baraka, but Hassan II failed to heed God's warnings and became more of a tyrant than ever. Yasin's epistle represents the king's last chance. It too is a warning from God. If Hassan II heeds it and repents, he can still be saved. If not, "Who will there be to protect you?"(Munson, 164-5)

The basic message of Yasin's epistle is simple and familiar. The Muslim's problems are due to their having deviated from Islam. If they return to the laws of God and stop imitating the West, the oppression of the poor by the rich will vanish. The state of terror in which Moroccans now live will vanish. Poverty will vanish. The squatter settlements ringing Morocco's cities will vanish. The caliph will be a man of the people instead of a potentate living indolently in his palaces. Everything that is bad will be good.

It is important to note, however, that Yasin's insistence on the contractual nature of the caliphate should not be confused with a commitment to democracy. Yasin's conception of an ideal Islamic polity is a thoroughly authoritarian one, with the masses seen as being in need of a "just imam" to guide them on the path of righteousness. Unlike many Salafi reformists, not to mention Morocco's principle political parties, Yasin ridicules democracy and advocates a "council elected in an Islamic manner" after all political parties have been banned. "The party of Satan," as Yasin calls people, who advocate a secular form of government, would not be allowed to participate in the elections for this council. Yasin contends that those who reject the idea of a strictly Islamic polity are entitled to "firm but humane solicitude." That is to say that they have the right to be taught the error of their ways.

After sending a copy for the king to the governor of Marrakesh province, Yasin reportedly prepared his burial shroud to prepare for the expected response of the king. While King Hassan II was of course infuriated by Yasin's epistle he was advised not to sentence him to death, but to place Yasin in a psychiatric hospital since only a lunatic could possibly address the king in such a way. Moreover, if Yasin would have been put to death it was assumed that he would appear to be a martyr who would clearly affect the king adversely. Subsequently, Yasin spent three and a half years in an insane asylum.

Once released from the asylum, Yasin resumed his campaign for a strictly Islamic polity in Morocco, but he no longer criticized the king directly. In 1979 he began publishing an Islamic review entitled al-Jama'a, "The Group," of which no more than three thousand copies were ever published. The government had obstructed the publication of this review for at least a year before the first issue was published. It was banned after the eleventh issue appeared in 1983. The government also forbade Yasin to preach in mosques. In December 1983, he tried to publish another newspaper, *al-Subh*, (*The Dawn*), but this too was immediately banned and he was sentenced to two years in prison.

After Yasin's release he transformed his home into a center for his movement to come and pray and here him preach. But, in 1987 Yasin attempted to establish an Islamic political party to participate in Moroccan elections to express the basic hostility toward the Morrocan electoral system. Although it is well-known that the elections were rigged Yasin's position was that the simple idea of a government based on the will of the people is contrary to Islamic law which presupposes that government should be based on the laws of God. The government paralyzed his movement by surrounding his home with police and arresting many of his followers. Although demonstrations were attempted to protest the government's hostility they met with very little success. In fact, except for the few who joined the protests most Moroccans were outraged by the inconveniences Yasin's movement had caused. To this day Yasin's group has had little impact on the social and political elements of the Moroccan state. Although the group is still in existence there remains virtually no threat to the current system by Yasin or his followers, or any other fundamentalist movement.

"The Commander of the Faithful": As Clifford Geertz argues in Islam Observed, the "strong-man" aspect of Moroccan kingship "inevitably clashed with and usually dominated the holy-man aspects" and that this is "both true and, for an understanding of the nature of the Moroccan state, critical."(Geertz, 53) The King of Morocco remains alone among his fellow heads-of-states in the region, having repeatedly renewed his links to a political system that has predated the protectorate. The Sharifian monarch, who rules in a very traditionalist society, is unique in that the Constitution by which the country seeks guidance designates a double leadership role that includes both temporal and spiritual powers.

The king knew better than anyone else how to preserve support in the field of religion. "From the force of its opposition, Islam, in fact, became the principal force of legitimating government power just after independence."(Leveau, 206) This privileged relationship, however, did not manage to halt a deep process of secularization of Moroccan society. But it did explain the natural reticence of the sovereign to allow the religion's place to be reduced in the field of politics and, thus, his ability to prevent any detraction from his religious legitimacy.

"As you know, I am the Commander of the Faithful," the successor of Mohammed V asserted: "I received this title at birth, without asking for it, without wanting it. That means that I am one of the descendants of the Prophet, which is not exactly common, and which means that as deeply rooted as I am in Morocco for generations, my original tribe is that of Mecca." This title, "Commander of the Faithful," for some, including the Iranians who have accorded such an importance to the question of the descent of the Prophet, does not meet with indifference. It is a title that imposes a great deal of humility and, all the same at certain times, great responsibilities.(Nouvel Observateur, Oct, 3, 1987)

Hassan II understands how to anchor the fundamentalist discourse within the heart of the state, reducing the territory left to the fundamentalism of protest. Fundamentalist-inspired measures largely counterbalance the few secular, modernist or ecumenical "provocations" made by the regime.

Contrary to the Tunisian legislation adopted at the same date, the code of civil status promulgated in 1957 was in strict conformity with Quranic prescriptions. Prayer in schools was made obligatory by the King, who in 1968 reintroduced the institution of Quranic schools. He repressed those who did not fast during Ramadan (800 imprisoned in 1965) and created a High Council of Ulemas (in 1980, seven years before Bourguiba thought of a similar measure), whose approval he took the precaution of obtaining for all the major decisions of his reign, even if nothing obliged him to do so. The monarch, whom certain of his own cadets felt was far too Westernized, was thus alerted at the start of the 1970's, and, far sooner than any of his peers, he went on the counter-offensive. Faced with the mounting current of popular Islamism which little by little began to take on the "look of a shrewd political protest" the monarchy's reaction consisted of effectively pushing official Islam's control as far as possible over the signs of vitality of popular Islam (Leveau, 206).

Thus, the rural structures of traditional Islam were mobilized, reinforced, and in some cases completely revived, in order to be given new means to watch over and control all the suspect forms of religious mobilization. (Bourgatt, 168-9) The centralization of the demonstration of official Islam was set up within the system to fulfill the need for a centralized Islamic system.

Favored by the structural fragility of the economy and the frustrations which it carried with it, the Islamist current has been deprived of the monopoly of protest. Islamic fundamentalist elements have had to contend with a political opposition and a labor movement endowed with a certain margin for maneuver and with the manipulation of a leftist discourse that remained more credible than in Algeria or in Libya.

CONCLUSION

No fundamentalist movement has gained widespread acclaim or support in Morocco since its independence for a number of reasons. First, the foundations of Islamic law that has provided a centralized religious structure in Morocco has not created the void typical of other countries in the Middle East whose predominantly Muslim society is denied a structured Islamic authority for guidance which fundamentalist movements promise to fill. Second, the all-powerful King Hassan II's repressive and coercive actions have successfully denied fundamentalism the ability to develop. Also, the constitutional law banning religious political parties legitimates the suppression of any Islamic opposition to the current regime. Finally, Moroccan society, although predominantly religious is not willing to deny itself the freedom to incorporate elements of other cultures and religions, particularly those of the west that may contradict traditional Islamic thought, yet are permitted by the more modern regime of King Hassan II.

Islamic fundamentalist movements are practically an anomaly in Morocco. The central Islamic foundations of the political and social system have provided the desired religious structure necessary to provide the Islamic foundations of this religious society. While other countries in the Middle East have established secular governments, fundamentalist movements predominate in their attempt to fill the religious void the state has neglected.

The strength of King Hassan II and his careful maneuvering to secure his powers has dissuaded any forceful opposition to his regime. As the Commander of the Faithful, and the head of state, the king has grounded his authority in law and used coercion and repression to undermine the forces of opposition that could potentially threaten his position of power.

Although Morocco is an Islamic state its relations with and influence from the West and its modern ideals has allowed for a more open society that often deviates from the traditional tenets of Islam. Clothing, food, education, traditions, and liberalization have been imported from the West and even the most traditional members of Moroccan society are willing to deny themselves of each of these. While maintaining the basic structure of Islam Morocco is developing and modernizing, and subsequently society is seeking greater personal freedom, that which fundamentalism generally denies. Fundamentalism contradicts modernization in the eyes of most Moroccans, and are subsequently looked down upon or generally ignored.

Neither the state nor society is willing to allow fundamentalism to impact Morocco. While no fundamentalist movement since the state gained its independence in 1956 has had an effective impact in Morocco it is difficult to assume that one will emerge successfully in the years to come. Fundamentalism, it is safe to suggest will not be a reality, at least during King Hassan II's reign.

7

Islam in Caucasus, Chicago, Brazil, Spain and Europe

INTRODUCTION

Many of the reports and analysis on the Caucasus often describe the conflicts as emanating from ancient hatreds, religious differences and as long-rooted. When describing the motivations and behavior of Muslims involved in the conflicts, such as Chechens and Azerbaijanis, the descriptions overwhelmingly assume that Islam is their primary collective identity, that their struggles are based on Islam, and that their religious beliefs make them prone to hate non-Muslims and to act in a violent way. For instance, Chechens are usually described as "Islamic insurgents", while the forces from Moscow are "Russian soldiers", described by their ethnic and state affiliation, but not by their religion. The conflict in Karabagh is frequently described as a dispute between Christian Armenia and Shi'i Muslim Azerbaijan, while religion plays little role in the conflict. Samuel Huntington explains the conflicts in the Caucasus as emanating from the location at a "fault line" between Orthodox Christianity and Islam, assuming that the coalitions in the area largely break down on a Christian/Muslim basis. Accepting these explanations of the origins of the conflicts assumes that the behavior of local elites and of external powers did not cause the conflicts, but that the religious differences and the history of interaction of the peoples of the Caucasus made these conflicts almost inevitable. Logical extension of this analysis of the inevitability of these conflicts is that little can be done to rectify the situation by way of changing the behavior of the external powers in the Caucasus region.

In contrast, evidence suggests that history of hatred and reasons for enmity exist almost everywhere, yet conflicts do not erupt in every region. Moreover, even in places where there is a history of positive interaction, mutual tolerance, and religious affinity, conflicts often breakout. It seems that these conflicts are not pre-determined by ancient hatred and religious differences, but shaped by current behavior and polices of local elites and regional powers. Moreover, in the case of the Caucasus, especially in the interaction between Armenians and Azerbaijanis, there is as much historical evidence of positive interaction as there is attesting to negative interplay, thus the chronicle of the relations of the two peoples has little to do with the conflict that emerged between them. Furthermore, different religious affiliations play only a small role in the conflicts currently waging in the Caucasus and specifically Islam plays no role in the Karabagh conflict with Armenia and only a minor role in the Chechnya war in Russia. In terms of the role of Islam in the conflicts in the Caucasus, a variety of assertions will be made:

Islam is not the primary collective identity of the majority of the Muslims of the Caucasus. Especially in the case of Azerbaijan, ethno-national identity is clearly stronger than Islamic identity. The major coalitions of states involved in the conflicts are not based on religious affinity. For instance, the Islamic Republic of Iran has joined in cooperation with Armenia and Russia to the disadvantage of Shi'i Azerbaijan.

Iran's policy toward the conflicts in the Caucasus is driven by its state geo-political interests, and little by Islamic ideology. Moreover, Iran engages in Islamic propagation in the Caucasus almost exclusively when it cannot damage its strategic interests in the area, and often uses Islam manipulatively in order to advance those interests, primary vis-a-vis Russia.

Collective identity exists on a variety of levels in the Caucasus: family or clan, regional grouping, ethnic group, religion, republic and, for some, a certain "Soviet" identity. Religious affiliation is only one of the multi-layers of identity of the residents of the region, and not necessarily the primary. Various collectives perform a role in the politics of the region. For instance, traditional groupings, such as extended family networks in Azerbaijan, have filled some of the functions no longer executed by the state and thus softened the blows of the shift to market economy and the collapse of the social net previously provided by the state. Furthermore, the relative lack of violence inside states like Azerbaijan, even during heightened political upheaval, can partially be explained by the functioning of the extended family representatives as a facilitator between parts of the government and the demands of the wider public.

Moreover, family ties are held with highest regard among most of the peoples of the Caucasus and greater Caspian region, and frequently there are family links between members of rival political camps, such as Heydar Aliyev and Abulfez Elchibey in Azerbaijan. Thus, often periods of instability and political upheaval in the region, such as those in Azerbaijan, are not marked with high degrees of violence. Family ties play a role in the political processes in the region, adding a dimension to ethnic ties. For instance, they play an important part in preserving the attachment between Azerbaijanis in the republic and beyond its border in Iran, as well as between Armenians in the state and in Karabagh and Georgia. The common primary allegiance to extended family members weakens the potential allure of other collective ideologies, such as Islam, although, of course, it is also present in the region. At the same time, these strong family allegiances also serve as an impediment to state-building and fostering national solidarity, which can be sources of stability.

In neighboring Central Asia, one of the important factors contributing to the relative internal stability in the new Muslim states since the Soviet breakup is the strength of the local, traditional power structures that have survived as a bulwark against major turmoil in the region, allowing continuity in leadership and reduced influence of external, radical forces. These local power structures, such as family and regional groupings endured in the Soviet period and the Soviet-era political elites in the region were most often grounded in these traditional structures. Their survival under the Soviet Union and their duration after its demise, explain why no "vacuum" was created that could have been utilized by foreign or other radical factors.

ISLAM IN THE CAUCASUS

For most of the Muslims of the Caucasus, Islam serves as a component of their ethnic and regional identity, but is not their primary collective identity. Solidarity on an Islamic basis with Muslims beyond the Caucasus is minimal, although beginning to emerge among small groups in the North Caucasus. Most members of the region hold in high regard their local cultures, and they are not particularly susceptible to chief identification with the broader Muslim world. Furthermore, Islam rarely serves as a unifying ideology of primary identity uniting the Muslim residents in the region, and many conflicts prevail among members of the same religion.

Outside forces have too easily labeled mass forms of dissent in the region as "Islamic." For example, when Azerbaijanis removed border posts in December 1989 in attempt to make contacts with their co-ethnics beyond the border in Iran, Western sources tended to interpret this as their desire for ties to "Khomeinism" in Iran. More recently, activity of Chechens involved in what they view as a national struggle for independence is predominately termed in the West as "Islamic" violence and activity, despite the fact that Islam plays a quite secondary role in the conflict. Islam in and of itself is not destabilizing and not all ethnic or regional conflicts in which Muslims are involved are inherently religious. Not all acts of violence and terror perpetrated by Muslims should be seen as Islamic terror.

The Islamic label and the Muslim origin of many of the peoples of the Caucasus is often manipulated for promotion of their own agendas by a variety of forces, both within and from outside the region. With Western audiences and at home, Moscow forthwith throws the Islamic label on movements of Muslims within its border demanding political independence or autonomy in order to cast aspersion on them and to attain American sympathy and acceptance of its policies against the insurgents. In the Soviet period, pious Muslims were generally referred to by the misnomer "Wahabbists", which had a more frightening association then simply observant. Russia has continued with this labeling of Muslim activists, despite the fact that few of the Muslims in the Caucasus are actually connected to Wahabbist movements. Muslim radicals in the Middle East also like to attach the Islamic stamp to uprisings in the Caucasus and Central Asia and often grant support to political movements in this area, even if the basic goal of the movement is not Islamic in nature, although in the long run, they can gain influence in this manner. Many of the fighters in the Caucasus, such as Shamil Bashayev, like to attach the Islamic label to their struggle in order to add an air of legitimacy and respectability to their often power-based struggles and violent behavior, when in their personal habits they show little signs of religious piety.

The overwhelming majority of the Muslims of the North Caucasus are Sunni, whereas the Azerbaijanis are predominantly Shi'i. However, the Shi'i factor has no influence on the Azerbaijanis' political orientation or activity, and actually Azerbaijan has tense relations with its Shi'i neighbor, Iran. In the region, Islam is predominately a cultural force, and scarcely a political force, especially in Azerbaijan. Islam forms the framework for major rites of passage, such as marking birth, death and marriages, but appears in few political contexts. In the northern Caucasus, Sufi Islam is very prominent and popular and does not traditionally aim for the formation of political or highly institutionalized frameworks, and as such can potentially contribute to fostering political moderation. Sufi Islam is as a whole highly condemned by

Wahabbist ideology, and does not seem to be good breeding ground this movement, further weakening Moscow' s claims of the Wahabbist basis of the Chechen movement.

Azerbaijan declared in its Constitution clear separation between religion and state and did not grant any special status to Islam. Moreover, religious parties are illegal and clerics may not run for office in Azerbaijan. As part of their drive for clear separation between religion and state, courts in Azerbaijan have demanded that women remove head coverings for photos for their official documents. Azerbaijan has a long tradition of secularism. With their inclusion in the Russia Empire, the Azerbaijanis were among the first Muslim groups to fall under European colonial rule. In keeping with Russian colonial policy, most of the powers of the Muslim clerical establishment were usurped. Freed from the constraints of the ulema, the Azerbaijanis and other Muslims in Russia became a bridgehead of secularism and proponents of modern education in the Muslim world.

In the north Caucasus, in contrast, some of the local regional governments have granted special status to Islam. However, local identity is very strong and it does not seem likely that the universalistic Islamic identity will surpass it as the primary collective identity of the different groups in the North Caucasus.

In Azerbaijan and in the north Caucasus, official clerical hierarchies, mosques and institutions of religious learning are functioning, predominantly in the attempt to control Islam and mobilize segments of its proponents in service of the regime. The official Islamic institutions have achieved varying degrees of success. In terms of the conflicts afflicting the region, the official clerical establishment in the Caucasus tends to promote stability and is adverse to any form of Islamic radicalism and most kinds of Islamic-based political activity. Moreover, these elements are viewed by the official clerics as their rivals for power and status. In many instances, such as in Chechnya and in connection to the Karabagh conflict, the establishment Muslim clerics have promoted moderation and attempted to advance conflict resolution. Nonetheless, it must be noted that due to their collaboration with the ruling state elites in the region, most of the establishment clerics are delegitimized in the eyes of the more radical and devout Muslims in the region and subsequently they have little influence over extremist Muslims in the area, and many influential independent clerics are operating in the region.

Not having undergone Western colonialism, many residents of the area do not harbor an anti-Western orientation, and many maintain an ambivalent relationship toward Moscow. Even enthusiastic supporters of independence of the region, often are willing to recognize the contributions of the interaction with Russia played in their national development. At the same time, some residents of the region are angered by the incursion on traditional local values and culture by the onslaught Western culture in the post-Soviet period, but it seems that Moscow is as blamed for that cultural assault as much, if not more so, than the West.

Political activity involving Muslims and the patterns of their struggles do not necessarily conform to the image of Muslim behavior associated with radical Arab movements in the Middle East. The absence of use by the Azerbaijanis of terror against civilian Armenian targets in the Karabagh conflict illustrates this point.

Religious based radical behavior seems most prevalent in the region in places where many people live outside their traditional places of residence. Affected by the alienation of new surroundings, often in large cities, without the welfare safety nets provided by their homes as well as the social constraints on their behavior, individuals are more susceptible to radical influences and prone to behavior of this type in their non-traditional settings.

In attempt to assess the extent of the hold of Islam on the population in the Caucasus region, it is important to separate between indicators of social conservatism and Islamic piety. In many parts of the region, social norms are in place, many pre-dating Islam's arrival to the region, that mandate strict behavioral codes in fields such as sexual activity and dress.

Many factors such as social segregation and occupational differentialization between the sexes, modest dress and the covering of the hair among the women have been interpreted by many researchers as external signs of Islamic religiosity and identity. Many Azerbaijanis, for instance, are secular in their outlook and do not observe many explicit Islamic laws (such as the prohibitions on alcoholic drinks and eating pork), even though they observe many conservative social customs. It seems that much of this traditional behavior is rooted in practices, which the practitioners did not necessarily associate with the Islamic religion when observing them.

Close-by examples of the results of wide political violence and Islamic radicalism, such as neighboring Afghanistan and Tajikistan, and the results of the Chechen conflict, serve as constant reminders to the residents of the Caucasus of the dangers of extremism of this type and even many religious people in the region have stated that radical Islamic-based political action must be avoided so that their country doesn't become "another Afghanistan."

In terms of export of Islamic radicalism to Caucasus, the most active external forces are from countries with a Western security orientation, such as Pakistan, Saudi Arabia and Turkey, although most of the Islamic groups are not associated with the ruling governments there and many are in opposition to the regimes, especially in Turkey. Ankara is also active in fostering its official version of Islam in the region through the institutions and employees of its Ministry of Religious Affairs, although many of these may not be actually promoting the agenda that their sponsor would like. Moreover, residents of the region have remarked that even Turkey's version of non-political Islam, is more religious that that which is prevalent in the region, and thus Ankara may inadvertently be promoting Islam through these programs. Moscow's recent actions in the name of combating potential Islamic terror against "Caucasians" residing in the capital and other major cities in Russia, booting them home to the Caucasus and depriving many of their livelihood, may bolster the potential supporters for Islamic and other radical politics and add to the instability of the region.

A source of potential instability in the region emanates from the "Afghani Arabs." This terms is used to refer to the Arab and other Muslim volunteers that came from outside Afghanistan and joined in the struggle in the 1980s against the Soviet Union. Service together in Afghanistan created an international network of Islamic radicals, sharing knowledge and experience in low-intensity warfare and terror. This network often offers assistance to different movements in the region and attempts to encourage them to undertake radical activity, and some of the local movements have accepted this aid. All in all, though, external elements have not been able to turn Islamic-based political activity to a major force at this juncture in the Caucasus.

IRAN AND THE CAUCASUS

Iran's policy in the region is largely guided by geo-political state interests and less by ideological goals, such as promotion of Islam. With the collapse of the Soviet Union, Iran grasped that a potentially conflict- laden zone had replaced its once stable northern border and that influences from the new states could permeate the internal Iranian arena. From the inception of their independence, Tehran took a very sober attitude toward the establishment of the new Muslim republics, seeing in this development the dangers that emanate from the internal ethnic factor in addition to the opportunities for expanded influence:

The first ground for concern from the point of view in Tehran is the lack of political stability in the newly independent republics. The unstable conditions in those republics could be serious causes of insecurity along the lengthy borders (over 2000 kilometers) Iran shares with those countries. Already foreign hands can be felt at work in those republics, especially in Azerbaijan and Turkmenistan republics, with the ultimate objective of brewing discord among the Iranian Azeris and Turkmen by instigating ethnic and nationalistic sentiments.

Iran is a multi-ethnic society in which approximately fifty percent of its citizens are of non-Persian origin. The largest minority group is the Azerbaijanis, which comprise close to a third of the population of Iran. Other major groups include the Kurds, Arabs, Baluch and Turkmen. Many of these groups are concentrated in Iran's frontier areas, and most have ties to co-ethnics in adjoining states, such as Azerbaijan, Turkmenistan, Pakistan, Iraq and Turkey. Thus, Iran's ethnic groups are especially subject to influence by events taking place in these bordering states, and the ethnic question is not merely a domestic matter. One of Tehran's chief goals in the region has been to prevent destabilization in Iranian Azerbaijan and a rise in ethnic-based activity among the Azerbaijanis in Iran.

Iran's cautious attitude toward the Caucasus is quite justified. Following the independence of the Republic of Azerbaijan, a flurry of activity associated with the probing of ethnic and national identity occurred among Azerbaijanis in Iran. The establishment of the Republic of Azerbaijan challenged the national identity of co-ethnics beyond the borders of the new state and served as a stimulant for many Azerbaijanis in Iran to identify with the Azerbaijani ethnic group though not necessarily with the new state itself. In the early 1990s, a significant rise in expressions of Azerbaijani ethnic identity in Iran has been observed, as well as important political manifestations of that identity. This rising Azerbaijani identity has generated few calls for the Azerbaijani provinces to secede from Iran and join the new republic, but rather for increased cultural rights within Iran.

Its close relations with Armenia illustrate the non-ideological nature of Iran's policy toward the region. Despite its rhetoric of neutrality in the Karabagh conflict, in and of itself inconsistent with the official ideology of a state that portrays itself as the protector and champion of the Shi'i in the world, throughout most of the post-independence period, Iran cooperated with Armenia despite its struggle with Shi'i Azerbaijan for control of Karabagh, evidently preferring overall that the Republic of Azerbaijan remain involved in a conflict, making it less attractive to Iran's Azerbaijanis and unable to allocate resources to stir-up 'South Azerbaijan.' Tehran adopted anti-Armenian rhetoric only at times when the results of the conflict directly threatened Iranian state interests. Yet, the non-ideological nature of Iran's policy toward the Karabagh conflict, for instance, has not strengthened the stability in the region. Rather, Iran's cooperation with Armenia and its tacit support in the conflict with Azerbaijan over Karabagh strengthened Yerevan's actual and perceived power and consequently may have lessened its sense of urgency to resolve the conflict.

Moreover, Iran's perception of fear of the Republic of Azerbaijan serving as a model for rising ethnic-based identity of its own Azerbaijani community has led it to have an interest in prolonging the Karabagh conflict, albeit on a low level of intensity. Iran has come to share an interest with Russia in protracting the strife; thus this factor has contributed to the cementing of Russian-Iranian cooperation in the Caucasus, additionally complicating conflict resolution here. Russia is interested in sustaining the conflict since it provides a means of influence and manipulation to promote Moscow's strategic, economic and political interests in the Caucasus, an area which it still considers a zone of highest importance, especially in the military and economic spheres. Moreover, the perpetuation of the conflict provides a means to preserve Yerevan's dependence on Moscow and thus its acquiescence to the stationing of Russian troops in its territory. External involvement and manipulation has been a major factor that has aggravated the Karabagh conflict and contributed to its protraction and escalation.

Moreover, the dispute over the rights of the Azerbaijani minority in Iran and Baku's often irredentist activities serve as a major factor of tension in the relations between the Republic of Azerbaijan and Iran which have led to an increase in Baku's sense of isolation and vulnerability. This tension has impeded cooperation between Iran and Azerbaijan and aversely affected wider regional cooperation, while contributing to Baku's drive to seek association with western security systems, advancing the projection of Iranian-American rivalry into the already troubled Caucasus region. Advancing of Western presence in the Caspian region has reinforced Iran's threat perception from these developments in an area that borders its territory, adding an element, which contributes to instability in the region.

Tehran's policy toward the Karabagh conflict is a good example of the diversity of opinions, which contrasts with its monolithic image, evident in the foreign policy-making process in Iran. The prevailing official Iranian foreign-policy establishment promoted tacit support for Armenia in the conflict and expanding cooperation with Yerevan, evidently as a counter to potential Azerbaijani irredentism. This policy was reflected in journals such as *Tehran Times*. This policy, set by overriding state interests, encountered open opposition from ideological steadfasts, who advocated adopting Islamic solidarity toward the Azerbaijanis in articles in *Jomhuri-ye Islami*. Even with the Iranian Foreign Ministry, there seemed to be diverging opinions over the fitting policy toward the conflict. Some actors, such as Deputy Foreign Minister, Va'ezi, seemed to have an institutional interest in Iran serving as a successful sponsor of the negotiation process between the conflicting sides and thus he seemed to play a candid role in conducting them in the early 1990s. Va'ezi's criticism of Russia as a spoiling factor in the negotiations at this time contrary to the evolving trend of Tehran-Moscow rapprochement is an indication of his apparent veracity in the negotiation process on his part that may not have reflected the prevailing Iranian policy.

Moreover, members of Iran's minorities- both Azerbaijanis and Armenians- lobbied and pressed for Iran's promotion of policies that favored their respective co-ethnics beyond Iran's borders and directly organized aid to their corresponding groups. This urging itself reflects that significant numbers of Azerbaijanis and Armenians in Iran identify with co-ethnics in the newly established republics, many evidently, parallel, to identifying as Iranians. The different viewpoints of various policy-making factors in Iran toward the conflict and relations with Azerbaijan and Armenia can partially explain some policy inconsistency and shifts in relating to Karabagh.

Iran's reactions to both the first and second Chechen

conflicts in the 1990s illustrate the non-ideological nature of its policy toward the Caucasus. Iran attaches high importance to its relations with Russia, who has become a major political ally and an important partner for both economic and military cooperation, thus was careful not to harm its relations with Moscow. Overall, the official Iranian statements and media was quite mild in its criticism of Russia in these wars, despite the Muslim background of the Chechen rebels, and Iranian officials frequently commented that the conflict was an internal Russian matter. Official Iranian condemnation was only aired at times that other issues in the state-to-state relations between Iran and Russia were in conflict over other issues. Moreover, Iran's complaisance on the Chechen issue was often rewarded by Moscow by a reaffirmation of its commitment to supply Tehran with its strongly sought after nuclear reactors.

The conflicts in the Caucasus have created interesting bedfellows, beyond the cooperation between Iran, Armenia and Russia, diverging from nominal lines of religious or "civilizational" affinity. For instance, Chechen activists assisted Moscow in aiding the Abkhaz in its struggle with Georgia. Furthermore, initially after the Soviet break-up, transports of food supplies to Armenia went through Turkish territory, often to the chagrin of Baku.

The use of religious labels to categorize the various sides to the hostilities in the Caucasus contributes little to understanding the roots of these conflicts and subsequently, finding appropriate solutions. Western relative lack of a business-like approach to the grievances of the Muslim peoples of the Caucasus and their assumptions concerning their motivations in the struggles can act like a self-fulfilling prophesy and push many of the Muslim peoples of the Caucasus into radical Muslim arms.

ISLAM IN CHICAGO

In 1996 the Greater Chicago area has over eighty Islamic organizations and most of them attached to an Islamic center or a mosque. The estimated population of Muslims in Cook and the collar counties is 350,000, almost 5% of the total population of the region. The Muslims have surpassed the population of Jews and many other ethnic groups. The nationalities of Muslims, wherever they have come from, includes Indo-Pak-Bangladesh subcontinent, Arabic speaking countries including the Middle East and North Africa, the East European countries of Albania, Bosnia and surrounding states, Turkey, Iran, Malaysia, Indonesia, Afghanistan and sub-Saharan Africa. In addition to white and Hispanic American Muslims, Chicago has the largest concentration of African-American Muslims in the U.S. It is a diverse community speaking a variety of languages, representing a variety of complexions and races, yet they are one community. The sense that all Muslims are one community is embedded in the Qur'anic teachings which make all Muslims one ethnic group, irrespective of their geographical origin, race and color.

The Muslim population of Greater Chicago is well educated and economically prosperous. A survey done a few years ago showed that the Indo-Pakistani Muslims, in particular, had perhaps the highest education level in the U.S. It was found that this community consisted of 16% medical doctors and 33% engineers, and overall 44% had doctorate degrees, 84% had at least bachelor's degrees and only 2% had less than a high school education. The average income of the Indo-Pakistani community was more than twice the average income level of the U.S. population.

The contribution of the Muslim professionals is beyond their proportion in number. Two of the skyscrapers of Chicago, the John Hancock Center and the Sears Tower, were designed by a Muslim architect, Dr. Fazlur Rahman. There is hardly a hospital without a Muslim doctor on its staff. There is hardly an engineering or electronic equipment manufacturer without Muslim engineers. Muslims are involved in the design, production and distribution of all American products and services. There are many Muslim teachers in Chicago public schools and professors in the universities. Chicago would have an extreme shortage of taxis if the Muslims pull out of taxi driving. There are many engineers, even rare medical doctors who are driving taxis either because they are preparing for board examinations or they enjoy freedom and self-employment.

Muslims also have political muscle which was demonstrated when Harold Washington won as a Mayor of Chicago with the slim majority provided by the Muslim vote. Since the early eighties the Muslim population has increased and they are becoming registered voters in increasing proportion. Only thirty years ago the Chicago Muslim population was very small with only one Islamic center which had a small congregation.

In social life, Muslims have almost no alcohol problems and drug use is rare among the Muslim young. There is rare dating because most marriages are still arranged by elders of the family. There is rarely a problem of adultery or homosexuality and there are no children out of wedlock. In general, Muslim youth are good students in their schools and motivated to excel. The divorce rate is relatively low and single parents are few. It is prohibited to show bare bodies, even bare legs, or tight clothing which makes exhibitionism and un-Islamic trait. Muslim men and women dress fully and modestly. Crime of any kind by the Muslims is a rare occurrence. In fact, Islam is playing a great role in the American prison system in reforming the prisoners. The reversion to crime of those prisoners who accept Islam during their incarceration is much lower than those who do not and a majority becomes productive citizens when becoming free.

Muslims are very tolerant people. It is in their grain to let other people know about Islam but not to go too far to make a person feel coerced or pressured to convert to Islam. The proof is in the history. Muslims ruled Spain for almost eight centuries yet they remained a minority and paid its price. Muslim ruled India for almost nine centuries yet remained a minority. Jerusalem was destroyed by Titus, a Byzantine general, who issued a decree forever forbidding Jews from entering the city. When the Muslims entered Jerusalem, victoriously without any battle or bloodshed, they allowed Jews and all other people to enter and live happily. Ever since

Jerusalem has remained a city open to the people of all religions and races until the State of Israel was established on Muslim-Palestinian land. Christian churches, Jewish synagogues or Hindu temples were never taken by force to convert them to mosques except under proper arrangements and at an agreed upon price with the owners or responsible caretakers.

Muslims have always lived with minorities or majorities of other religions except, occasionally, when rotten apples among Muslims were in power for short periods of time. It is obvious that many Christian churches, Jewish synagogues, Hindu temples and places of worship of other religions are in existence all over the Muslim lands from the ancient times. In fact, whenever Jews were slaughtered in European countries they found a safe refuge in the Muslim lands of North Africa, Turkey and East Europe. In North America and Europe Muslims have no friction with Jews or Christians? Even now, Christians and Jews are living happily together in all Muslim lands except the lands under the control of Israel. Who should be blamed for troubles in lands under the control of Israel? Why should weaker people risk their lives when they are living happily as in Skokie, Illinois? Muslims have been peaceful people throughout the history.

It is worthwhile to look closely at the Muslim community of America because it has a potential of becoming a model community for all Americans.

ISLAM IN BRAZIL

Brazil is the largest country in Latin America. Although there are no official statistics, the Muslim population in Brazil is estimated to be approximately 1 million people, with a total population of more than 170 million. This number includes converts to Islam, Arab immigrants and their descendants. Brazilian converts make up for no more than 1% of this number, about 10,000 people. Therefore, within a population of over 170 million, the small numbers that make up Brazilian converts to Islam have very little power.

Islam is the fastest growing religion in the world. However, in Latin America, and specifically in Brazil, this is not the case. Why?

One could argue that this is due to the strong influence of the Catholic Church. Brazil is considered to be the largest Catholic country in the world. However, a closer look proves that this is not true. Despite its strong presence, Catholicism has been losing followers in Brazil to other religions.

The argument has also been made that it is due to the Latin culture, which encourages Brazilians to always be playing, dancing and engaging in activities that are not lawful in Islam. As such, it is assumed that Brazilians simply aren't fit to be Muslims. This is generally the excuse used by those responsible for Dawah work in Brazil for their failure. It is, of course, not true. Brazilians are, by nature, very religious and have in the past been an easy prey to all sorts of innovative religious movements. So, what is really happening?

Through the statement of Sheikh Khalil Saifi, coordinator of the Center of Divulgation of Islam to Latin America, we can easily identify the real problem. The Center is located in Sao Bernardo do Campo, in the most important state of Brazil: Sao Paulo. Its president is Mr. Mohammed Saifi, a Lebanese immigrant who came to Brazil several years ago. Mainly his relatives and close friends compose the Center's staff. In an interview with "Istoé" magazine, one of the most important magazines in the country, Sheikh Khalil Saifi said: "Our main concern is to attend to the Muslims who descended from Arabs to help them preserve their link to their language and culture." And, continuing in his statement: "The Brazilians who come to us come through the contact with Muslims out there." Based on such statements, we are lead to conclude that a group of persons, who are supposed to make "Dawah," have decided who has the right to be Muslim or not.

When a Brazilian decides to go against their "plans," he or she is treated as an intruder in the Arab-Muslim community. All his/her misbehaviors concerning religious teachings are highlighted and pointed out, even if the same mistake is occurring among the Arab-Muslims. Normal mistakes due to lack of experience in the religion are presented as "proof" of an "incapacity" to practice and understand the religion. Little attention is given to the fact that the right teachings are not easily available to converts.

The new converts then have to fight alone against the criticism of his/her family, friends, the Brazilian society and worst: fight against the criticism of their own fellow Muslim brothers and sisters. The feeling of isolation leads some to abandon Islam after a while. Others keep insisting and all these difficulties just increase their faith and search for knowledge.

For those who persevere, they face another problem- the lack of good books about Islam available in the Portuguese language. The other Latin people are Spanish speakers and can depend on good works translated to Spanish. However, Brazilians are the only Portuguese speakers among Latinos and this fact increases their difficulties. The Center of Divulgation of Islam to Latin America provides the few books available. The books that have been chosen for translation are often of poor content quality. When a good book choice is made, a bad translation often destroys the work of its author. And even these few and badly translated books are difficult to find.

The lack of interest in spreading Islam is quite clear when one observes that the institution which is responsible for "Dawah" not only in Brazil but in all Latin America, doesn't maintain a website about Islam. When such a resource is available nearly for free to everyone and day-by-day more and more Muslim individuals and institutions are using the Internet to inform about the Islamic teachings, this attitude is undoubtedly proof that the Center fails to fulfill its most vital function.

BRAZIL: A MUSLIM HISTORY

Next April, Brazil will celebrate 500 years of its discovery, and a major controversy is surrounding the event. In traditional Brazilian history, the discovery of the country is attributed to a Portuguese navigator named Pedro Alvarez Cabral. New historical sources however, seem to offer another fact: that the discoverer might have been a Spanish navigator.

More and more historians, both Muslim and non-Muslim, are becoming aware of the strong Muslim presence in the early Americas. Many evidences of the Muslim presence in Brazil, including inscriptions with the name of Allah, have being found. In the language of the Native Americans, words of Arabic origin have been identified and even the names of some Brazilian cities were supposed to be related with the native American language, seems to have Arabic origins. If all this information is confirmed and introduced officially as part of Brazilian history, it means that faithful Muslims were the first ones to discover Brazil more than 500 years ago.

Also, through the Muslim slaves brought from Africa, we can easily identify the influence of the Islamic culture, although greatly distorted nowadays. This is especially evident in the northeast region of the country.

All of this proves that Islam is not an alien to the Brazilian culture. It's indeed an important part of it. Presenting Islam to the Brazilian people in a comprehensive manner is important not just to preach one religion; it is also to help them to restore their original culture, carefully erased due to political and religious interests in the past.

Unfortunately, political and personal interests in the present coming this time from Muslims themselves seem to be preventing or at least delaying such tasks. Let us hope and pray to Allah that faithful Muslims of the present could "rediscover" Brazil and give to its people the chance to know the beauty and wisdom of Islam.

ISLAM IN SPAIN

When the Arab and Berber armies crossed from North Africa into Spain in the eighth century, they thought they'd discovered heaven on earth.

By the time they were finally driven out in 1492 they'd actually created an earthly celebration of paradise- the Alhambra palaces and gardens in Granada. For desert Arabs, water is luxury. And in the melting snow of the Sierra Nevada Mountains they found what they wanted. By a series of intricate channels they directed water into the palace grounds and onto the dusty plains below.

Still today at the Alhambra you get a glimpse of paradise. Small streams take the water hither and thither to innumerable fountains and ponds- at one point rushing down channels in the balustrades of a stone stairway. Everywhere, splashing and gushing water. And great splashes of colour under the conifers- roses, lilies and sweet-smelling jasmine.

Not to mention the luxury of the palaces themselves with their courtyards shaded by trees and cooled by fountains and with the walls decorated by elaborate Arabic inscriptions and patterned tiles.

When the Christians recaptured Granada, they burnt all 80,000 books from the palace library- as if to expunge the memory of Islamic rule. Then they built a cathedral on the site of the great mosque and put a baroque facade around the main palace.

Today the Alhambra is marketed very much as a major Spanish tourist site. One Spanish guidebook says that the Alhambra is to Granada what St Peter's is to Rome or St Mark's Square is to Venice.

What the guidebook doesn't say is that the Alhambra is a legacy of nearly eight centuries during which the Arabs not only occupied Spain but also introduced into Europe mathematics, philosophy and Greek scholarship. Furthermore, the Arabs brought into Spain oranges, lemons, rice, sugar, date palms, cotton and much more.

And then there was the elaborate irrigation system, bringing water to the plains of Andalusia and giving it the landscape it has today. Even when the Arabs had been expelled en masse, two families were required to stay in each village to operate the irrigation system.

In other words, the Christians of Europe were happy to inherit the legacy of the Arab occupation of Spain, but were reluctant to acknowledge its Islamic origin. The American traveller, Washington Irving, noticed this when he visited Granada at the beginning of the nineteenth century. The Spanish, he said, considered the Muslims nothing more than "invaders and usurpers". And that still seems to be the case today.

But escapism can't hide the fact that the Arabs as a whole feel they've lost their way and lost their self-esteem. They live, for the most part, under corrupt and incompetent regimes, and- as they see it- in the shadow of the West.

"The West calls the tune to which we dance," Rabee Dejani, a Palestinian businessman in Jordan told me, "We hate the tune and we hate ourselves for dancing".

The accumulation of this resentment is creating new generations of Arabs who are hostile to the West. With no political platform on which to vent their anger, they're increasingly turning for comfort to Islam and to Islamic fundamentalism. And the violent acts that militants carry out blacken the name of Islam in the West.

Thus the anti-Muslim slogans daubed on the walls of the ancient *caravanseria* in the centre of Granada- and the look of anxiety and suspicion on the face of Hassan, the caretaker of the small centre nearby, when I knocked on the door.

Mutual suspicion is increasing. It's a vicious circle that won't easily be broken. But a start would be for the West to give credit where it's due.

Yes, the Alhambra is a tangible legacy of a great Islamic civilisation. But there are many other intangible legacies from the days of Arab rule in Spain, ingredients of our daily lives that we take for granted. If those debts were acknowledged, Arabs, I believe, would still go to their mosques in large numbers. But they'll be less attracted than they are now by the angry rantings of anti-Western fundamentalists.

ISLAM IN EUROPE

There's standing room only in a converted warehouse in the decaying industrial hinterland north of central Paris. It's mid-October, just days after the first U.S. bombs fell on Afghanistan, and the French magazine La Médina- which serves as an outlet for the country's Muslim population- has organized a public meeting on the significance for Islam of the September 11 attacks and their aftermath.

The atmosphere is electric. The men are in jeans and sportswear, while most of the women wear scarves over their heads. With few exceptions, the audience is made up of North Africans in their mid-20s. On the podium, 39-year-old Swiss university professor Tariq Ramadan- whose grandfather founded Egypt's Islamic revival movement the Muslim Brotherhood in 1928 begins to speak. "Now more than ever we need to criticize some of our brothers," he tells the packed hall. "My dignity depends on saying, 'You're unjustified if you use the Koran to justify murder.'" The French establishment- with its traditional mistrust of religion-views Ramadan with suspicion, but tonight he sounds like the voice of reason.

Then a young woman steps up to the microphone. With her black hijab she could be from almost anywhere in the Muslim world, but her accent is unmistakable- it's pure northern Parisian: "It's urgent for Muslims today to do everything they can to make the truth about their religion understood." The crowd bursts into thunderous applause.

Although most media have focused on a hard-core fringe calling for armed struggle against America, the overwhelming majority of Europe's Muslims see their religion as a moderate one. A survey carried out by the Mori agency for Eastern Eye, Britain's biggest selling Asian newspaper, shows that 87% of the Muslims polled are loyal to Britain, even though 64% oppose the U.S.-led strikes against Afghanistan.

These people and thousands of others like them are crafting a new strand of Islam, one that aims to reconcile the basic tenets of the faith- such as social justice and submission to the will of God- with the realities of contemporary European life. Though this process has been under way for some time, the events of Sept. 11 and afterward have lent it new urgency.

For many of Europe's 12.5 million Muslims, now is the time to redefine Islam in the context of their identities as believers who were born and bred in Europe. The result is a kind of Euro-Islam, the traditional Koran-based religion with its prohibitions against alcohol and interest-bearing loans now indelibly marked by the "Western" values of tolerance, democracy and civil liberties. This new vision could well end up influencing the world these young Europeans' grandparents left behind.

For this new generation, Euro-Islam is not a zero sum game: it is possible to be Muslim and European at the same time. In fact, unlike that of their Christian neighbors, the religious faith of Europe's Muslims is getting stronger. A survey published by French newspaper Le Monde in October shows that people from Muslim backgrounds are praying more, attending mosques more often and observing the Ramadan fast more assiduously than they did in 1994, when the survey was last conducted. The increased devotion is particularly marked among those who have been to university. In Britain, more women are wearing the hijab today than 10 years ago.

Euro-Islam is a bridge between two cultures, providing young believers with a way of respecting inherited traditions while living in a different world. It also gives them the confidence to practice their religion more openly, unlike their parents or grandparents who thought their sojourn in Europe was temporary and so were content to express their faith in private. Their children view Europe as their home and see no reason not to worship more publicly.

During Ramadan, the holy month of fasting, Ahmid- a Moroccan-born imam at an Islamic cultural center in Rome- was selling Korans and cassettes of Muslim preachers at his stall outside the central mosque. A practicing Muslim back in Morocco, Ahmid has become more devout since arriving in Italy 13 years ago. "The immigrant turns to religion for support," he says. "Muslims have always gone anywhere in the world and adapted to learn to live as they must- and let others live their lives."

As Ahmid suggests, the story of Islam in Europe is a story of immigration. During the Continent's reconstruction after

World War II, Britain and France turned to their former colonies in South Asia and North Africa to fill their manpower shortages, while Germany opened its doors to "guest workers" from Turkey. Most of these guests never went home again, and their children were born and grew up as Europeans. Today, the Muslim communities in these three countries are the biggest in Europe: 5 million in France, 3.2 million in Germany and 2 million in Britain. These numbers have been augmented by more recent waves of immigration to countries like Spain, the Netherlands, Italy, Belgium and the Scandinavian region.

But Islam itself is nothing new in Europe. After advancing as far as Tours in 732, the Arabs remained in Spain until 1492, when they were driven from Granada. Over those centuries they bequeathed the Spanish their distinctive pronunciation of the letter J as well as masterpieces of Moorish architecture. The Islamic scholars Ibn Sina and Ibn Rushd reintroduced Greek philosophy to the West during the middle Ages, while Arab mathematicians revolutionized science with the invention of algebra. And when the Ottoman armies pushed west through the Balkan peninsula in the 14th century, they established Muslim communities in Central Europe that still exist today.

In Sarajevo, the imams' calls to prayer from reconstructed mosques blend with the chimes of bells from Orthodox Christian medieval churches and 19th century cathedrals. "I have more in common with Bosnian Serbs than Muslims from Pakistan and Afghanistan," says former Bosnian Interior Minister Muhamad Besic. His words offer striking testimony of the strength of Islam's historic roots on the Continent, given that not 10 years ago his city was under siege from those same Bosnian Serbs. But they also speak of an assimilation that even war could not affect.

What's different now is that for the first time in their 14-century history, Muslims are living as minorities in secular societies. Traditional Islamic theology divides the world into two zones: the dar al-Islam, or house of Islam, and the dar al-harb, or house of war. This world view assumes that Muslims will never be able to practice their religion properly in non-Muslim lands and so should not settle there. But second and third-generation Muslims in Europe quickly discovered that this was a false opposition. Fresh ideas were needed, such as the dar ash-shahada, or house of testimony: a new concept referring to any place where Muslims can make their profession of faith and live according to the precepts of their religion.

Tariq Ramadan is one of the most prominent exponents of this new thinking. "As a Muslim I can be at home anywhere I'm safe and where the rule of law protects my freedom of conscience and my freedom to worship," he says. "In this new environment, my responsibility is to bear witness to the message of my faith."

European Muslims don't necessarily differ from other Muslims when it comes to the basic tenets of that faith, but according to Dilwar Hussain, a research fellow at the Islamic Foundation in Leicester, they do have "greater flexibility, greater awareness of the wider society and more liberal attitudes." Witness the growing number of Muslim girls contacting the Rutgers Women's Health Foundation in the Netherlands for abortion advice.

Hussain says that Europe's liberal attitudes are forcing the faithful to reassess their own beliefs. "The younger Muslims are going back to the text and asking: 'What my parent used to do, is that really part of my faith or is that part of their cultural tradition?' Drawing that distinction between faith and culture is very important. You may find some things in the Islamic texts, and then the cultural setting can lead to a particular interpretation. When the cultural setting changes, those interpretations will naturally change" says Lhaj Thami Breze, president of the Union of Islamic Organizations of France: "We're forging our own way of practicing Islam, and it's going to be different from the way it's done in Morocco, Algeria or Saudi Arabia. Islam needs to free itself from imported customs."

For Yakob Mahi, 36, a Moroccan imam living in Belgium, adapting Islam to new environments has been central to the development of his faith. He cites the concept of Shari'a, the way of life ordained by God for mankind, which he says many countries have turned into a code of punishment- even though less than 1% of the Koran consists of penal rules. In Europe, Mahi says, "We can see Shari'a not as law, but as a path to be understood in its context. When we transform it into daily European life, we see that Shari'a doesn't mean cutting off the hand of a thief. Rather it's a spirit present in many things we enjoy in Europe: the principles of democracy, the rule of law, the freedoms of expression and association." That innovative interpretation makes Muslim law compatible with its Western secular counterparts. So Mahi advocates a doctrine of "spiritual citizenship" in which Muslims "respect the laws [of the secular state] but try to give a spiritual impulse to everything they do."

In Europe, Muslims must also confront social questions- such as euthanasia, abortion and sexuality- that are suppressed in many Islamic countries. Nowhere is this confrontation more obvious than in the assertive roles being claimed by women. After all, the 7th century doctrines of the Prophet Muhammad considerably improved their lot, forbidding the then common practice of female infanticide and making the education of girls a sacred duty. "It's not the religion that holds back women but the culture-and the men," says Fatma Amer, head of education and interfaith relations at the London Central Mosque. "It's up to the women to organize themselves and not accept everything their communities tell them they must do."

One area in which both women and men are asserting themselves more vigorously is marriage. In Britain, increasing numbers of young women are resisting arranged marriages to cousins back in Bangladesh or Pakistan. In France, too, young people are clashing with parents who always assumed their children would marry someone from their own village in Morocco or Algeria. "We want to choose the person we marry," says Fouad Imarraine, who runs the Tawhid Cultural Center in the Paris suburb of Saint-Denis. "It doesn't matter what color their skin is as long as we're of the same faith."

Imarraine describes how the attitudes of Europe's Muslims have changed. "When we went back to North Africa on holiday, we realized we had deeper ties in France," he says, sipping coffee in a café nestled at the foot of concrete tower blocks. "Very few of my generation made it to university and Islam provided us with a refuge from failure at school and feeling shut out of society. But there's now a younger generation using Islam as a way of establishing the universal values they have in common with those around them. Defining their own identity as Muslims is a way of interacting with the rest of society."

This generation has grown up thinking of Europe as home, even if it has often seemed inhospitable. Schoolgirls have been expelled for wearing the hijab in France, while in British Islamic communities like the one in Luton; Muslims are twice as likely to be unemployed as other townsfolk. But for this new generation, being Muslim and European means their faith has become a matter of individual choice rather than social constraint.

"Younger Muslims are far more individualistic in the way they interpret the Koran, but that doesn't necessarily mean they're any less devout," says Mustapha Oukbih, a 36-year-old journalist who lives and works in the Hague. The Dutch website Maghreb.nl, for example, has hosted chat rooms to discuss whether it's okay for Muslim newlyweds to have oral sex. "They want to decide for themselves how to live their lives," Oukbih says. This emphasis on personal choice is providing many Muslims with a new vision of politics, too.

"Strictly religious problems are becoming more marginal," says Hakim El Ghissassi, editor of *France's La Médina*, referring to the widespread availability of mosques and religious instruction. "Young people today are more concerned with resolving the social issues facing Muslims: employment, equality in the labor market, political representation and the way that history is taught in schools. Muslims are going to make their voices heard more and more on these issues. They're going to want to take part in government at the local, national and European level."

For the moment, though, Muslim political representation is

small. With a Muslim population of 800,000, the Netherlands has seven Muslim M.P.s. Britain has only two, and France none. Yet people like Bassam Tibi, a professor of international relations at the University of Göttingen who coined the term Euro-Islam, insist that the integration of Europe's Muslims depends on the adoption of a form of Islam that embraces Western political values, such as pluralism, tolerance, the separation of church and state, democratic civil society and individual human rights. "The options for Muslims are unequivocal," says Tibi. "There is no middle way between Euro-Islam and a ghettoization of Muslim minorities."

In Britain, that view is shared by the writer and critic Ziauddin Sardar, who came to the country with his Pakistani parents as a child in the 1960s. "If there is a sociological change there will be a theological change as well," he says. "In Islam, law and ethics are the same thing. If you change the ethics, you change the law. There will be a new interpretation of Islam."

This new interpretation is taking shape in different places at different speeds. Although non-Muslims often view Islam as a monolithic bloc, the religion is characterized by its diversity. With over a billion believers scattered across every continent, as well as separate Shi'ite and Sunni traditions, the Muslim community (or ummah) has long been a philosophical construct rather than a demographic reality. That's true in Europe, where Muslims are divided by country of residence as much as by country of origin. "The problems Muslims are facing here are deeply influenced by the institutions of the countries where they live," says Farhad Khosrokhavar, a professor at Paris' School of Post-Graduate Studies in Social Science. "But the influence of democracy and religious tolerance is bringing about a meeting of minds."

And that influence could well spread to the Muslim world as a whole. For Zaki Badawi, chairman of the Imams and Mosques Council of Britain, Muslims in the West are helping to answer the question that has haunted Islam for the past century: how to reconcile tradition and modernity. "Islam, like any other society, finds modernity challenging," Badawi says. Although that challenge is felt more acutely in the developing world, intellectuals in those countries don't have the freedom to analyze the problem and find effective solutions. "The tension between Islam and modernity will be answered by thinkers in the West," Badawi says, "and transferred back to our native countries."

It would be symbolically and historically fitting if the next great reform of Islam came from the diaspora in the West. After all, the starting point of the Muslim calendar is not the year of Muhammad's birth but the day 1,379 years ago when the Prophet led his followers from his birthplace in Mecca to found a new community in Medina. "The very foundation of Islamic civilization was built on diaspora, on the move from Mecca to Medina," says British Muslim writer Sardar. "This is where the diaspora is very important: in creating a truly moderate tradition for the future." The new diaspora of Muslims in Europe already has that task in hand.

8

Islam in Arab and Middle East

ISLAM IN ARAB: AN INTRODUCTION

If there is one foreign leader whose views were validated by the painful events of September 11, 2001, it is Tunisia's President Zine El Abidine Ben Ali. For years he has conducted a no-holds-barred battle against Islamism in Tunisia. And unlike in Algeria, Tunisia's neighbor to the east, Ben Ali has largely won.

One price of the extirpation of Islamic militants in Tunisia prior to September 11 has been an incessant barrage of foreign (often French) press criticism for various human rights violations. Watchdog NGOs like Human Rights Watch piled it on as well. While he kept up the heat at home, Ben Ali often found that Islamist exile leaders had been given a pass, finding comfortable perches in London or Frankfurt. Ben Ali chided Western countries as early as 1994 for "serving as rear bases for fundamentalist terrorists", pointing to laissez faire attitudes toward the political activities (and worse) of Islamic exiles in London, Frankfurt and Paris.

September 11 swiftly softened the public criticism. French Foreign Minister Hubert Vedrine was dispatched to Tunis soon after September 11 to express solidarity with Tunisia's efforts. Shortly thereafter, French President Jacques Chirac visited to praise Ben Ali's long-term struggle against terrorism and Islamic fundamentalism, underscoring that Tunisia's position of "refusing religious intolerance and fundamentalism is completely exemplary." In November 2001, the French magazine *L'Express* repented its targeting of human rights violations in Tunisia, pointing out that "democracy is not built in a single day." In the United States, Assistant Secretary of State for Near Eastern Affairs William Burns spoke of Tunisia's "record of moderation and tolerance in the region."

The Tunisian approach to combating terrorism has taken three forms. First, the country has refused to cede ground on Islamic theology to fundamentalist clerics. Second, since 1990 the country has conducted a "war" against Islamic fundamentalism, an approach that America only began after September 11. When it comes to the security aspects of fighting Islamic fundamentalism, the Tunisians, to borrow an Algerian term, are eradicateurs. Third, Tunisia has understood that economic development is vital to the task of drying the pools of fundamentalist support in the country. And it has remembered a vital corollary as well: for the sake of social stability, attention must be paid to the social well-being of those temporarily left behind by economic rationalization.

COOPERATION OF CHURCH AND STATE

Tunisia sees itself as a state of Muslims, but not an Islamic state. At the same time Tunisia offers its own vision of Islam-one based on strict limits on the public role of religion and a strong focus on tolerance as part of Islam itself. While the constitution describes the country as a predominantly Muslim nation, this empirical fact of demography does not lead to the conclusion that Tunisia is an Islamic state.

True, Tunisia does not follow a Western model of strict separation of church and state. Habib Bourguiba, the country's first president, dropped state support for Islamic seminaries and institutions. After his ascension to power in 1987, Ben Ali tempered this course somewhat, giving more prominence to the rituals of faith. Thus, the call to prayer could once again be heard on state-run radio and television. Furthermore, while in Tunis some years ago during the Prophet's birthday, the entire cabinet was expected to join President Ben Ali at Zeitouna, the country's main mosque.

Tunisia's divergence from a model of strict secularity is designed to promote a form of Islam consistent with tolerance and respect for religious difference. Jalloul Jerabi, Minister of Religious Affairs and former head of the Tunis Zeitouna University (its religious university), has suggested that the traditional rule requiring the reconquest of dar al-Islam (lands of Islam) lost to the dar al-harb (lands of darkness) is no longer applicable. This rule, he told me over lunch in a Tunis Kosher restaurant, was applicable in the 7th century, when Islam was a struggling religion, but not today, when it is a growing religion of over one billion adherents. Zeitouna, in the words of its President Muhammad Toumi, stresses the Quran's "125 verses that insist on religious freedom and that ask Muslims to respect others." Thus, Tunisia rejects the view of Islam as a religion that ineluctably captures all of a society's social and political space, a principle further reflected in its ban on Islamic parties.

Because graduates of Zeitouna staff the state's Islamic institutions, the faithful of Tunisia hear a very different message at Friday prayers than their co-religionists in Egypt, Saudi Arabia or East Jerusalem. So do secondary school students in religious classes taught by Zeitouna graduates. As Mohammad Charfi (himself a critic of Ben Ali) has underscored, These subjects, as well as modern science, are all taught as part of- not in contrast to- the values of an enlightened Islam.

This past November, Ben Ali announced creation of an "International Prize for Islamic Studies" in order to enrich interpretive (ijtihad) thinking that believes in dialogue and openness and rejects exclusion and fanaticism. This focus on Islamic values of tolerance may be not only Tunisia's most important weapon against Islamic fundamentalism, but also its greatest contribution to a Western counter-terrorism policy designed to win "hearts and minds."

Further evidence of Tunisia's efforts to influence Islam includes its actions overriding sharia law in the matter of the status of women. When Tunisia gained its independence from France in 1956, the new republic's first major social reform was the Code of Personal Status, banning polygamy and establishing basic equality. Most recently, a 1998 presidential decree created a national fund to protect the rights of divorced women whose husbands refuse to pay alimony. Women are fully integrated into the workforce and compose 52 percent of students enrolled in university. In terms of women's rights, Tunisia is a rare phenomenon in the Arab world.

LES ERADICATEURS

The rejection of Islamic fundamentalism is total. President Ben Ali first reached out to the Islamists directly after coming to power in 1987, but after Rachid Ghannouchi's Al-Nahda (Renaissance) Islamist party turned to terrorism- placing bombs in tourist hotels in the late 1980s, attacking the ruling party office in the Tunis suburb of Bab Souika in the early 1990s and conspiring during that time in an Islamist coup- Ben Ali cracked down. Since then, Tunisia has been unwavering in its approach toward Islamists, outlawing its institutions and jailing its followers (such as they are).

In the late 1990s, many foreign analysts felt that the Al-Nahda threat had been stanched. Indeed, some, like Professor John Entalis of Fordham, have called Al-Nahda a "mainstream group" (together with the Muslim Brotherhood in Jordan and in Egypt!) and labeled its exiled leader Rachid Ghannouchi "a moderate voice." This is the same Ghannouchi who signed a 2002 call "to end any discourse with Israel" and described Operation Iraqi Freedom as "a war against Islam", arguing that "struggling against this war is a compulsory duty for every Muslim."

Still, Tunisia did not wait until September 11 to strike hard against Islamic terrorism. Between 600 and 1,000 Islamists are currently imprisoned for extended terms. The Tunisian state has used military courts to give prison terms to 34 Tunisians found guilty of recruiting for Al-Qaeda. In November 2002, Muhammad Saidani received a twenty-year jail sentence for leading an Islamist cell in Italy. Not surprisingly, Amnesty International has complained about the use of military courts to levy these and other harsh penalties.

Recent years have witnessed an increasing concern over joint activity between Al-Nahda and the secular Left. A London satellite television station that broadcasts to Tunisia provided these strange bedfellows airtime to attack the regime. And for a time, Al-Nahda and Mouvement des Democrates Socialistes (MDS) representatives (one of the seven legal opposition parties) joined to create a "demonstrative front" against Ben Ali.

The April 11, 2002 bombing deaths of 21 people at the El-Gribba synagogue in Djerba makes clear that the danger of Islamism in Tunisia has not dissipated. At first, the government claimed the explosion, caused by a gas truck driving directly into the synagogue, was an accident. But after a reality check, the Ben Ali government moved with great dispatch. German investigators (many of the dead were German tourists) were invited to cooperate. Further, Ben Ali moved to shake up his anti-terror apparatus, removing from office both the interior minister and Djerba's police chief. The Tunisians will not brook failure in the fight against terrorism.

ECONOMIC GROWTH

In contrast to most Arab states, you cannot visit the cities of Tunisia (big cities at least) and not be aware of its economic progress. New skyscrapers, bustling stores and privately-owned automobiles abound. Objective statistics also tell the tale. GDP growth reached 4.3 percent in 2002 and is forecast at 5.89 percent in 2004 (world recession and tourist drought notwithstanding). Inflation has stabilized at fewer than 3 percent. Only 4.2 percent of the population falls below the poverty line (the number was almost one third in the 1960s). Tunisia's per capita GDP already equals that of Eastern European countries like Bulgaria or Romania.

The World Economic Forum recently named Tunisia the most competitive country in Africa. The Global Corruption Report for 2001 found Tunisia to be not only the least corrupt nation in North Africa (a dubious distinction, to be sure) but also the third least corrupt state in Africa as a whole. Foreign investment, around $400 million in 1997, topped off at $1 billion in 2000 before falling back to $700 million in 2001.

Nor has human development been ignored in favor of GDP growth: 91 percent of the minor population is literate, and the rate of population growth has been held to 1.15 percent. (Contrast this number with Syria at 2.5 percent, Jordan at 2.9 percent and Morocco at 1.68 percent.) Over 80 percent of the population owns their own homes. The life expectancy of 72.4 years is the highest in Africa. All citizens have government health insurance. About 6 percent of Tunisian GDP is allotted to education, 99 percent of children eligible for primary school attend and 75 percent of secondary school age children are enrolled. Notwithstanding its Francophone past, English is compulsory in schools after age 13, and computer training is offered in most schools.

Still, the economic challenges are significant. Unemployment hovers around 15 percent and will stay so for the next three years. The tourist boom has collapsed, and the anemic world economy has increased pressures on the export economy. In particular, the textile sector, which comprised over 40 percent of the export economy in past years, has drastically suffered.

In 1998, Tunisia began to implement the Euro-Tunisian Association Agreement that was designed to drop all customs duties between Tunisia and the EU by 2010. Specifically, Tunisia is committed to a structural adjustment program, the so-called mise a niveau. This will require it to meet EU manufacturing and service industry quality standards and improve both the quality and competitiveness of Tunisian manufacturers. The EU agreement demands painful introspection by the Tunisian business and manufacturing community. One commentator has suggested that "the portion of industrial production threatened by the removal of import controls from the EU has been estimated at 60 percent." Still, Tunisia leads the pack of EU Mediterranean "partners" in meeting its structural adjustment benchmarks; notwithstanding the pressures such economic rationalization places on the economy.

Tunisia's concern for social stability makes it acutely sensitive to the costs (and often real pain) of the "structural readjustment" so often required by economic modernization. A good example is the National Solidarity Fund. The 2626 Fund, as it is informally called, was created in 1992 to involve all members of society in the fight against poverty. The fund consists of voluntary (although strongly encouraged) contributions and a government stipend. The fund makes grants for infrastructure and employment projects in impoverished, usually rural areas. The success of the 2626 program led the UN to set up a World Solidarity Fund based on the Tunisian model.

Concern over structural unemployment led to the creation of the Solidarity Bank in 1997. Designed to promote entrepreneurship, the bank makes loans of up to 33,000 dirhams (with a specified grace period and subsidized interest rates) to those with a university diploma (US$1=D1.2825). It focuses on unemployed and underemployed university graduates, such as waiters with doctorates who might indulge in social unrest. The bank was funded by over 232,000 shareholders who paid in D18.5 million. The state added D11.5 million to bring bank capitalization to D30 million. From March 1998 to May 2001, the bank funded some 42,000 projects that generated almost 60,000 jobs. Thus, the Bank serves the twin purposes of reducing the costs of the EU economic rationalization campaign and lessening its potential to cause political instability.

Tunisia has also focused on supporting entrepreneurship among the "working poor." Following the model of the Grameen Bank in Bangladesh, in October 1999 the Solidarity Bank introduced a micro-credit program to assist entrepreneurs in rural development areas. The program makes loans of D1,000 at 5 percent interest with a repayment period of three years. By 2001, almost 9,000 such loans had been made. Only four loans had fully defaulted.

To further encourage entrepreneurship, Ben Ali recently announced a program to grant leaves of absence to civil service employees and managers who wish to start their own business in the country's less-developed regions. During these one year (renewable) leaves, the government will pay half their salaries. The hope, of course, is that this "safety net" will encourage entrepreneurs to go out on their own.

The conventional wisdom is that Tunisians have been offered a Faustian bargain, whereby they thrive economically but abandon politics to the political class. This simplistic trade-off is unfair to the vast majority of Tunisians, who have not chosen lucre over liberty. Rather, the photos of fundamentalist carnage in next door Algeria have sensitized them to the threat of violent anarchy and the need to guard against it. They may not embrace the restrictions, but they accept them.

Tunisia is first and foremost a homogeneous society with little ethnic division (contrasted to the Berbers in Algeria and Morocco). It has a long tradition of relatively centralized, personal authority- be it by the Bey of Tunis or the French Resident-General. Further, it is a society with a high premium on stability and consensus, as its relatively bloodless independence reflects. And so it is that the ruling party, the Rassemblement Constitutionelle Democratique (RCD), possesses the vast portion of the nation's political energy. It has 2 million members and 7,800 branches nationwide and won 91.59 percent of the vote in the October 1999 elections. One-party state or not, the RCD would likely win a fully fair and free election if held today. The seven legal opposition parties are anemic at best. If democracy is to take hold, it may be that the ruling authorities will have to force-feed the opposition.

Ben Ali has in fact done just that (confident that, for the foreseeable future at least, the opposition lacks both bark and bite). In July 2001, he announced an initiative to enlarge the pool of those eligible to run against him in the next presidential elections. And while the opposition holds 34 of the 182 seats in the Chamber of Deputies, these are all seats given to the opposition on a proportional basis, and it holds those seats only because Ben Ali passed a law that ensured the opposition parties at least 20 percent of the seats, no matter how few votes they actually received. The same is true for municipal councils. In Ben Ali's view, these actions "consecrate political pluralism."

These developments reflect Ben Ali's view that "the development of democracy is very much a matter of education and of progressing step by step." He fears that in societies without historical democratic roots, opening the floodgates of political discourse can easily lead to extremism and instability. While he encourages opposition, it is responsible or "loyal" opposition. The "hard" Left and Islamic perspectives are banned outright. Ben Ali views the legal opposition as part of the national consensus and meets with their leaders regularly to promote national unity. Nevertheless, the political space the legal opposition covets is securely held by the RCD.

The recent round of constitutional reforms adds considerably to the country's formal democratic structure. It creates a second parliamentary chamber, gives new prerogatives to the elected Constitutional Council and installs a two-round presidential electoral process in cases where no candidate wins an absolute majority in the first round (as in the French system). It also requires periodic oral questioning of elected officials (as in the British parliament). In Tunisia, where the government has an overwhelming parliamentary majority, this becomes one of the few ways available to foster government accountability.

But these significant structural reforms have been overshadowed by the controversy surrounding the constitution's revised term limit provisions. Ben Ali would have bumped up against the three-term limit when his term ran out in 2004, but the very thought of succession-planning was a non-starter for the ruling party. (Indeed, many Tunisians may well have been frightened by the thought.) Thus, it came as no surprise when Ben Ali proposed a constitutional amendment abolishing such term limits. After further changes by parliament, the proposal raised the maximum age of presidential candidates to 75, thus allowing Ben Ali, at 74, to run for a fifth term in 2009. (In the resulting constitutional referendum, 99.52 percent of the electorate ratified the changes.) Ben Ali's populatiry notwithstanding, the symbolism of the term limit waiver is undeniable. Thus, for Tunisian political institutions, the challenge of succession has been postponed but not resolved.

Political scientists have begun to realize that elections alone are not a sufficient definition of democracy. Democracy assumes a competitive electoral arena with multiple strong political parties. Opposition parties cannot be created ex nihilo; instead they must reflect the variety of political, geographical and class interests of the population. Tunisian elections do not yet include, in Joseph Schumpeter's words, "a competitive struggle for the people's vote." While Tunisia possesses the grammar of pluralist democracy, its oversized ruling party crowds out not only political competition but other elements of civil society. The problem of how the party relates to the state and the state to the party is one of the most significant challenges facing Tunisia. It has been avoided rather than addressed.

THE CHALLENGE OF HUMAN RIGHTS

Just as the war on terrorism raises human rights issues so does Tunisia's war on Islamic fundamentalism. The government has arrested hundreds of suspected Islamists, passed laws making it a crime to incite religious fanaticism and clamped down harshly on any suggestion of an association with Al-Nahda. At times this zeal has spilled over to members of outlawed secular groups like the Parti Communiste Ouvrier Tunisien (PCOT). It ought, therefore, to be no surprise that Tunisia is heavily criticized by human rights organizations for a variety of misdeeds ranging from prison conditions to political prosecutions for defaming the government to refusal to allow political activists exit visas. These charges should not be minimized, though they are often overstated by NGOs. They certainly pale in comparison to the level of human rights violations by its neighbors to its east and west- let alone by the "axis of evil" states.

The government's response to these criticisms is to point

to the concrete threat of fundamentalism. Sadok Chaabone, a former justice minster, has argued, "When we started, we had 1,000 people in the prisons.... But it's better than 100,000 dead, like in Algeria." At the same time, the government has embraced the normative grammar of human rights. It has restructured cabinet portfolios to raise the profile of human rights concerns through a Ministry of Justice and Human Rights (now held by Bechir Takkari). Indeed, Tunisia even has its own human rights league (the Arab world's first): the Ligue Tunisienne des Droits de L' Homme (LTDH), which it continually pressures but steadfastly recognizes. In a recent Republic Day speech, the President affirmed "the supremacy of the law", underscoring that "the foundations of the republican system include the protection of the right to differ."

At the same time, senior magistrate Mokhtar Yahyaui- who was suspended without pay in July 2001 when he complained about the "total lack of independence" in government- was restored to office. A torture victim, Ali Mansouri won a court case against government officials and received $210,000 in compensation. In May 2001, President Ben Ali pardoned Nejib Hosni, a legendary Tunisian lawyer and civil rights advocate. In January 2002, Mohammed Mouda, head of the opposition socialists, was conditionally released after a hunger strike and is back at the helm of MDS. Hamma Hammani, the leader of the barred PCOT, who was jailed after coming out of hiding last February, was recently released on health grounds. And in August 2002, former Prime Minister Muhammad Mzali returned from 15 years in exile to praise Tunisia's economic and social stability within the context of a movement toward democratic pluralism.

There is no doubt that the government would prefer to control the human rights debate. It tried to "stack" the membership of LTHD (presumably to influence its policies), and it has refused official recognition to a second, competing human rights group: the Civil Liberties League, which leaves its membership open to prosecution. Indeed, its efforts to ward off criticism have led to a unique and humorous moment in human rights advocacy: the battle of competing human rights websites. After a series of critical reports by Amnesty International, a pro-government website went online with the confusing address of *www.amnestytunisia.org*. Amnesty cried foul, charging that the government was creating a deceptive website. Tunisian officials claimed ignorance of the entire affair. The faux website was eventually moved to *www.rights-tunisia.org* and is not currently operational. The bad blood between the government and the international human rights community has colored perceptions on all sides. And even when the government is responsive to human rights complaints, as when it set up a commission of inquiry on jail conditions, it gets little credit.

The big civil liberties issue up for grabs, however, is freedom of expression and freedom of the press in particular. State officials seem to take personal offense to attacks in the press and react harshly when criticized. Tunisia has found itself afoul of press freedom groups worldwide. To the government, this is largely the result of a vendetta by the left-wing French press, especially *Le Monde* and *L'Express*. Many in the government, however, have begun to appreciate the foolishness of barring foreign media who air negative news stories when more and more homes have satellite dishes. Besides *Al-Jazeera* in Dubai, *Al Musta Killah*, a London based cable network, has specific Tunisian-focused programming. Its weekly no-holds-barred talk show, Le Grand Maghreb, offers discussion with dissidents of various stripes.

In April 2001, the Tunisian parliament revised the country's press code, eliminating the charge of "defaming public order" and removing the possibility of prison sentences for falsely presenting advertising material as news items and other selected code violations. The period of suspension was shortened from six to three months. And in May 2001, the president spoke out on press freedom, calling on journalists to "write on any subject you choose. There are no taboos except what is prohibited by law and press ethics." The following year, however, Zouhair Yahyaoui, publisher of a webzine, was jailed for two years. His crime: "putting out false news." Another journalist, Hedi Yahmed, was similarly charged when he published a critical report on the country's prisons. His case has not yet been adjudicated.

Tunisia remains a North Africa success story. One can point to its economic growth, political stability, integration of women into the workforce, successful war on terrorism and support for a moderate Islam as elements of that success. Still, its challenges in the coming decade are great. First is the continuing challenge of social stability, which it is far better positioned than its neighbors to achieve. Second is continued economic development, including the ultimate challenge of free trade with the EU. Here, too, Tunisia is progressing past its Maghreb neighbors and looks likely to meet its EU target of full free trade by 2010. Third is the continuing challenge of Islamic fundamentalism that is often propelled by regional developments.

Finally, there is the challenge of democracy and human rights. Ben Ali has staked his country's survival on a philosophy of gradualism, one in which economic and social stability provides the basis for what one of his closest advisors has called "the road to pluralism" and respect for law. Gradualists are inherently open to the criticism of not moving fast enough. If the language of democracy is not fortified by pluralistic politics, the hopes for a democratic civitas can easily atrophy. Further, there is a real danger that the very restrictions on democracy and freedoms designed to ensure stability can themselves create instability. By choosing a top-down, drawn out process of democratization, Tunisia may well find itself riding the proverbial tiger, forced to choose more authoritarian solutions to ensure stability because the democratic aspirations of the moderate center are being too slowly fulfilled. To paraphrase former Solicitor-General Archibald Cox: Once loosed, the idea of liberty is not easily cabined.

1. Ben Ali came to power in 1987 in a bloodless coup known as "The Change." It was directed against the government of Habib Bourguiba, the leader who had achieved

Tunisia's independence in 1956 but who had grown increasingly erratic in his later years.

2. "Ben Ali contre Bin Laden", L'Express, November 8, 2001.
3. Tunisia is a country rich with political heritage. While nominally under Ottoman suzerainty in 1861, it produced the Arab world's first written constitution. This document followed on the 1857 ahd al-aman (Charter of Faith), which provided legal protections to the country's non-Muslims.
4. Phase 1 of the EU agreement from 1996-2001 allowed Tunisia to subsidize the restructuring process of manufacturing firms. This "loop-hole", the period of which can be extended by prior agreement between the two countries, fits Tunisia's dirigiste history, particularly its concern for social stability. Thus, the government has acted to contain the damage of bankruptcy (using a law that asserts that the survival of firms takes priority over debt repayment) and the unemployment that might ensue. While the government has continued the privatization process (26 firms were slated for sale in 2002), it has done so cautiously, resisting IMF pressure to speed up economic liberalization due to its continued sensitivity to the perceived danger of social unrest.

ISLAM IN MIDDLE EAST

INTRODUCTION

The globalization of international commerce and the technological revolution of the 1990s have posed serious challenges for developing countries, including those in the Middle East.

International markets are now harsher and more competitive while political reform and democratization have become indispensable for the long-term successful integration of developing countries into the global political economy. Stabilization and adjustment programs demand substantial administrative capacity and political skill. In this regard, the primary problem with governments in the Middle East remains the persistence of traditional political structures. Political elites and entrenched interests continue to resist political reforms and economic adjustment policies that they perceive as threatening the status quo.

At the same time, the powerful distributive conflicts unleashed by economic change threaten the legitimacy and stability of incumbent regimes. In light of fiscal constraints and growing opposition to the existing state systems by Islamic groups, intellectuals, professionals, and the growing middle class in varying degrees in different countries, Middle Eastern regimes have tried a number of different ways to introduce political reforms without seriously jeopardizing the political status quo.

John Waterbury has noted that heavily statist economies give rise to similar forms of property rights and interest group coalitions, underlining the importance of technocratic "change teams" within the state to implement reforms. Middle Eastern countries either enter "the democratic-technological-scientific race, invests [sic] heavily in R&D, and `endure the information economy' metamorphosis or [they] become unimportant, unexploited and unexploitable."

Political reforms at home are necessary for progress in this area. The emergence of a vibrant and effective civil society, capable of checking the authoritarian tendencies of the state, can help free the economic activities of individuals, groups and associations from their political constraints, and facilitate the long-term socioeconomic and political development and eventual integration of these states into the global economy.

The persistence of authoritarian rule and the marginality of popular politics in the majority of Middle Eastern countries have largely been a product of the domestic socioeconomic and political environment, not external manipulation. Ultimately, the state monopoly over resources and the decision-making process, outside of the purview of civil society, hinders popular participation in fostering the long-term economic success of the country.

THE GLOBAL CONTEXT

Despite the primacy of internal factors, the impact of a spreading global political economy has already been felt by individual countries in the Middle East. The region has continuously attracted foreign intervention, in one shape or another. External influences, however, have for the most part helped bolster the state in the region: the Western powers have in the past 50 years promoted the political status quo in the Middle East through support for conservative oil-producing authoritarian states, arms sales to friendly but autocratic regimes, and direct and indirect intervention. The long term impact of globalization on the state in the Middle East, and elsewhere in the developing countries, through a whole range of economic, cultural and political (including human rights or democracy) interactions may have a reverse effect. Globalization may actually help the cause of civil society and democracy by weakening the state's control of the economy and society on the whole. However, the state in the Middle East hitherto remains dominant in politics and the economy.

After more than four decades of development efforts, the majority of the Middle East's population still lives in poverty, and the political system remains for the most part authoritarian. Professor Howard Wiarda recently described the Middle East in the following terms: "In the political realm all these regimes remain authoritarian. Economically, they have done reasonably well lately not because they are efficient or self-sufficient but because of oil, foreign subsidies, or proximity to wealth that rubs off on them."

Maintaining the status quo costs the state and society more in the 1990s than it did previously. Political instability, radical Islamic fundamentalism, and external threats to the state have helped justify arms purchases by the governments in the region. But as a consequence of their high defense spending, Middle Eastern governments have made fewer investments in the economic and social development (e.g., education, health) of their countries.

External support has also fallen. With the threat of Communism evaporated, the United States and Europe are less interested in addressing the long-term development concerns of the region, even if they are involved in the Arab-Israeli peace process. Sanctions against Iraq or Iran have regional economic costs. Low oil prices also inhibit Middle Eastern development while the abundant supply of cheap oil helps fuel European and American economies. The level of economic protectionism, through tariffs, quotas, and other such mechanisms, vis-a-vis the West remains relatively low. This is especially true in the Gulf States.

Ghassan Salame has observed that the Middle East and North Africa "are viewed in Europe primarily as geo-strategic rather than economic or political issues, while pan-European institutions are far from being equipped, let alone ready, to devise a strategic approach." Even while Europe shows more independence from U.S. policy in setting its positions on the region-including opposition to sanctions against Iran, Iraq, and Libya-European concerns focus on regime stability in Saudi Arabia and the oil-rich Gulf states, regardless of their political system and orientation, the containment of "rogue" states like Iran, Iraq, the Sudan and Libya, and an end to the Arab-Israeli conflict. Fundamental democratic reform is of lesser importance. Important questions such as whether European countries will coordinate Middle Eastern policy as a bloc or will compete with one another for influence in the region remain unanswered.

NEW WORLD, OLD TRENDS

Despite a wave of coups bringing radical regimes to power in the 1950s and 1960s, and despite the success of efforts to preserve regimes in other countries, the political structure in most Middle East states remains underdeveloped, with a high degree of traditionalism and a low level of political institutionalism. Family ties and kinship, informal decision making and social cleavages, for example, are as important, if not more important, as institutional and formal avenues to power and decision making.

Lebanon, Saudi Arabia and the Gulf States are primary examples of Arab societies, where patrimonial sources of social and political prestige and power still coexist with modern institutional and formal avenues to power. Opposition political parties are either nonexistent (e.g., Saudi Arabia and the Gulf

States, Iraq, Syria and Libya) or are used by governments to legitimate elite domination (e.g., the Sudan, Egypt, and Morocco). Only governments in Israel and Turkey have allowed competitive political contests by opposition parties.

Similarly, labor unions are either non-existent or remain largely ineffective in their bargaining position vis-a-vis the state and business interests, with the notable exceptions of Israel and, to a lesser degree, Turkey, Egypt and Tunisia. Although on the surface political institutions give the appearance of being modern, where they exist they are organizationally weak. With the exception of Israel and to some degree Turkey, viable opposition political parties are rare in the Middle East. Political parties, where they exist (e.g., Egypt, Jordan, Morocco, Tunisia), are dominated by powerful individuals, lack a strong organizational base at local and provincial levels, and do not have viable party platforms to unite their members and to address the economic and social needs of the population at large. In other words, they are organizationally weak and parochial. Governments themselves are bloated with large bureaucracies where nepotism and favoritism play as much of a role as merit in hiring and promotion. As Nazih Ayubi puts it, in the Middle East, "most Arab rulers find in the machine bureaucracy a useful control device, and most executives find it a means of acquiring authority and exercising influence. Most Arab rulers and executives want to see their bureaucracies play a part in developing their countries, but in their real order of priorities, power often comes before development."

Public officials have become rent-seekers, and "state-owned enterprises have become a net drain on public finances." Government bureaucrats and their allies, including public sector managers, civil servants and their ministers, and labor and business representatives with ties to the government, prefer to preserve their own interests rather than cooperate with the opposition to benefit the country on the whole. John Waterbury, for example, observes in the cases of Egypt and Turkey that "coalitions of interests dependent on public enterprise can create arduous obstacles to reform. But, these same coalitions are often weak and fragmented, unable to resist the fundamental restructuring through privatization in which governments have attempted to remove public enterprise from the reach of politics." While Turkey and Egypt have had limited success in crushing old coalitions, prospects for success in other Middle Eastern countries, given the entrenched interest coalitions of a diverse range of groups in the public sector, and weak civil societies, are not promising.

Waterbury has suggested that economic crises could serve as catalysts for reform. That is, if economic "crisis itself is of sufficient severity, it provides the element of discontinuity that allows incumbents to restructure their power bases." Governments in the region have so far repeatedly demonstrated their resistance to reforms that threaten themselves and their constituencies. However, an economic crisis, if accompanied by a severe political crisis (e.g., loss of legitimacy, factionalism within government) could lead to structural reform.

In Iran, for example, the ideological and political factionalism within the state and the government's inability to fight the persistent economic crisis has put the state on the defensive. Now, the Islamic republic must either tolerate increasing political participation and to eventually democratize, or face increasing social unrest. In Algeria, the failure of successive governments to resolve severe economic problems and the lack of representative political institutions helped the electoral victory of the Islamic National Salvation Front (FIS). However, the Algerian elites, headed by the military decided to unite to crush the opposition, despite disagreements over the course of privatization the country had embarked upon since the 1980s. The Algerian government has thus far resisted giving concessions to the Islamic opposition, with the open conflict costing close to 100,000 lives since 1992.

THE MISSING LINK

The economic performance of both oil producers and non-producers has been unimpressive in recent years. This was partly due to the Middle East's parochial and underdeveloped political systems and processes. Though the region as a whole enjoyed relatively high levels of economic growth in comparison with the rest of the world in the 1960s and up to the mid-1970s, recent economic performance tells a different story. The annual average growth rate of the Middle East in the 1962-1975 period was 4.91 percent, well above the average world growth of 3.15 percent. However, in the years between 1975-1990, when average world growth registered at a low .58 percent, Middle East economies grew at (-.75) percent, the lowest in the world. The percentage economic growth for Africa (-.57), the Western hemisphere (-.29), Asia (1.95), the developed world (1.95), and East Asia/Pacific (3.43) were all higher. The average economic growth for the 1962-1990 period for the region stood at 2.14 percent. The world growth for this period registered at 1.8.

The economic growth of the region is even less impressive once population growth is considered. The population of the Middle East grew 2.33 percent between 1962-1975 and 3.08 percent in the 1975-1990 period. Thus, the rate of population growth for 1962-1990 stood at 2.61 percent, higher than the economic growth of 2.14 percent for the same time period. So, a partial explanation for the overall poor regional performance between 1962 and 1990 is the high rate of population growth, especially in the post-1975 periods. Table 8.1 summarizes the percentage rates of the gross national product (GNP) and population growth for the world and different regions, as well as the percentage difference between the two (Percentage GNP growth- Percentage population growth) for the 1962-1990 period. Although economies around the world experienced slower economic growth after the 1973 oil price hikes, the Middle East's economic performance was exceptionally poor, lagging behind all other regions of the world, except Africa.

Regional economic performance and the level of population growth in the 1990s remained similar to the 1980s. The percentage of gross national product per capita (GNP/PC) average annual growth for the region in 1985-1995 stood at-.03, as compared to Asia's 5.05, Latin America and the Caribbean's 0.3, high-income countries' 1.9, and Sub-Saharan

Africa's-1.1. Again, Middle East economic performance lagged behind all other regions of the world, except Africa. Furthermore, the percentage of average annual population growth for 1990-1995 for the Middle East was 2.7, as compared to Asia's 1.6, Latin America and Caribbean's 1.7, high income-countries' 0.7, and Sub-Saharan Africa's 2.6. Thus, the Middle East surpassed all other regions in population growth, effectively meaning that the region's meager economic performance was even worse than the negative growth of .03.

Table 8.1

Comparison of Economic Performance of Six Regions (1962-1990) Minus (-)

	% GNP Growth	% Pop. Growth	% Pop. Growth
World	1.8	1.63	.17
East/Pacific	4.04	1.70	2.34
Developed	2.58	.55	2.03
Western Hemisphere	1.13	1.49	-.36
Asia	1.89	2.46	-.57
Africa	.80	2.19	-1.39
Middle East	2.14	2.61	-.47

Although external forces have played a big role in generating or exacerbating conflicts and instability, stagnant regional regimes bear the burden of responsibility for the Middle East's dismal economic performance. Governments in the region, regardless of their size, are faced with a tremendous challenge: either makes the necessary political and economic adjustments in order to compete with other regions, or continue with the status quo and be undermined by growing markets in East Asia, Latin America and Europe.

The decline in economic growth, partially because of lower oil and gas prices and foreign aid-particularly for Egypt and Jordan-has forced some states in the Middle East to "liberalize" their economies and withdraw from such sectors of the economy as education, health, and welfare. However, the state's control of the national economy (e.g., government's high level share of the total expenditures in the economy as a percentage of Gross National Product) remains largely intact. The present private sector's marginal share in the national economies of most countries in the region will not expand without the blessings of the state, given its overwhelming control of the market. Furthermore, the state's dominant presence in all aspects of the social and political lives of citizens makes it very resistant to sharing political power with the opposition. For, example, as Emmanuel Sivan points out, the "powerful interventionist state" remains the "structural factor" responsible for the absence of democracy in the Arab World.

The record shows that fundamental structural reforms cannot be achieved without the emergence of civil society. Professors Muhammad Muslih and Augustus Richard Norton have pointed out that civil society exists where "clubs, organizations, and groups act as a buffer between state power and the life of the citizen." In the absence of such groups and associations, the state dominates socioeconomic and private affairs, and authoritarian tendencies intensify. The Iranian revolution, the rise of Islamic movements in the 1980s, and declining oil prices led to increased optimism for the creation of civil society in the Middle East in the 1980s and 1990s. The consensus is that, "Today most scholars confidently affirm that both intermediate powers and autonomous social groups exist in the Middle East."

But such expectations, especially in the post-Cold War era, must be viewed with caution. The civil society debate in the Middle East has focused on changes in formal procedures of governance rather than substantive change in state-society relations. The emergence of state-controlled, quasi-pluralism in countries like Egypt or Jordan is seen as a shift from one-party rule to pluralism (ta'addudiya), involving the rise of numerous political parties and associations. Despite the proliferation of some interest groups like lawyers, teachers and womens' associations, and the rise of Islamic political opposition since the early 1970s, the state's monopoly in politics continues. Therefore, political participation by pro-government parties or individuals in national elections should not be considered as a serious move toward pluralism, but as an attempt by the ruling elites to maintain the status quo.

For example, in the November 1995 elections in Egypt, the government's National Democratic Party and its allies, the Independents, won 431 of 444 available seats. The opposition, including, the Wafd party, the leftist Tagammu party, the Nasserite party and Ahrar party were left with no real power in the Majlis. In Jordan, at least 12 political parties competed for political office in the November 1997 elections, but the independent candidates won 75 of the 80-seat in the Majlis. The Jordanian Democratic Union Party, Arab Land Party, the Jordanian Arab Ba'ath Socialist Party and the National Constitutional Party (NCP) together mustered 5 seats. The political opposition in Jordan is thus neutralized by divisions among Jordanian candidates for political office, and the absence of an effective political party, capable of unifying individual candidates around a party platform. And yet in another example, while 16 political parties participated in the November 1997 parliamentary elections in Morocco, electoral blocs, reflecting three major pro-government political tendencies, captured all but 26 of the 325-seat House.

The augmentation of political parties in the region may thus be more a result of states adjusting to pressure from Islamic groups and their allies than a genuine political opening. Political parties in the Middle East remain for the most part ineffective and play mostly a ceremonial role that serves to legitimate state policies, without change in the composition of the ruling elites. For example, in all national elections in the Middle East since 1980, only in Iran (1989, 1997), Turkey (1991, 1995) and Israel (1992, 1996 and 1999) did a change in the government actually occur. In all other cases, the ruling government political parties maintained their control over the state. There are mechanisms for maintaining a political monopoly that include "restrictions on voter and candidate eligibility, gerrymandering, choice of electoral system and legal constraints on political parties. Many governments [in the Middle East] adopt or change laws between elections in order to produce different results." Moreover, embryonic associations, although they exist, are poorly organized and remain dependent on patrons within the state. As Carrie Rosefsky Wickham of Emory University puts it, regarding Egypt: "The emergence of independent sites of social and political expressions within an authoritarian setting is not the same as the emergence of civil society at least not in its liberal conception." In the final analysis, the emergence of an effective civil society in most countries of the region in the foreseeable future is not very promising.

The inadequacies of viable and productive capitalism in the region remain largely due to inefficient rent-seeking and the monopolistic nature of the state, exacerbated by foreign influence and control. The state's domination of the economy has led over the years to bloated governments with inefficient bureaucracies. The state, unwilling or unable to initiate political reforms to free it from tribal, landed, religious and merchant/commercial elites, has proven incapable of dealing with the intricacies of privatization and the open market. This, combined with external financial and political pressure for expansion of free trade and democracy, has left the state with incentives to continue resorting to oppression rather than cooperation to resolve political and economic problems.

The ruling elites have a great deal to lose in the long run. With the cost of labor higher, and the ratio of skilled to semi-skilled to unskilled labor lower, than in other regions, prospects for foreign capital investments in the near future are not promising. As Waterbury tells us: "If exploitative private economic behavior, both indigenous and foreign, could be throttled or eliminated, if the proliferation of middlemen with their attendant usury, speculation, monopolies, and short-term horizons could be halted, then a dynamic, carefully and rationally planned state enterprise sector could, as farsighted helmsman of the economy, mobilize scarce resources, stimulate markets, adopt new technologies, and rapidly lift the entire economy to a level of self-sustaining industrial growth. Governments in the region can either become efficient in the management of their economies and societies or face stronger opposition from the populace and Islamic groups. Failure to enact political reforms today can result in severe economic crises that in all probability will exacerbate political instability in the region tomorrow. This will deter foreign investments, further weakening the economic status of the region in the international political economy.

The post-Cold War international political economy has intensified economic competition among developed countries. But for developing countries, the new economic and political arrangements are far bleaker. With the threat of Communism and a world war weakened, most developing countries have found themselves outside of global political economy.

In the Middle East, oil revenues, expanded militaries, and the emergence of a sub-class of state bureaucrats, technocrats and professionals had increased the capability of the state. On the other hand, declining oil revenues in the 1980s and the 1990s forced the oil-producing states in the region to attempt some structural economic adjustments without serious attempts at political reform.

These economic adjustments have come through some limited privatization, as in Jordan and Syria, reduction in government subsidies in the cases of Iran and Iraq, and/or increased reliance on international actors for borrowing or aid, as is evidenced in Lebanon, Jordan, Egypt and Iran. Nonetheless, the state's financial and coercive power in the region remains strong and far superior to the resources available to its rival social, economic and political opposition. The challenge to the state by the Muslim Brotherhood in Egypt, Jordan, and Syria, and the National Salvation Front in Algeria, for example, has failed to force serious changes in the domestic and foreign policies of the state.

The Middle East is second only to Africa as the least developed region in the world. It has already lost much of its strategic importance since the Soviet Union's demise and with the price of oil at its lowest level in recent memory; prospects for continued sustained development do not look promising.

Most Middle Eastern states might, and probably do, possess the necessary technocratic and professional personnel to run state affairs in an efficient and modern manner. What is not present is the willingness or ability of the elites in charge to disengage the old coalitional interests that dominate governments in these countries. Whatever the new international order is, it is surely more competitive, and it punishes political rhetoric and stagnation. Those interested in serious reform and regional stability must recognize that reality and adopt their policies accordingly.

9

Islamism and Post-Islamism in Sudan

INTRODUCTION

Islamism has been defined as 'political Islam' or a 'politicized Islam.' It emerged as the major Western diagnostic reference for 'extremism' in Muslim nations after terms such as Islamic "revival," "resurgence," or "militance" was generally abandoned. Oliver Roy (1992) argued that Islamism- defined as the populist and often revolutionary ideology with the goal of the establishment of an Islamic state and governance according to Islamic principles- peaked in the 1970s with the Iranian Revolution, and thereafter declined. Notable other experiments in Islamism include contemporary Iran (from 1979, preceding Sudan by four years- why does Gallab argue for the Sudan being the "first" Islamist Republic?), Afghanistan under the Taliban, and most of the history of Saudi Arabia. Post-Islamist theory emerged in the early 1990s as the differing outcomes of various Islamist experiments were examined in Europe. Sudan was not one of the cases reviewed, perhaps due to its historic liminal status. One important indicator of post-Islamism is the shift toward evolution of the Islamic state away from models of state-imposed Islamist rule by militarist or autocratic regimes, such as in Sudan in 1983 and 1989.

Key to Islamist the goal of an Islamic state is Shari'a as the main instrument. Sudan is indeed one of the major examples of Islamism and Shari'a was the engine of mobilization for its Islamic state. Gallab dates the "first Islamic Republic" from the 1983 mandate of Shari'a as national law. Sudan is the only African state to apply Shari'a comprehensively as a national law, a well-known move that figured importantly in its second period of civil war from 1983 to 2005. Moreover, Shari'a was the major symbol of northern intransigence and the major stumbling block to a negotiated peace agreement from Abuja I and II in the early 1990s until the 2003 Machakos breakthrough of "one country-two systems"- Shari'a in the North and secularism in the South. With the signing of the historic Comprehensive Peace Agreement (CPA), Shari'a was officially withdrawn as state law in Sudan, ending its 22 years as national law, and thus beginning the transition to post-Islamism.

However, the disengagement of Islamism has not been clear or decisive as implementation of the CPA has slow and lacking in political will. Withdrawal of Shari'a from non-Muslims in the North has been partial, and the CPA-mandated Commission on their status in the capital city was delayed for two years.

Post-Islamism has been analyzed as (Lauzière 2005, 241):

1. Post-Islamists who evolve more modest agendas.
2. Post-Islamists who create a secular space by re-routing religious activism away from the state, such as the revival of Sufi orders.
3. Post-Islamists who employ reformist theology.

If the case is to be made for post-Islamism in Sudan, it would be the first example, a regime that has evolved a more modest i.e. less extremist-agenda. Gallab argues that the Muslim Brotherhood movement- later the NIF and NCP, in other words Sudan's Islamist movement- has undergone remarkable evolution. Whether they used multi-partyism or militarism, they always seek the shortest path to power. Turabi led the movement for 40 years and his downfall in 1999 signaled a shift from idealistic MB Islamism to rank opportunism. The question today is how far from the levers of power and for how long has been Turabi's fall from power? His ability to opportunistically reinvent himself is legend, and his role as an instigator and backer of JEM and of internally divisive Darfur-national politics is clear. A further question is whether this is a new stage in Sudan's Islamism, shifting the political base from the center to the West, or simply a new game in the old rivalry among the unchanging national elite power base?

Gallab argues that the fall of the Islamist regime was marked by the split in the movement after Turabi's fall in 1999. Further he says that the party shift from totalitarianism to authoritarianism is in transition now, and we may be witnessing the passing of the Islamist order. Some scholars whom I interviewed in Sudan refer to the present era as "post-extremist." Sudanese and Sudanist scholars in the West may be reluctant to accept the post-CPA period as 'post-Islamist' as so much anti-regime rhetoric is invested in the abuses associated with its pursuit of an Islamist agenda. Moreover, international press coverage of incident such as the "Teddy bear named Muhammad" with the arrest and detention of a British teacher, as well as Bashir's references to the "Crusaders and Zionists" behind the troubles in Darfur, leave western observers and Sudanese in the Diaspora cool to the idea of 'post-Islamism.' The few active Western researchers and the Sudanese who have returned after, in some cases decades of exile, are seeing a different-and in many ways a transformed- reality on the ground. This new reality needs further exploration and analysis.

Gallab concludes that the Sudanese Islamist model is actively being contested. However, this space has been opened more by the historic CPA than by the internal politics of the 'fall' of Islamism. As with the collapse of other colonialist and authoritarian regimes in Africa- such as the end of Portuguese rule and apartheid in South Africa- the potential for liberation among the communities of the oppressed is a fortunate by- product of the successful struggles by the oppressed. The democratic space opened by the CPA in the demographically transformed North is at least an important factor (or one of many factors) in the evolving Sudanese polity as are the squabbles and rivalries of the core elites.

Assessing post-Islamism is a vital part of the analysis of the future of Sudan- as a less or more peaceful unified state with a more restrained Shari'a, or as conflict- ridden and divided into two or more nations, de facto in the short term and de jure after 2011.

Islamism has been critiqued by both Muslim and non-Muslim scholars for its apparent focus on the faith of Islam as the source of the alleged extremism and resulting abuses in Islamist states. These critics observe that a comparable use of "Christianism" for extremist advocates of Christian values or rule in a state has not been applied, thus Islam has been singled out as having a particular penchant for religious extremism.

THE COMING TRANSFORMATION OF THE MUSLIM WORLD

Like the printing press in sixteenth-century Europe, the combination of mass education and mass communications is transforming the Muslim majority world, a broad geographical crescent stretching from North Africa through Central Asia, the Indian subcontinent, and the Indonesian archipelago. In unprecedentedly large numbers, the faithful-whether in the vast cosmopolitan city of Istanbul, the suburbs of Paris, or in the remote oases of Oman's mountainous interior are examining and debating the fundamentals of Muslim belief and practice in ways that their less self-conscious predecessors in the faith would never have imagined.

Buzzwords such as "fundamentalism," and catchy phrases such as Samuel Huntington's "West versus Rest" or Daniel Lerner's "Mecca or mechanization," are of little use in understanding this transformation. They obscure or even distort the immense spiritual and intellectual ferment that is taking place today among the world's nearly one billion Muslims, reducing it in most cases to a fanatical rejection of everything modern, liberal, or progressive. To be sure, such fanaticism-not exclusive to Muslim majority societies-plays a part in what is happening, but it is far from the whole story.

A far more important element is the unprecedented access that ordinary people now have to sources of information and knowledge about religion and other aspects of their society. Quite simply, in country after country, government officials, traditional religious scholars, and officially sanctioned preachers are finding it very hard to monopolize the tools of literate culture. The days have gone when governments and religious authorities can control what their people know, and what they think.

MASS HIGHER EDUCATION AND COMMUNICATION

What distinguishes the present era from prior ones is the large numbers of believers engaged in the "reconstruction" of religion, community, and society. In an earlier era, political or religious leaders would prescribe, and others were supposed to follow. Today, the major impetus for change in religious and political values comes from below. In France, this has meant an identity shift from being Muslim in France to being French Muslim. In Turkey, it means that an increasing number of Turks, especially those of the younger generation, see themselves as European and Muslim at the same time. And some Iranians argue that the major transformations of the Iranian revolution occurred not in 1978-79 but with the coming of age of a new generation of Iranians who were not even born at the time of the revolution. These transformations include a greater sense of autonomy for both women and men and the emergence of a public sphere in which politics and religion are subtly intertwined, and not always in ways anticipated by Iran's formal religious leaders.

If "modernity" is defined as the emergence of new kinds of public space, including new possible spaces not imagined by preceding generations, then developments in France, Turkey, Iran, Indonesia, and elsewhere suggest that we are living through an era of profound social transformation for the Muslim majority world.

Distinctive to the modern era is that discourse and debate about Muslim tradition involves people on a mass scale. It also necessarily involves an awareness of other Muslim and non-Muslim traditions. Mass education and mass communication in the modern world facilitate an awareness of the new and unconventional. In changing the style and scale of possible discourse, they reconfigure the nature of religious thought and action, create new forms of public space, and encourage debate over meaning.

Mass education and mass communications are important in all contemporary world religions. However, the full effects of mass education, especially higher education, only began to be felt in much of the Muslim world since mid-century and in many countries considerably later. In country after country including Morocco, Egypt, Turkey, and Indonesia- educational opportunities have dramatically expanded at all levels. Even where adult illiteracy rates in the general populace remains high, as in rural Egypt and Morocco, there is now a critical mass of educated people able to read, think for them, and react to religious and political authorities rather than just listen to them. Women's access to education still lags behind that of men, although the gap is rapidly closing in many countries.

Both mass education and mass communications, particularly the proliferation of media and the means by which people communicate, have had a profound effect on how people think about religion and politics throughout the Muslim world. Multiple means of communication make the unilateral control of information and opinion much more difficult than it was in prior eras and foster, albeit inadvertently, a civil society of dissent. We are still in the early stages of understanding how different media-including print, television, radio, cassettes, and music-in fluence groups and individuals, encouraging unity in some contexts and fragmentation in others, but a few salient features may be sketched.

At the "high" end of this transformation is the rise to significance of books such as al-Kitab wa-l-Qur'an [The Book and the Qur'an] (1992), written by the Syrian civil engineer Muhammad Shahrur. This book has sold tens of thousands of copies throughout the Arab world in spite of the fact that its circulation has been banned or discouraged in many places. Its success could not have been imagined before there were large numbers of people able to read it and understand its advocacy of the need to reinterpret ideas of religious authority and tradition and apply Islamic precepts to contemporary society. On issues ranging from the role of women in society to rekindling a "creative interaction" with non-Muslim philosophies, Shahrur argues that Muslims should reinterpret sacred texts and apply them to contemporary social and moral issues.

Shahrur is not alone in attacking both conventional religious wisdom and the intolerant certainties of religious radicals and in arguing instead for a constant and open re-interpretation of how sacred texts apply to social and political life. Another Syrian thinker, the secularist Sadiq Jalal al-'Azm, debated Shaykh Yusifal-Qaradawi, a conservative religious intellectual, on Qatar's *Al-Jazira* Satellite TV in May 1997. For the first time in the memory of many viewers, the religious conservative came across as the weaker, more defensive voice. *Al-Jazira* is a new phenomenon in Arab language broadcasting because its talk shows, such as "The Opposite Direction," feature live discussions on such sensitive issues as women's role in society, Palestinian refugees, sanctions on Iraq, and democracy and human rights in the Arab world.

Such discussions are unlikely to be rebroadcast on state-controlled television in most Arab nations, where programming on religious and political themes is generally cautious. Nevertheless, satellite technology and videotape render traditional censorship ineffective. Tapes of the *Al-Jazira* broadcasts circulate from hand to hand in Morocco, Oman, Syria, Egypt, and elsewhere. *Al-Jazira* shows that people across the Arab world, just like their counterparts elsewhere in the Muslim majority world, want open discussion of the issues that affect their lives, and that new communications technologies make it impossible for governments and established religious authorities to stop them.

Other voices also advocate reform. Fethullah Glen, Turkey's answer to media-savvy American evangelist Billy Graham, appeals to a mass audience. In televised chat shows, interviews, and occasional sermons, Glen speaks about Islam and science, democracy, modernity, religious and ideological tolerance, the importance of education, and current events.

Religious movements such as Turkey's Risale-i Nur appeal increasingly to religious moderates, and in stressing the link between Islam, reason, science, and modernity, and the lack of inherent clash between "East" and "West," promote education at all levels, and appeal to a growing numbers of educated Turks. Iranian, Indonesian, and Malaysian moderates make similar arguments advocating religious and political toleration and pluralism.

As a result of direct and broad access to the printed, broadcast, and taped word, more and more Muslims take it upon themselves to interpret the textual sources-classical or modern of Islam. Much has been made of the opening up of the economies of many Muslim countries, allowing "market forces" to reshape economies, no matter how painful the consequences in the short run. In a similar way, intellectual market forces support some forms of religious innovation and activity over others. In Bangladesh, women's romance novels, once a popular secular specialty, now have their Islamic counterparts, making it difficult to distinguish between "Muslim" romance novels and "secular" ones.

The result is a collapse of earlier, hierarchical notions of religious authority based on claims to the mastery of fixed bodies of religious texts. Even when there are state-appointed religious authorities as in Oman, Saudi Arabia, Iran, and Egypt- there no longer is any guarantee that their word will be heeded, or even that they themselves will follow the lead of the regime. No one group or type of leader in contemporary Muslim societies possesses a monopoly on the management of the sacred.

THE EMERGING PUBLIC SPHERE

Without fanfare, the notion that Islam should be the subject of dialogue and civil debate is gaining ground. This new sense of public space is shaped by increasingly open contests over the use of the symbolic language of Islam and increasingly discussions in newspapers on the Internet on smuggled cassettes and on television cross-cut and overlap, contributing to a common public space.

New and accessible modes of communication have made these contests increasingly global, so that even local issues take on transnational dimensions. The combination of new media and new contributors to religious and political debates fosters awareness on the part of all actors of the diverse ways in which Islam and Islamic values can be created. It feeds into new senses of a public space that is discursive, performative, and participative, and not confined to formal institutions recognized by state authorities.

Two cautions are in order. The first is that an expanding public sphere need not necessarily indicate more favorable prospects for democracy, any more than civil society necessarily entails democracy. Authoritarian regimes are compatible with an expanding public sphere, although an expanded public sphere offers wider avenues for awareness of competing and alternate forms of religious and political authority. Nor does civil society necessarily entail democracy, although it is a precondition for democracy.

Publicly shared ideas of community, identity, and leadership take new shapes in such engagements, even as many communities and authorities claim an unchanged continuity with the past. Mass education, so important in the development of nationalism in an earlier era, and a proliferation of media and means of communication have multiplied the possibilities for creating communities and networks among them, dissolving prior barriers of space and distance and opening new grounds for interaction and mutual recognition.

10

Liberal Islam
Prospects and Challenges

Although the focus of research and public perception in the West has been on radical Islamic thought and movements, many Muslims adhere to principles which could be described collectively as "Liberal Islam." This refers to interpretations of Islam that have a special concern regarding such issues as democracy, separating religion from political involvement, women's rights, freedom of thought, and promoting human progress. In each case, the argument is that both Muslims and religious piety itself would benefit from reforms and a more open society. These attitudes parallel those of liberalism in other cultures and also of liberal movements in various religious faiths.

It is quite possible that these tendencies will grow more important in the future, perhaps even coming to be the dominant orientation in the years to come. Such a trend could happen because of local factors, modernization and development in Islamic societies, and reasons similar to those that brought about such an evolution in the West.

THE TROPES OF LIBERAL ISLAM

Liberalism in the Islamic world and liberalism in the West may share common elements, but they are not exactly the same thing. They may both support multi-religious coexistence, for example, but go about it in different ways. Within the Islamic discourse, there are three main tropes:

1. The "liberal shari`a"
2. The "silent shari`a"
3. The "interpreted shari`a"

Shari'a is the body of Islamic guidance and precedent that has been handed down from the time of the Prophet Muhammad in 7th century Arabia.

The "liberal shari`a" argues that the revelations of the Qur'an and the practices of the Prophet command Muslims to follow liberal positions. For example, in the case of Ali Bula (Turkey, born 1951) quotes Sura 109, Verse 6 of the Qur'an: "To you your religion, to me my religion." He goes into great detail describing the "Medina Document," a treaty signed by the Prophet Muhammad with the Jewish tribes of Medina in the first moments of the Islamic era: "The urgent problem of the day was to end the conflicts and to find a formulation for the co-existence of all sides according to the principles of justice and righteousness. In this respect, the Document is epochal....A righteous and just, law respecting ideal project aiming for true peace and stability among people cannot but be based on a contract among different groups (religious, legal, philosophical, political etc.)....This is a rich diversity within unity, or a real pluralism." (Pages 170-174)

Chandra Muzaffar (Malaysia, born 1947) quotes Sura 49, Verse 13: "O mankind! We created you from a single pair of a male and a female, and made you into nations and tribes, that ye may know each other, not that ye may despise each other." (Page 157) Mohamed Talbi (Tunisia, born 1921) quotes Sura 5, Verse 48: "To each among you, have we prescribed a Law and an open way. And if God had enforced His Will, He would have made of you all one people." (Page 164) Hostile and discriminatory forms of inter-religious relations, according to this trope, are un-Islamic. In the words of Subhi Mahmassani (Lebanon, born 1911): "There can be no discrimination based on religion in an Islamic system." (Page 23)

Mohamed Talbi (Tunisia, born 1921) quotes Sura 5, Verse 48: "To each among you, have We prescribed a Law and an Open Way. And if God had enforced His Will, He would have made of you all one people." (Page 164) Hostile and discriminatory forms of inter-religious relations, according to this trope, are un-Islamic. In the words of Subhi Mahmassani (Lebanon, born 1911): "There can be no discrimination based on religion in an Islamic system." (Page 23)

The second trope, the "silent shari`a," holds that coexistence is not required by the shari`a, but is allowed. This trope argues that the shari`a is silent on certain topics not because divine revelation was incomplete or faulty, but because the revelation intentionally left certain issues for humans to choose.

For example, Humayun Kabir (India, 1906 -1969) argues that the precedent of the early period of Islam does not apply automatically to later periods: "The situation changed as the Muslim empire spread rapidly through large areas of Asia and many different peoples were brought within its fold. Many practical problems arose and Muslim political thinking had to find a place for non-Muslim subjects in a Muslim State. ... [In India, today, for example,] Muslims have condemned compulsion in religion and admitted that different religions must be given due respect." (Pages 148, 152)

Syed Vahiduddin (India, born 1909) quotes the same Qur'anic verse as Mohamed Talbi: "In a pluralistic and multi - religious society one cannot do better than to ponder on the Qur'anic vision of human conflicts: To every one of you we have appointed a right way and open path. If Allah had willed, He would have made you one community...." (Sura 5, Verse 48) But Vahiduddin interprets this verse within the context of the changing needs of an evolving Islamic community: the late 20th century, he writes, is a period, "When Muslims are tempted to take an extremely static view of religion. Their preoccupation with issues which are not of capital importance has made them uncompromising not only in inter -religious dialogue but also in inter -Islamic dialogue." (Pages 22 -23)

Similarly, Abdurrahman Wahid (Indonesia, born 1940), leader of the world's largest Islamic organization, calls the 1945 Indonesian constitution better suited than an exclusively Islamic state for the particularly multi-cultural setting of contemporary Indonesia. "[T]here is a need for steps to be taken to resist the deterioration of relations between the different religions and faiths in Indonesia," he writes, and the first of these steps is the defense of democratic freedoms: "First of all, efforts to restore the attitude of mutual respect among people from different faiths should be based on the fundamental legal principles of freedom of speech (even for very small minority groups), the rule of law and equality before the constitution."

The first trope of liberal Islam holds that the shari'a requires democracy, and the second trope holds that the shari'a allows democracy. But there is a third trope that takes issue with each of the first two. This trope is "interpreted Islam." According to this view, "Religion is divine, but its interpretation is thoroughly human and this-worldly." (Abdul-Karim Soroush, Iran, born 1945) (Page 246):

"The text does not stand alone, it does not carry its own meaning on its shoulders, it needs to be situated in a context, it is theory-laden, its interpretation is in flux, and presuppositions are as actively at work here as elsewhere in the field of understanding. Religious texts are no exception. Therefore their interpretation is subject to expansion and contraction according to the assumptions preceding them and/ or the questions enquiring them ....We look at revelation in the mirror of interpretation, much as a devout scientist looks at creation in the mirror of nature ... [so that] the way for religious democracy and the transcendental unity of religions, which are predicated on religious pluralism, will have been paved." (Pages 245, 251)

Farid Esack (South Africa, born 1959), cites the words of 'Ali ibn Abi Talib, fourth caliph and son-in-law of the Prophet: "this is the Qur'an, written in straight lines, between two boards [of its binding]; it does not speak with a tongue; it needs interpreters and interpreters are people." Esack translates this into contemporary terms: "Every interpreter enters the process of interpretation with some preunderstanding of the questions addressed by the text- even of its silences-and brings with him or her certain conceptions as presuppositions of his or her exegesis." Esack's pre-understandings emerge from the multi-religious struggle against apartheid in South Africa. He argues that this commitment resonates with the spirit of early Islam, when an "emerging theology of religious pluralism was intrinsically wedded to one of liberation."

Similarly, Hassan Hanafi (Egypt, born 1935) wrote: "There is no one interpretation of a text, but there are many interpretations given the difference in understanding between various interpreters. An interpretation of a text is essentially pluralistic. The text is only a vehicle for human interests and even passions. ... The conflict of interpretation is essentially a socio-political conflict, not a theoretical one. Theory indeed is only an epistemological cover-up. Each interpretation expresses the socio-political commitment of the interpreter." (Page 26)

Amina Wadud-Muhsin (United States, born 1952) argues in a similar vein that "when one individual reader with a particular world-view and specific prior text [the language and cultural context in which the text is read] asserts that his or her reading is the only possible or permissible one, it prevents readers in different contexts from coming to terms with their own relationship to the text." (Page 130)

Abdullahi An-Na'im (Sudan, born 1946) said: "there is no such thing as the only possible or valid understanding of the Qur'an, or conception of Islam, since each is informed by the individual and collective orientation of Muslims...."

This third trope suggests that religious diversity is inevitable, not just among religious communities but within Islam itself.

THE SOCIAL LOCATION OF LIBERAL ISLAM

INCREASING ADVANCED EDUCATION

Widespread higher education has broken the traditional

religious institutions' monopoly on religious scholarship. Millions of autodidacts now have access to texts and commentaries, such as non-clerics with secular educations: engineers such as Muhammad Shahrour (Syria, born 1938) and Mehdi Bazargan (Iran, 1907-1995); philosophers such as Muhammad Arkoun (Algeria-France, born 1928) and Rachid Ghannoushi (Tunisia, born 1941); and sociologists such as 'Ali Shari'ati (Iran, 1933-1977) and Chandra Muzaffar (Malaysia, born 1947).

For example, Fatima Mernissi (Morocco, born 1940), trained in sociology rather than theology, examined the hadith (tradition of the Prophet), "Those who entrust their affairs to a woman will never know prosperity!" Consulting a variety of ancient sources, she discovered that the hadith was attributed to Abu Bakra (died circa 671)-born a slave, liberated by the Prophet Muhammad, who rose to high social position in the city of Basra. He is the only source for this hadith, and he reported it 25 years after the Prophet's death. Mernissi suggests that this hadith, though included in Muhammad ibn Ismail al-Bukhari's collection of traditions, *Al-Salih* (The Authentic) and widely cited in the Islamic world, is suspect for two reasons.

First, when placed in context, Abu Bakra's relation of the hadith seems self-serving. He was trying to save his life after the Battle of the Camel (December 656), when, to quote Mernissi, "all those who had not chosen to join `Ali's clan had to justify their action. This can explain why a man like Abu Bakra needed to recall opportune traditions, his record being far from satisfactory, as he had refused to take part in the civil war. ... [Although] many of the Companions and inhabitants of Basra chose neutrality in the conflict, only Abu Bakra justified it by the fact that one of the parties was a woman." (Pages 116-117)

Second, Abu Bakra had once been flogged for giving false testimony in an early court case. According to the rules of hadith scholarship laid out by Imam Malik ibn Anas (710-796 A.D.), one of the founders of the science of hadith studies, lying disqualifies a source from being counted as a reliable transmitter of hadith. "If one follows the principles of Malik for fiqh [Islamic jurisprudence], Abu Bakra must be rejected as a source of hadith by every good, well-informed Malikite Muslim." (Page 119)

Thus, in the world of CD-ROMs and global internet access, anyone literate in Arabic with a personal computer, like Mernissi, can investigate the sources of Islamic law and question the reigning interpretations.

INCREASED INTERNATIONAL COMMUNICATION

International technologies of communication-newspapers, telegraph lines, and international trade-as well as radio, television, telephones, and the internet, are bringing educated people from around in the world into ever-closer contact. The ideals of Western liberalism, like other Western notions such as nationalism, have entered people's homes around the world. People in Gabon, West Africa, for example, watched the fall of Communism in eastern Europe and started demanding democracy themselves, prompting that country's dictator to comment derisively on the "wind from the east [i.e., the Communist Eastern bloc] that is shaking the coconut trees."

Another example: Nurcholish Madjid (Indonesia, born 1939) defends freedom of thought by quoting the famous U.S. judge Oliver Wendell Holmes (1809-1894): "The ultimate good desired is better reached by free trade in ideas-that the best test of truth is the power of thought to get itself accepted [in the] competition of the market ..." Madjid goes on to say: "Among the freedoms of the individual, the freedom to think and to express opinions are the most valuable. We must have a firm conviction that all ideas and forms of thought, however strange they may sound, should be accorded means of expression. It is by no means rare that such ideas and thoughts, initially regarded as generally wrong, are [later] found to be right. ... Furthermore, in the confrontation of ideas and thoughts, even error can be of considerable benefit, because it will induce truth to express itself and grow as a strong force. Perhaps it was not entirely small talk when our Prophet said that differences of opinion among his umma [community] were a mercy [from God]." (Page 287)

A further example of how technology is inducing change in the Islamic world is the tremendous Internet activity surrounding the arrest of former Malaysian deputy prime minister Anwar Ibrahim (born 1947), whose trajectory from youthful Islamist militant to liberal reformist coincided with his increasing use of quotations from William Shakespeare and other cross-cultural sources. Ibrahim's political career began with a communalist Islamism that scapegoated Chinese Malaysians. In recent years, Ibrahim had become an outspoken proponent of multi-religious co-existence, both in Malaysia and at the global level: "The experience of contemporary Islam in Southeast Asia has much to contribute not only to Muslims in other regions but possibly also to the world at large. This is due to the fact that the devout Southeast Asian Muslim practices his religion in the context of a truly multicultural world. Especially in Malaysia, a Muslim is never unaware of the presence of people of other faiths; as friends, colleagues, collaborators, partners or even competitors."

Supporters of Ibrahim's reform movement contributed to international communication through Web sites such as Anwar Online (*http://members.tripod.com/~Anwar_Ibrahim*), Anwar Ibrahim One (*http://www.anwaribrahim1.com*), Gerakan Reformasi (*http://members.xoom.com/Gerakan*), ADIL (*http://members.easyspace.com/reformasi*), Reformasi Dot Com (*http://www.reformasi.com*, quoting poetry by Rabindranath Tagore), and Ibrahim's wife's official web site, *http://www.anwaribrahim.org*.

Some of these sites registered hundreds of thousands of visitors in two or three months. As one flashing pro-Ibrahim Web site noted in halting English: "Welcome to J's Reformasi Online, the site of the oppressed and depressed!! In the name of Allah, most gracious, most merciful."

Some countries, like Saudi Arabia and Iran, have tried to block foreign ideas from entering their countries precisely because they fear these sorts of inter-cultural interactions. But blocking foreign ideas, to quote U.S. President Woodrow Wilson out of context, "is like using a broom to stop a vast flood." Few countries will be able to keep up this level of sweeping for long.

THE FAILURE OF ISLAMIC REGIMES

A third factor in the rise of liberal Islam is the failure of alternative ideologies. In particular, there appears to be a growing sense that Islamic regimes have not lived up to their promise. The Sudan and Pakistan, for example, have proved to be no less corrupt after the Islamization of the government than before. Taliban rule in Afghanistan horrifies most Muslims.

The number one disappointment for "fundamentalist" Muslims, however, is Iran. The Iranian Revolution of 1979 raised tremendous hopes among Islamists in Malaysia, Africa, and throughout the Islamic world. Iran was to be the showpiece of the Islamist movement. For the first time since the seventh century, a truly Islamic society was to be constructed. It has been painful for these people to find that dream unfulfilled.

There are many examples of this painful disillusionment and the liberal outcome that resulted. Consider 'Abdul-Karim Soroush, a man who wholeheartedly favored the Islamic Republic in the early years. Soroush participated actively in the revolutionary reorganization of the universities in Iran, which involved getting rid of many fine professors in the name of ideological purity. Yet even this staunch supporter of the Islamic Republic eventually had his doubts.

By the mid-1980s he had started to distance himself from official committees on which he had served. By the late 1980s he came to realize that the Islamic Republic was not ushering in a new era of justice and righteousness. Soroush started to criticize the government and began to call for a reinterpretation of Islamic law and for academic and intellectual freedoms that his university reorganization had disregarded in the early 1980s. These themes, along with his impressive erudition and his talent for public speaking, made Soroush one of the most popular public speakers in Iran in the early 1990s. He spoke at mosques and universities and on the radio, always to big audiences. Naturally the Iranian government found his words threatening, and Soroush has since been barred from speaking publicly in Iran. He now speaks outside of Iran, when he is allowed to travel, addressing international audiences, mainly in Europe and North America, stressing the commonality of his views with Western interpretations of religion. But the pain of Soroush's break with the Islamic Republic and his disillusionment are apparently so great that he literally cannot deal with his own former hopes and aspirations. In interviews, Soroush denies that he was a supporter of the Cultural Revolution in Iran or that he was active in the reorganization of the universities. The Islamic Republic in Iran appears not only to be generating liberal ideas, but may even be erasing the memory of Islamist ideals.

CHALLENGES TO LIBERAL ISLAM

Although there are Muslims who find common ground with Western liberals, liberal Islam is not without its detractors. Some claim that liberal Islam is inauthentic, that it is a creation of the West and does not reflect "true" Islamic traditions. "Authenticity movements" have been increasing globally over the past quarter-century, from religious authenticity movements such as Islamism or the B.J.P. Hindu nationalist party in India, to ethnic authenticity movements such as tribal hostilities that have resulted in gruesome massacres in central Africa. The emphasis on authenticity is not limited to the Islamic world.

One of the crucial characteristics of this renewed interest in authenticity is the idea that one can take a culture and draw a box around it; that a culture can be defined as a discrete entity, separate from other cultures, with well-defined boundaries. In reality, these boundaries are rarely so precise. In Uzbekistan, for example, the government insists that the Now Ruz New Year's celebration was invented in Central Asia, not in Iran- as if cultural practices would be less valuable if they were imported from elsewhere.

The flip side of this increasing need for cultural ownership is a flurry of criticisms against things or people for not being authentic enough. Because liberal Islam shares concerns with Western liberalism, critics claim, it must not be a valid interpretation of the religion-if X is Western, it cannot be Islamic. This binary opposition ignores the tremendous history of cultural borrowings and influences that permeated the supposed border over the centuries.

If the first charge is that liberal Islam is inauthentic, and therefore somehow wrong, the second charge argues that liberal Islam should not be tolerated whether or not it is wrong. For example, Gai Eaton, a British Muslim, calls liberal Muslims "Uncle Toms." ("Uncle Tom" is a derisive term used by African-Americans to describe a Black person who is grotesquely servile to whites.) In essence, Eaton is calling liberal concerns treasonous to the cause of Islam. Not only are these concerns wrong, according to Eaton's way of thinking, but right or wrong, raising these concerns publicly weakens the Islamic world in its struggle with the West. It is like a team sport, where each side demands loyalty from its members and sees any internal critique, any self-critique, as aiding and abetting the other team.

In Iran, for example, the feeling of being besieged by foreign, especially American, hostility is so strong that in order to survive, politicians must prove that they are not "soft" on the "Great Satan." Iranian politicians, who wish to negotiate with the West, or to raise concerns about democracy, human rights, or other issues, are immediately labeled by their political opponents as "soft on Satan." This pattern is so common and so damaging to liberal concerns, that even Iran's moderate president, Muhammad Khatami, engaged in liberal-bashing during his campaign in 1997, perhaps in order to ward off similar criticism of him. In one speech, on May 4 at Tehran University, Khatami sounded liberal themes such as: "The government should provide a safe environment for the people so that they may express their opinions on internal issues and economic affairs," and "We should study the West, a fountain of all transformations." At the same time, he accused some liberal oppositionists of having "fallen in the lap of foreigners," of not being a legitimate political party, and of not coming "from inside society."

Western ignorance poses yet another challenge for liberal Islam. For centuries, the West has constructed an image of Islam as "the Other," identifying Islam with its most exotic elements. Islamic faith has been equated with fanaticism, as in Voltaire's Mahomet, or Fanaticism (1745). Islamic political authority has been equated with despotism, as in Montesquieu's intentionally redundant phrase "Oriental despotism." And, Islamic tradition has been equated with backwardness and primitiveness, as in Ernest Renan's inaugural lecture at the College de France (1862):

"Islam is the complete negation of Europe; ... Islam is the disdain of science, the suppression of civil society; it is the appalling simplicity of the Semitic spirit, restricting the human mind, closing it to all delicate ideas, to all refined sentiment, to all rational research, in order to keep it facing an eternal tautology: God is God."

Aside from bias, Western policy must better understand the distinctions within Islamic movements. An example is the recent history of Algeria. *The Front de Salvation Islamique* (FIS) was divided into liberal and radical factions. During the elections of late 1991 and early 1992, the liberal wing was in the ascendant; its leaders were setting the group's policy, its candidates were running for office, and it stood a great chance of actually coming to power.

'Abbasi Madani, the leader of the liberal faction, made a number of statements aimed at calming the fears of Algerians and Westerners about the intentions of the FIS, such as: "Pluralism is a guarantee of cultural wealth, and diversity is needed for development. We are Muslims, but we are not Islam itself. We do not monopolize religion. Democracy as we understand it means pluralism, choice, and freedom." The FIS had won 81 percent of the first-round elections in December 1991 and was poised to do equally well in the second round in early January 1992 when the Algerian military, supported by France and the United States, canceled the elections, banned the FIS, and arrested its leaders. The result was that the liberals within the Islamic movement were thoroughly discredited for having proposed an effort to win within the rules of democracy. The radical wing prevailed and even murdered liberal Islamic activists who objected to terrorism, such as Mohammad Sa'id and Abderrazak Redjam who were killed in 1995. The Western inability to believe that there might be such a thing as liberal Islam proved a self-fulfilling prophecy.

There is a growing number of Muslims who share common concerns with Western liberalism, one of which is peaceful multi-religious co-existence. There are three Islamic approaches in this context which, while still very much minority views, seem to be growing. In the "liberal shari`a" school, Islamic scholars base their arguments on injunctions in the Qur`an and on precedents from the early years of Islam.

Using an argument that might be called the "silent shari`a," Islamic scholars argue that the shari`a does not speak about certain topics-not because the revelation is incomplete or imperfect, but because these matters have been intentionally left to human invention.

The third approach is the "interpreted shari`a," where Islamic scholars argue that the revelation is divine, but interpretation is human and fallible and inevitably plural.

These liberal approaches to multi-religious co-existence have been stimulated by three historic shifts of the past quarter century: the rise of secular higher education in the Islamic world, which has broken the monopoly of the seminaries over religious discourse; the growth of international communications, which has made educated Muslims more aware than ever of the norms and institutions of the West; and the failure of Islamic regimes to deliver an attractive alternative.

These liberal approaches face serious challenges, including accusations of treason and inauthenticity, and a Western ignorance about the existence and importance of this internal Islamic debate.

Bibliography

Abraham, A. J. *Islamic Fundamentalism and the Doctrine of Jihad.* Lima, OH: Wyndham Hall Press, 2002.

AbuKhalil, As'ad. *Bin Laden, Islam, and America's New 'War on Terrorism'.* Open Media Pamphlet Series. New York: Seven Stories Press, 2002.

Ahmed, Nafeez Mosaddwq. *The War on Truth: 9/11, Disinformation and the Anatomy of Terrorism.* Northampton, MA: Olive Branch Press, 2005.

Aho, James. *Politics of Righteousness: Idaho Christian Patriotism.* Seattle, WA: University of Washington Press, 1995.

Alexander, Yonah. *European Terrorism Today & Tomorrow.* Brassey's Terrorism Library. Washington, DC: Brassey's, 1992.

Alexander, Yonah. *Middle East Terrorism: Current Threats and Future Prospects.* International Library of Terrorism; 5. New York: G.K. Hall & Co., 1994.

Alexander, Yonah. *Middle East Terrorism: Selected Group Profiles.* Washington, DC: Jewish Institute for National Security Affairs, 1994.

Alexander, Yonah. *Palestinian Religious Terrorism: Hamas and Islamic Jihad.* New York: Transnational, 2002.

Alexander, Yonah. *Terrorism in Europe.* New York: St. Martin's Press, 1982.

Alexander, Yonah. *Usama bin Laden's al-Qaida: Profile of a Terrorist Network.* Ardsley, NY: Transnational Publishers, 2001.

Alexander, Yonah; Latter, Richard, editors, *Terrorism and the Media: Dilemmas for Government, Journalists and the Public.* Washington, DC: Brassey's, 1990.

Bartholomeusz, Tessa J. *Buddhist Fundamentalism and Minority Identities in Sri Lanka*. New York: State University of New York Press, 1998.

Barton, Greg. *Indonesia's Struggle: Jemaah Islamiyah and the Soul of Islam*. Sydney, Australia: University of New South Wales Press, 2004.

Cateura, Linda Brandi. *Voices of American Muslims: 23 Profiles*. New York: Hippocrene Books, 2005.

Catholic Institute for International Relations, *Guatemala, Never Again*. Maryknoll, NY: Orbis Books, 1999.

Davies, Barry. *Terrorism: Inside a World Phenomenon*. London: Virgin Books, 2003.

Devji, Faisal. *Landscapes of the Jihad: Militancy, Morality, Modernity*. Ithaca, NY: Cornell University Press, 2005.

Devji, Mantoshe Singh. *The Mad Messiah: Osama bin Laden and the Seeds of Terror*. Scottsdale, AZ: Inkwell Productions, 2002. Emerson, Steven. *American Jihad: The Terrorists Living Among Us*. New York: Free Press, 2002.

Esposito, John L. *Islam: The Straight Path*. 3rd edition. New York: Oxford University Press, 1998.

Esposito, John L. *The Islamic Threat: Myth or Reality?*. New York: Oxford University Press, 1992.

Esposito, John L. *The Oxford Dictionary of Islam*. New York: Oxford University Press, 2003.

Esposito, John L. *Unholy War: Terror in the Name of Islam*. New York: Oxford University Press, 2002.

Etzioni, Amitai. *How Patriotic is the Patriot Act? Freedom Versus Security in the Age of Terrorism*. New York: Routledge, 2004.

Fandy, Mamoun. *Saudi Arabia and the Politics of Dissent*. New York: Palgrave, 2001.

Farah, Douglas. *Blood From Stones: The Secret Financial Network of Terror*. New York: Broadway Books, 2004.

Gardell, Mattias. *Gods of the Blood: The Pagan Revival and White Separatism*. Durham, NC: Duke University Press, 2003.

Gerges, Fawaz A. *The Far Enemy: Why Jihad Went Global*. New York: Cambridge University Press, 2005.

Habeck, Mary R. *Knowing the Enemy: Jihadist Ideology and the War on Terror*. New Haven, NY: Yale University Press, 2006.

Hoffman, Bruce. *Holy terror: The Implications of Terrorism Motivated by a Religious Imperative*. Santa Monica, CA: RAND, 1993.

Howard, Russell D. *Defeating Terrorism: Shaping the New Security Environment*. Guilford, CT: McGraw-Hill, 2004.

Jaimoukha, Amjad M. *The Chechens: A Handbook*. New York: Routledge Curzon, 2005.

Karawan, Ibrahim. *Islamic Impasse*. New York: Oxford University Press, 1997.

Miniter, Richard. *Losing Bin Laden: How Bill Clinton's Failures Unleashed Global Terror*. Washington, DC: Regnery, 2003.

Mishal, Shaul. *The Palestinian Hamas: Vision, Violence, and Coexistence*. New York: Columbia University Press, 2000.

Napoleoni, Loretta. *Modern Jihad: Tracing the Dollars Behind the Terror Networks*. Sterling, VA: Pluto Press, 2003.

Noorani, A. G. *Islam & Jihad: Prejudice versus Reality*. New York: Zed Books, 2002.

Nusse, Andrea. *Muslim Palestine: The Ideology of Hamas*. Amsterdam: Harwood Academic Publishers, 1998.

O'Ballance, Edgar. *Islamic Fundamentalist Terrorism: 1979-95*. Basingstoke: Macmillan, 1997.

Ojeda, Auriana. *Islamic Fundamentalism*. San Diego, CA: Greenhaven Press, 2003.

Randal, Jonathan C. *Osama: The Making of a Terrorist*. New York: Knopf, 2004.

Rapoport, David C. *The Rationalization of Terrorism.* Frederick, MD: University Publications of America, 1982.

Scheuer, Michael. *Through Our Enemies Eyes: Osama bin Laden, Radical Islam, and the Future of America.* Rev. ed., 2nd ed.. Washington, DC: Potomac Books, 2006.

Taheri, Amir. *Holy Terror: Inside the World of Islamic Terrorism.* Bethesda, MD: Adler & Adler, 1987.

Venske, Ben. *The al-Qaeda Threat: An Analytical Guide to al-Qaeda's Tactics & Targets.* Alexandria, VA: Tempest Publishing, 2003.

Venzke, Ben. *The al-Qaeda Threat: An Analytical Guide to al-Qaeda's Tactics & Targets.* Alexandria, VA: Tempest, 2003.

Waardenburg, Jacques. *Muslims and Others: Relations in Context.* New York: Walter de Gruyter, 2003.

Wiktorowicz, Quintan. *Global Jihad: Understanding September 11.* Falls Church, VA: 2002.

Zacharias, Ravi K. *Light in the Shadow of Jihad.* Sisters, OR: Multnomah Publishers, 2002.

Index

R

S

T

U

W